T0341764

TALKING
BACK
TO THE
INDIAN ACT

TALKING
BACK
TO THE
INDIAN ACT

CRITICAL READINGS IN
SETTLER COLONIAL HISTORIES

Mary-Ellen Kelm and Keith D. Smith

UNIVERSITY OF TORONTO PRESS

Toronto Buffalo London

Library and Archives Canada Cataloguing in Publication

Kelm, Mary-Ellen, 1964–, author
    Talking back to the Indian Act : critical readings in settler colonial histories / Mary-Ellen Kelm and Keith D. Smith.

Includes bibliographical references and index.
Issued in print and electronic formats.

ISBN 978-1-4875-8735-2 (softcover). – ISBN 978-1-4875-8736-9 (hardcover).
ISBN 978-1-4875-8737-6 (HTML). – ISBN 978-1-4875-8738-3 (uPDF).

    1. Canada. Indian Act. 2. Native peoples – Legal status, laws, etc. – Canada – History – Sources. 3. Native peoples – Canada – Government relations – Sources. 4. Native peoples – Canada – History – Sources. I. Smith, Keith D. (Keith Douglas), 1953–, author II. Title.

KE7709.2 K45 2018   342.7108'72   C2018-901475-X
                                                 C2018-901476-8
KF8205 K45 2018

We welcome comments and suggestions regarding any aspect of our publications—please feel free to contact us at news@utphighereducation.com or visit our Internet site at utorontopress.com.

North America
5201 Dufferin Street
North York, Ontario, Canada, M3H 5T8

2250 Military Road
Tonawanda, New York, USA, 14150

ORDERS PHONE: 1-800-565-9523
ORDERS FAX: 1-800-221-9985
ORDERS E-MAIL: utpbooks@utpress.utoronto.ca

UK, Ireland, and continental Europe
NBN International
Estover Road, Plymouth, PL6 7PY, UK
ORDERS PHONE: 44 (0) 1752 202301
ORDERS FAX: 44 (0) 1752 202333
ORDERS E-MAIL: enquiries@nbninternational.com

Every effort has been made to contact copyright holders; in the event of an error or omission, please notify the publisher.

The University of Toronto Press acknowledges the financial support for its publishing activities of the Government of Canada through the Canada Book Fund.

This book is printed on paper containing 100% post-consumer fibre.

Printed and bound by CPI Group (UK) Ltd, Croydon, CR0 4YY

Contents

Figures, Tables, Illustrations, and Maps

Maps

Map 0.1: Ontario Communities of the Grand General Indian Council of Ontario and Quebec

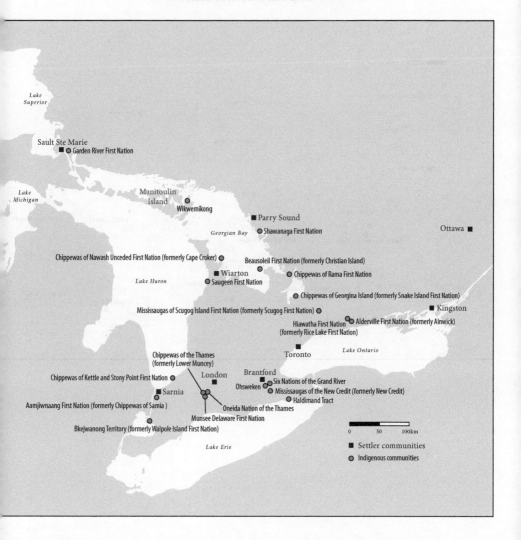

Lake Superior

Sault Ste Marie
Garden River First Nation

Lake Michigan

Manitoulin Island
Wikwemikong

Parry Sound

Georgian Bay
Shawanaga First Nation

Ottawa

Chippewas of Nawash Unceded First Nation (formerly Cape Croker)
Beausoleil First Nation (formerly Christian Island)

Wiarton
Chippewas of Rama First Nation

Lake Huron
Saugeen First Nation

Chippewas of Georgina Island (formerly Snake Island First Nation)

Mississaugas of Scugog Island First Nation (formerly Scugog First Nation)

Kingston

Hiawatha First Nation
(formerly Rice Lake First Nation)
Alderville First Nation (formerly Alnwick)

Toronto
Lake Ontario

Chippewas of the Thames
(formerly Lower Muncey)

Chippewas of Kettle and Stony Point First Nation
London
Brantford
Ohsweken
Six Nations of the Grand River
Mississaugas of the New Credit (formerly New Credit)

Sarnia
Haldimand Tract

Aamjiwnaang First Nation (formerly Chippewas of Samia)
Oneida Nation of the Thames

Munsee Delaware First Nation

Bkejwanong Territory (formerly Walpole Island First Nation)

Lake Erie

0   50   100km

■ Settler communities
◉ Indigenous communities

Map 0.2: The North-West

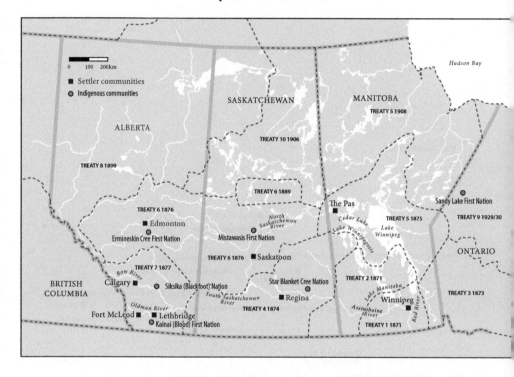

Map 0.3: Treaty 7 Communities

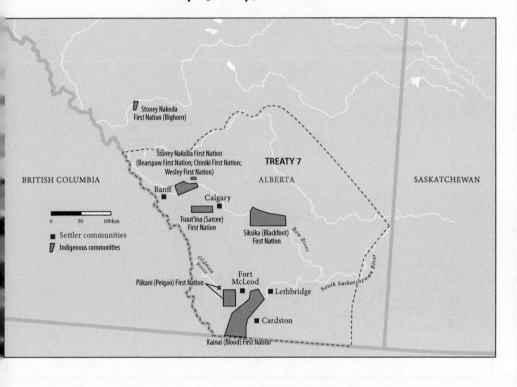

Stoney Nakoda
First Nation (Bighorn)

Stoney Nakoda First Nation
(Bearspaw First Nation; Chiniki First Nation;
Wesley First Nation)

TREATY 7

BRITISH COLUMBIA

ALBERTA

SASKATCHEWAN

Banff

Calgary

0   50   100km

Tsuut'ina (Sarcee)
First Nation

Siksika (Blackfoot)
First Nation

Bow River

■ Settler communities
▨ Indigenous communities

Oldman River

Piikani (Peigan) First Nation

Fort
McLeod

■ Lethbridge

South Saskatchewan River

■ Cardston

Kainai (Blood) First Nation

Map 0.4: Haudenosaunee Territories

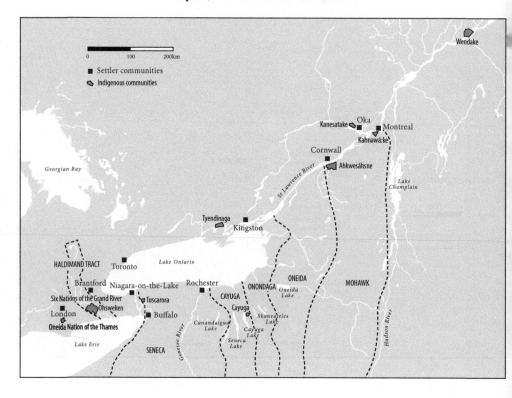

Introduction

Historians do more than simply read sources; we converse with them. We listen intently to the stories they tell and the silences they allow. We think deeply about the conversations and interchanges that brought our sources into being—the questions and anxieties, the common sense assumptions, the motives of authors and audiences. We ask questions not so much to call our sources out as false or falsifying but rather to lay bare the remnants of the past embedded within them.[1] We ask our sources to speak to us, from the context of their times, and we talk back to them from the context of our own. We can ask our sources to tell us how we got here, and we can look to our sources to reveal the pathways not taken, the roads we did not even know existed.[2] As the Truth and Reconciliation Commission (TRC) taught us, history tells us a great deal about the truths with which we live today. In order to answer fully the TRC's 94 calls to action, we must understand better Canada's historical relationship with Indigenous peoples.[3] To do so we must bring minds attuned towards historical thinking and skills developed for critically reading texts of various kinds. This textbook will offer you an opportunity to develop methods of engaging with documents in more sophisticated and sensitive ways. We take as our example in this text the Indian Act—one of the most enduring and significant pieces of legislation in Canadian history. Passed in 1876, and still in force today, the Indian Act set the course for Canada's relationships with Indigenous peoples, relationships that are embedded within the structures of settler colonialism. Settler colonialism is a variant of imperialism in which the

---

1 Ann Laura Stoler, *Along the Archival Grain: Epistemic Anxieties and Colonial Common Sense* (Princeton: Princeton University Press, 2009), 3.

2 Lynn Fendler, "The Upside of Presentism," *Paedagogica Historica* 44, no. 6 (December 2008): 677–90.

3 Truth and Reconciliation Commission (TRC), *The Final Report of the Truth and Reconciliation Commission of Canada*, vol. 1, *Canada's Residential Schools: The History, Part 1, Origins to 1939* (Montreal and Kingston: McGill-Queen's University Press, 2015).

settlers come to stay, to seek out lives and identities grounded in the colony and for whom Indigenous people, their rights to land and resources, are obstacles that must be eliminated.[4] For nearly a century and a half and through countless amendments, the Indian Act has sought to do just that—to eliminate Indigenous people through its own defining powers, to sever their connections to lands and to their families and communities, to disrupt Indigenous systems of governance, and to silence protest. Among the other settler colonies, including the United States, Australia, New Zealand, and South Africa, Canada is the only one to use a single piece of legislation to order its affairs with Indigenous people.[5] As such, the Indian Act reveals much about Canadian politics and what was acceptable to generations of Canadian parliamentarians and the Canadian people who elected them. The Indian Act is, therefore, central to Canadian history.

The Indian Act is also the most important piece of Canadian legislation affecting Indigenous people. It defines who is and who is not considered as Indian under the law. As Métis scholar Chris Andersen has written, the Indian Act has contributed to race-based policy in Canada. By labelling Métis and indeed any family seen as "half-breed" as "non-status," it defined "status Indian" as racially pure without regard for the complexity of Indigenous peoples' communities or kinship networks.[6] Although most of its interventions target those it defines as Indian, that very definition impacts all Indigenous people in Canada whether they are considered Indian or not.

The Indian Act has used gender as its primary mechanism of defining Indian status. The act, until 1985, passed Indian status through the father (patrilineally) and for over a hundred years forcibly removed status and membership in reserve communities from women who married non-Indian men. Children of non-Indian men were no longer considered Indians. Revisions to the Indian Act, intended to end the gender discrimination within it, came in 1985, but even after that date, children of women who had married non-status men before 1985 passed on a category of band membership (referred to as 6(2)) that was different than those of children of men who had married non-status women; they received

---

4 TRC, *The Final Report*, 1: 3; Adam J. Barker, "Locating Settler Colonialism," *Journal of Colonialism and Colonial History* 13, no. 3 (Winter 2012); Audra Simpson, *Mohawk Interruptus: Political Life Across the Borders of Settler States* (London and Durham: Duke University Press, 2014), 7; Bonita Lawrence, *"Real" Indians and Others: Mixed-Blood Urban Native Peoples and Indigenous Nationhood* (Vancouver: University of British Columbia Press, 2004), 7; Patrick Wolfe, *Settler Colonialism and the Transformation of Anthropology: The Politics and Poetics of an Ethnographic Event* (London and New York: Cassell, 1999); Lorenzo Veracini, *Settler Colonialism: A Theoretical Overview* (London: Palgrave Macmillan, 2010); Taiaiake Alfred, *Peace, Power, Righteousness: An Indigenous Manifesto*, 2nd ed. (Toronto: Oxford University Press, 2009), 27.

5 Lawrence, *"Real" Indians and Others*, 27; J. R. Miller, *Lethal Legacy: Current Native Controversies in Canada* (Toronto: McClelland & Stewart, 2004), 33.

6 Chris Andersen, "Mixed Ancestry or Métis," in *Indigenous Identity and Resistance: Researching the Diversity of Knowledge*, edited by Brendan Hokowhitu, Nathalie Kermoal, Chris Andersen, Anna Petersen, Michael Reilly, Isabel Altamirano-Jimenz, and Poia Rewi, 23–36 (Dunedin: University of Otago Press, 2010), 23–36, see pages 29–30; Lawrence, *"Real" Indians and Others*, 88.

6(1) status.[7] People with 6(2) status who married non-status people could not pass status on to their children. The "two-generation cut off clause," remained in place until 2010 when Bill C-3 provided a new and complicated process to apply for reinstatement.[8] Bill C-3 still excluded many from status, including grandchildren born before September 4, 1951, of those status women who married out; descendants of status women who had co-parented with non-status men in common law unions; and illegitimate children of status Indian men.[9]

In 2016, the Liberal government under Justin Trudeau introduced Bill S-3, An Act to Amend the Indian Act in response to the court case *Descheneaux v. Canada*. In *Descheneaux* (August 2015), the Superior Court of Québec agreed with plaintiffs that the Indian Act, as amended by Bill C-3, still discriminated against the descendants of Indigenous women. During legislative review, the Senate called for amendments to S-3 that would ensure that all descendants of Indigenous men and women would be entitled to full 6(1) status. The House of Commons, at first, refused to accept this amendment, but the Senate responded that it would not pass the bill by the Quebec court-imposed deadline of December 22, 2017. Faced with this stand off, the House of Commons crafted its own amendment that would end sex discrimination in the Indian Act after consultation with First Nations. That consultation period was not, however, defined. Bill S-3 passed the House of Commons on December 4, 2017 despite continued concern raised by the opposition that it would still not effectively eliminate sex discrimination. We continue to await the results of consultation and the opportunity to review the impact of Bill S-3 on Indigenous women and their descendants.[10]

7 Chelsea Vowel explains that while women who were reinstated under Bill C-31 were granted 6(1), their children were granted 6(2) status. If a 6(1) person married a 6(2) person, their children had 6(1) status; if two 6(2) people married, their children had 6(1) status; and if two 6(1) people married, their children had 6(1) status. If a 6(1) person married a non-status person their children were 6(2); if a 6(2) status person married a non-status person, their children would not have status. Therefore, as Vowel puts it, "Two generations of out-marriage. That is all it takes to completely lose status." See Chelsea Vowel, *Indigenous Writes: A Guide to First Nations, Métis and Inuit Issues in Canada* (Winnipeg: Highwater Press, 2016), 30. See also Figures 4.1 and 4.2 in Chapter 4 on the effects of bills C-31 and C-3. The *McIvor* case (included in this volume) dealt with the way that the gender discrimination of the Indian Act persisted under these membership provisions of C-31.

8 Thomas King, *The Inconvenient Indian: A Curious Account of Native People in North America* (Toronto: Doubleday Canada, 2012), 167–69.

9 Sharon McIvor to members of Parliament, May 18, 2010, in *Strange Visitors: Documents in Indigenous-Settler Relations in Canada from 1876*, edited by Keith D. Smith (Toronto: University of Toronto Press, 2014), 334–36; see also Pam Palmater, "Updated—Bill C-3—Gender Equity in Indian Registration Act," March 12, 2010, http://www.pampalmater.com/updated-bill-c-3-gender-equity-in-indian-registration-act/ (accessed on January 4, 2018).

10 Bill S-3, An Act to Amend the Indian Act in Response to the Superior Court of Quebec Decision in *Descheneaux c. Canada* (Procureur General), 1st Sess, 42nd Parl, 2017 (assented to December 12, 2017). Available online from *Openparliament.ca:* https://openparliament.ca/bills/42-1/S-3/ (accessed on January 4, 2018). See also Government of Canada, Indigenous and Northern Affairs Canada, "Are You Applying as a Grandchild of a Woman who Lost her Indian Status through Marriage?" https://www.aadnc-aandc.gc.ca/eng/1308068336912/1308068535844 (accessed on January 4, 2018); For a review of Bill S-3's process and background, see Pamela Palmater and Sharon McIvor, "The People Left Behind by Trudeau's Promised Nation-to-Nation Relationship," *Maclean's*, June 9, 2017, http://www.macleans.ca/news/canada/the-people-left-behind-by-trudeaus-promised-nation-to-nation-relationship/ (accessed January 4, 2018).

The goal of Indian Act policies of voluntary and enforced enfranchisement was to reduce the number of Indigenous people considered Indian. Indeed, even today, one of the government's stated concerns about S-3 has been that the number of Indigenous people considered status Indian would grow exponentially, from around 750,000 to as high as 12 million (though Indigenous and Northern Affairs admits that that figure is likely inflated).[11] Indigenous legal scholar Pamela Palmater writes that a 1992 study affirmed that, if the Indian Act were not amended again (this following the 1985 amendment), the people with Indian status would become extinct as a legally defined people.[12] This is what settler colonial scholars call the "logic of elimination."[13] Canadian census figures indicate the success of the Indian Act in this regard: in 2011, only 45 per cent of all people who identified as Aboriginal had Indian status.[14]

Offers of enfranchisement from the mid-nineteenth century onwards worked towards this goal. As early as 1857, the government of the combined colonies of Canada West (Ontario) and Canada East (Quebec) devised mechanisms by which Indigenous men could request citizenship provided they were sober, able to speak and write in either English or French, debt free, and willing to cease being a member of their own community—to cease being an Indian under the law. In exchange, such an individual would receive 20 hectares of land in freehold tenure from his former reserve. Only one man chose to enfranchise under this provision.[15] The Indian Act enfranchised status Indians who obtained a university degree, were admitted to the bar as lawyers, or joined the Christian clergy, as well as veterans and those who worked away from their reserve for over five years. Then, in 1920, a new amendment allowed for forcible enfranchisement. This time it was Indigenous leaders that government officials had their eye on. For example, Indian Affairs investigated F. O. Loft, Mohawk leader, veteran of World War I, and founder of the League of Indians of Canada, in an attempt to force his enfranchisement and hence to invalidate his leadership of the league. Amendments made in 1922 that eliminated these provisions prevented the government's action against Loft, but forcible enfranchisement was

11 Gloria Galloway, "Senate Backs Down from Standoff over Indian Act Amendment," *The Globe and Mail*, November 13, 2017, https://www.theglobeandmail.com/news/politics/senate-backs-down-from-standoff-over-indian-act-amendment/article36901420/ (accessed January 4, 2018).

12 Palmater and McIvor, "The People Left Behind."

13 Glen Coulthard, *Red Skin, White Masks: Rejecting the Colonial Politics of Recognition.* (Minneapolis: University of Minnesota Press, 2014), location 306, Kindle; Patrick Wolfe, "Settler Colonialism and the Elimination of the Native," *Journal of Genocide Studies* 8, no. 4 (2006): 387–409.

14 Vowel, *Indigenous Writes*, 28.

15 Canada, Royal Commission on Aboriginal Peoples, *Report on the Royal Commission on Aboriginal Peoples*, vol. 1, *Looking Forward, Looking Back* (Ottawa: The Commission, 1996), chapter 9. This chapter, entitled "The Indian Act," is available online at http://www.collectionscanada.gc.ca/webarchives/20061209130351/http://www.ainc-inac.gc.ca/ch/rcap/sg/sgm9_e.html (accessed October 15, 2016). Future notes to the Royal Commission on Aboriginal Peoples will use RCAP.

back in the Indian Act in 1933 and stayed until 1951.[16] At that time, a register of Indians was established that codified the previous generations' history of enfranchisement.[17]

The Indian Act also sought to break down extended family ties, community bonds, and Indigenous collective identities. To this end, the Indian Act invalidated Indigenous systems of inheritance and of community membership.[18] Such systems include matrilineal or bilateral descent, clan affiliation that might transcend or bisect other political or social organizational membership, and robust mechanisms of adoption. Extended families had no place in the world legislated by the Indian Act.[19] The Indian Act interfered with inheritance by making the superintendent of Indian Affairs responsible for probating the wills of status Indians. This power was immense, as it allowed Indian Affairs officials to determine who had rights of kinship and to deny wives the right to inherit moveable property from their husbands, thus impoverishing them. From birth, when being registered as an Indian determined one's life course, to death, when the government supervised inheritance, the Indian Act oversaw and intervened intimately in the lives of Indigenous people defined as Indian.

The Indian Act has been used to determine how lands reserved for status Indians could be allocated, used, or alienated. No one but an "Indian of the band" could live on a reserve without government permission. No private enterprise could place a lien on reserve land, and no provincial or municipal government could tax that land. Individuals could not sell or give any portion of their reserve away.[20] These provisions protected the reserve land base from individual settler intrusion. As Secwepemc leader George Manuel put it, "The main value of the Act from our point of view was that it was the one legal protection of our lands, and spelled out the basic rights and privileges of living on the reserve. But it also included a price tag."[21] That price tag was government control over the use and alienation of reserve lands.

The federal government held considerable power over how reserve lands could be used. For example, Indian Commissioner for the North-West Territories Hayter Reed thought that Indigenous people should learn to farm but not

16 RCAP, vol. 1, chapter 9; John Leslie and Ron Maguire, *The Historical Development of the Indian Act* (Ottawa: Indian and Northern Affairs, 1978), 118–25.

17 Miller, *Lethal Legacy*, 37–38; Lawrence, *"Real" Indians and Others*, 53–63.

18 After 1985, band councils have been able to set up their own membership rules, but this process remains controversial, in part because of the contested nature of band governance more generally and in part because Indigenous people contend that the individuals making these rules are affected by over a century of colonization and missionization and do not necessarily make rules that reflect traditional forms of governance and membership. See Andersen, "Mixed Ancestry," 29–30.

19 Kim Anderson, *Life Stages and Native Women: Memory, Teachings, and Story Medicine* (Winnipeg: University of Manitoba Press, 2011), 29; John Leslie and Ron Maguire, *The Historical Development of the Indian Act*, 118–25; RCAP, vol. 1, chapter 9.

20 RCAP, vol. 1, chapter 9.

21 George Manuel and Michael Posluns, *The Fourth World: An Indian Reality* (Don Mills: Collier-Macmillan Canada, Ltd., 1974), 123, cited by RCAP, vol. 1, chapter 9.

with the modern machinery of the late nineteenth century. So he prohibited Indian bands on the Prairies from cultivating more than a few acres to obviate the need for machinery and to make sure that they would not be in a position to sell their surplus in competition with local settler farmers.[22] The Indian Act still contains archaic provisions that demand government permission for minor matters affecting the use of the land—for example, preventing the sale of topsoil by reserves.[23] Even worse, while the Indian Act prohibited individuals from selling reserve land, amendments after 1894 gave the federal government authority to alienate reserve lands as it saw fit under certain conditions. An amendment to the Indian Act in 1894 allowed the superintendent general of Indian Affairs to lease any land being held by a widow, orphan, or physically incapacitated Indian without their consent. In 1906, the Indian Act facilitated the surrender of reserve lands adjacent to a municipality, and in 1911 appropriation of reserve land was allowed without the consent of the band council, for any land needed for the development of public works, or by a judge, for any land thought too close to a municipality with a population of 8,000 or more. In 1919, the superintendent of Indian Affairs could grant mining companies the surface rights to reserve lands even if the band council had refused. That same year, Indians returning from World War I could also be granted a location ticket to lands on their reserve in lieu of the 160 acres promised to non-Indian veterans in the Soldier Settlement Act. By governing reserve lands, the Indian Act had the power to both protect and break up that land base.[24]

The Indian Act undermined Indigenous sovereignty in other ways as well, attacking both collective and individual self-determination. Determined to break Indigenous collective resistance, the Indian Act sought to remake Indigenous governance completely and to place it under the control of the superintendent general of Indian Affairs and the Department of Indian Affairs' staff. It legislated an elected band council system on Indigenous people east of the Great Lakes in 1884, having already stipulated that wherever an elected band

---

22   Sarah Carter, *Lost Harvests: Prairie Indian Reserve Farmers and Government Policy* (Montreal and Kingston: McGill-Queen's University Press, 1990); Sarah Carter, "Two Acres and a Cow: 'Peasant' Farming for the Indians of the Northwest, 1889–1897," in *Sweet Promises: A Reader in Indian-White Relations in Canada*, edited by J. R. Miller (Toronto: University of Toronto Press, 1991), 353–80, see page 80.

23   For an artful depiction of the kinds of limitations the Indian Act puts on the uses of reserve lands see CBC's *8th Fire: Aboriginal Peoples, Canada and the Way Forward*, which can be found online at http://www.cbc.ca/8thfire//2011/11/tv-series-8th-fire.html (accessed June 29, 2018).

24   John L. Tobias, "Protection, Civilization, Assimilation: An Outline History of Canada's Indian Policy," in *Sweet Promises: A Reader on Indian-White Relations in Canada*, edited by J. R. Miller (Toronto: University of Toronto Press, 1991), 127–44; Leslie and Maguire, *The Historical Development of the Indian Act* 114; Keith D. Smith, *Liberalism, Surveillance and Resistance: Indigenous Communities in Western Canada, 1877–1927* (Edmonton: Athabasca University Press, 2009), 228–29.

council was in place, traditional leaders would have no authority.[25] Only men were given the right to vote in band council elections (in 1884, only elected band council members could vote for the chief). This effectively eliminated women from any decision-making authority and excluded the traditional political entities of the confederacy or the clan from playing an official political role. Eventually, the elected band council system was forced onto treaty and status Indians in Western Canada. The terms of band governments were (and are) limited, and the scope of their authority even more so. Told in 1876 to make rules enforcing public health measures, for example, band councils were given little authority to enforce such rules. Later amendments provided for the levying of fines and imprisonment, but with the appointment of Indian agents, authority continued to rest principally in the hands of government officials.[26] On the Prairies, Indian agents virtually appointed band councils. Everywhere, the Indian Act empowered agents to depose any elected official they did not like, though the wishes of Indian agents were sometimes turned down by their Indian Affairs superiors.

Through the Indian Act and the powers it granted them to enforce Canadian law, Indian agents had unprecedented authority in the lives of Indigenous peoples. By enforcing the vagrancy laws of the Criminal Code and the trespass provisions of the Indian Act, they could expel anyone they considered a non-resident from the reserve. They applied rules prohibiting drinking alcohol, going to pool rooms, participating in local festivities, and dressing in ceremonial attire. After 1920, the act made residential schooling compulsory, and Indian agents along with police constables were the ones to collect and transport unwilling students.[27] Anishinaabe legal scholar John Borrows writes of the limestone brick house of the Indian agent on his Saugeen reserve, of its two-sided porch and impressive architecture, meant to symbolize and facilitate the agent's surveillance of the reserve, its residents, and its chief, who lived on the opposite side of the harbour.[28]

---

25 Legislation was only part of the story, however; enforcement was uneven and Indigenous leaders responded to attempts to shape governance creatively. Martha Elizabeth Walls, *No Need of a Chief for This Band: The Maritime Mi'kmaq and Federal Electoral Legislation, 1899–1951* (Vancouver: UBC Press, 2011); Gerald F. Reid, "To Renew Our Fire: Political Activism, Nationalism, and Identity in Three Rotinonhsionni Communities," in *Tribal Worlds: Critical Studies in American Indian Nation-Building*, edited by Brian Hosmer and Larry Nesper (Albany: State University of New York, 2013), 37–64.

26 Leslie and Maguire, *The Historical Development of the Indian Act*, 66; "Grand Indian Council of the Province of Ontario Held at Sarnia, June 27th, 1879," *Wiarton Echo*, August 15, August 29, September 5, September 12, September 19, 1879; Chandra Murdock has shown that the government was much more willing to heed the demands of Indian agents for legislation that granted them more powers than to Indigenous leaders who expressed desire for more local control over their affairs. Chandra Murdoch, "Reactions to Enactment: Suggestions from Reserves to Amend the *Indian Act* and the Expansion of Legal Power for Indian Agents, 1858–1906" (unpublished paper presented to the Canadian Historical Association, Ryerson University, Toronto, 2017, cited with permission of the author).

27 Keith D. Smith, *Liberalism, Surveillance, and Resistance*, 105–108.

28 John Borrows, *Drawing Out Law: A Spirit's Guide* (Toronto: University of Toronto Press, 2010), 18.

Finally, the Indian Act sought to undermine Indigenous governance and sovereignty by prohibiting the ceremonies through which leadership is affirmed, wealth redistributed, and healing accomplished. In 1884, an amendment thus outlawed the potlatch and the tamanawas, or winter dancing. Though scholars tell us that prosecuting communities and individuals for these practices was difficult and at times impossible, in 1922, Kwakwaka'wakw Dan Cranmer and 49 others were convicted of violating the Indian Act by hosting a potlatch on Village Island (Memkumlis). The convicted were sentenced to six months of Oakalla prison, and Indian Agent William Halliday brokered a deal, contrary to any existing legal process, with some family members to barter their potlatch regalia in exchange for reduced sentences. Even when prosecutions did not occur, Indigenous people nevertheless changed the nature of their ceremonies in order to avoid attracting the attention of the Indian agent. Potlatches and sun dances (outlawed in 1895 by an amendment to section 114 of the Indian Act) became abbreviated, movable feasts; watchmen were posted outside the longhouses to alert winter dancers of the approach of colonial authorities.[29] Others simply turned their backs on the old ways. Having learned the lessons taught in residential schools and by missionaries, they simply ceased resisting the pressure to conform, to assimilate. The Indian Act infiltrated every aspect of Indigenous peoples' lives.

Yet the act remains surprisingly understudied, resistant to substantial revision, and largely unknown to non-Indigenous Canadians. This too is connected to the logic of elimination, for Canadians exhibit a particular blindness towards Indigenous people and the policies our government has directed toward them—as Tragically Hip frontman Gord Downie put it, they are the people "that we were trained our entire lives to ignore."[30] Political scientist Michael Morden argues that everyone associated with the Indian Act—Indigenous leaders who now owe their authority to it and even those sincerely attempting to reform it—are tainted by the anger and frustration it provokes.[31] The Indian Act has produced an enduring social order and identities for those covered by this legislation, those excluded by it, and those who benefit from it.[32] It is as deeply Canadian

---

29 Tina Loo, "Dan Cranmer's Potlatch: Law as Coercion, Symbol, and Rhetoric in British Columbia, 1884–1951," *Canadian Historical Review* 73, no. 2 (1992): 125–65; Katherine Pettipas, *Severing the Ties that Bind: Government Repression of Indigenous Religious Ceremonies on the Prairies* (Winnipeg: University of Manitoba Press, 1994); Douglas Cole and Ira Chaikin, *An Iron Hand Upon the People: The Law Against the Potlatch on the Northwest Coast* (Vancouver: UBC Press, 1990).

30 Andree Lau and Ron Nurwisah, "Gord Downie Uses Tragically Hip Concert to Spur Trudeau on First Nations," *Huffington Post Canada*, August 20, 2016, http://www.huffingtonpost.ca/2016/08/20/gord-downie-trudeau-first-nations-aboriginal_n_11635148.html (accessed October 15, 2016); Barker, "Locating Settler Colonialism."

31 Michael Morden, "Theorizing the Resilience of the Indian Act," *Canadian Public Administration* 59, no. 1 (2016): 113–33, see page 126.

32 Taiaiake Alfred and Jeff Corntassel, "Being Indigenous: Resurgences Against Contemporary Colonialism," *Government and Opposition* 40, no. 4 (2005): 587–614.

as it comes, and as Indigenous studies scholar Bonita Lawrence wrote, "almost entirely naturalized."[33] The Indian Act begs for historical analysis.

We also chose the Indian Act for this textbook because it generated so many other historical sources. Administering the Indian Act produced an enormous archive. Indian agents wrote countless letters to the Department of Indian Affairs asking for clarification, reporting on how they were implementing the act, and complaining when their attempts to do so went awry. Indigenous people protested the act, composing letters, petitions, and radio addresses explaining their concerns and participating in government-appointed bodies set to review and revise the legislation. Indigenous women brought the government to court over the gender bias of the Indian Act. Indigenous people were prosecuted under the Indian Act, and these cases resulted in police and court records. Missionaries, schoolteachers, merchants, and landowners, amid a host of other ordinary Canadians, all had, and expressed, opinions about the Indian Act when they became aware of it. Administering the Indian Act required an immense amount of surveillance of Indigenous people, and those observations were recorded and archived.[34] If there was ever a single piece of legislation that would generate enough records to keep historians, and history students, busy reading and analysing for years to come, we thought it was the Indian Act.

In this text, we are putting the Indian Act, not Indigenous people, under the microscope. But it is not a history of the Indian Act, either. Rather, we are organizing a set of lessons in interpretation around sections of the Indian Act and the documents that it generated. In particular, we are bringing together historical thinking, Indigenous methodologies, and intersectional analysis (taking into consideration gender and other social cleavages) to help students develop sophisticated methods for reading the archives of settler colonialism in Canada.

Good Things to Think With: Historical Thinking, Intersectionality, and Indigenous Methodologies

In response to the question "What does it mean to think historically?" historian educators Thomas Andrews and Flannery Burke listed five concepts that are the keystones to historical understanding. These are change over time, context, causality, contingency, and complexity—the 5 Cs. Questions that use these concepts as springboards inspire our own interpretations of the past and offer a quick checklist to students interested in developing their own analysis of primary sources. At the beginning of each grouping of documents that follows in this text, we will provide some specific questions that will guide interpretation

---

33 Lawrence, *"Real" Indians and Others*, 25.
34 Jean M. O'Brien, "Historical Sources and Methods in Indigenous Studies: Touching on the Past, Looking to the Future," in *Sources and Methods in Indigenous Studies*, edited by Chris Andersen and Jean M. O'Brien (New York and London: Routledge, 2017), 15–22, see pages 19–20.

and, where necessary, additional information to help answer those questions. For now, we want simply to provide some illustrative examples of how the 5 Cs can aid us in understanding better the Indian Act and its place in settler colonial Canada and in the lives of Indigenous peoples.

Change over Time

One of the aspects of the history of the Indian Act that is so important, given that we tend to think of the order it has produced as almost natural, is that it *has* changed over time. Indeed, if we consider the nearly constant stream of amendments over the years, the Indian Act appears to be constantly changing. What does this string of amendments signify? Most certainly, they were the result of dissatisfaction with the act, either because it went too far or because it did not go far enough, fast enough. On the matter of enfranchisement, for example, the act went too far for Ontario members of Parliament. They noted, in 1879, that giving voting rights to enfranchised Indians in their province violated the Ontario Election Act, which prevented all Indians from voting, whether they held fee simple property or not.[35] And yet, on the same issue, legislation had been too sluggish a mechanism. Indigenous resistance to assimilation was met by the granting of greater authority for officers of the Indian Affairs Department, and so amendments in 1881 extended their judicial powers so that they became ex-officio justices of the peace and magistrates with jurisdiction over reserve communities.[36] Aware of mounting tensions in the north-west, in 1884 the government amended the Indian Act to prohibit the "sale, gift or other disposal" of fixed ammunition or ball cartridges to Indigenous people "in the Province of Manitoba . . . or in the North West" and punished those with jail sentences who were proven to have incited a riot or to have dealt with an agent of the government in a "riotous, routous, disorderly or threatening manner." Also in 1884, the Macdonald government added new clauses prohibiting the potlatch and the tamanawas (winter dances) in an effort to suppress Indigenous cultures and governance in British Columbia. This was done at the behest of missionaries who sought to use the new legislation to enforce the cultural change they could not accomplish through mere suasion.[37] The nearly annual amendments to the Indian Act offer us an opportunity to study the government's shifting response to conditions, to mark out the limits of its control, and to discern Indigenous peoples' resistance, through the language of anxiety expressed by government officials and their amendments. But just as we must ask about change over time, Cherokee writer Thomas King reminds us not to lose sight of the continuity in Indian policy. Throughout all these changes, the eliminatory intent of government stayed the same. So too did its claim to

---

35 Leslie and Maguire, *Historical Development of the Indian Act*, 75. Fee simple property is recognized in law as being held through the most absolute type of ownership.

36 Leslie and Maguire, *Historical Development of the Indian Act*, 79; Smith, *Liberalism, Surveillance, and Resistance*, 108–10.

37 Leslie and Maguire, *Historical Development of the Indian Act*, 75–83.

have the authority to control the reserve land base, the definition of "Indian," and reserve governance.[38] As we examine our sources, we need to be alert to both change and continuity.

Context

The Indian Act did not come out of nowhere, and its context, at least initially, was one of failure and anxiety. Previous acts, including the Gradual Civilization Act of 1857 and the Gradual Enfranchisement Act of 1869 had done little to encourage Indigenous people to integrate into Canadian society. In the 1870s, British Columbia obstreperously refused to get in line with Ottawa's dictates on Indian land, and unrest on the Prairies was a reminder that Métis and First Nations had their own ideas of sovereignty and land rights, which were quite at odds with the provisions of the British North America Act that gave the federal government sole responsibility for Indigenous peoples and their lands.

Macdonald's rise to power and Confederation itself rested on the promise of a continental rail link and land opened for settlement across the Prairies. His successor, Alexander Mackenzie, elected in 1873, sought to mark out his own path in Indian policy and yet was equally committed to Confederation and western settlement. An overarching Indian Act that would be the legislative expression of Ottawa's primacy in matters relating to Indigenous people seemed appropriate.

There were contradictions, too, in the Indian policy that the federal government enacted at this time. The Indian Act was passed in the midst of treaty talks on the Prairies, talks that First Nations understood as recognizing their sovereignty and asking them to share their land and resources with incoming settlers. We can only imagine their surprise when they learned that, under the Indian Act, they had become wards of the state. Yet treaty making, with all its promises of support to Indigenous people as they transitioned to new economies, also motivated the government to try to limit the scope of those promises by restricting who might be considered an Indian. One of the most immediate limitations came through the 1879 amendment and the 1880 Indian Act that established separate policies for Indian and Métis people and encouraged any Métis who might have been included in a treaty to withdraw from it and to receive scrip instead. Receiving scrip annulled the government of any further obligations.[39] Further mechanisms of enfranchisement similarly reduced the number of people for whom the government had responsibility for the provision of schools, relief, and other services, including health care.

Widening the lens of context and casting our gaze beyond Canada's borders reveals the uniqueness of the Indian Act among settler colonies. Though

---

38 King, *The Inconvenient Indian*, xi.
39 Leslie and Maguire, *Historical Development of the Indian Act*, 77. Scrip can be defined as a document certifying that the recipient is owed something; in this case, it was comparable to an IOU issued by the government, documenting that the government owed public land to the recipient.

Australia and the United States both developed rules to determine Aboriginal or Indian status, no other country used a single act to govern the lives of Indigenous people so totally. As we consider this transnational context, we can ask ourselves why Canada took this approach. Historians use context to help them understand why events occurred the way they did, and we will help you ask questions that will set the documents included below in context.

Causality

Sketching context, however, is not the same as understanding causality. Historical actors have choices, and they are not blindly driven by circumstances. There are not always straight lines between cause and effect in history, and, as often as not, actions are caused by a number of sometimes contradictory factors. Considering causality allows us to think about the intentions of policymakers and the choices they had, or thought they had, before them. Canadian policymakers had two precedents from which they could choose at the time the Indian Act was framed—British and American.[40] British policy, best articulated in the North American colonial context through the Royal Proclamation of 1763, was that all land cessions by Indigenous people had to be made solely to the Crown, preferably in advance of settlement. Through the British North America Act (1867), the Crown's authority to treat with Indigenous people and to administer their affairs rested with the federal government. They could choose to exercise that power through treaty making and overarching administration or not.

Policies pursued south of the border offered other choices. In the United States, settlement proceeded in advance of treaty making, resulting in conflict that cost thousands of Indigenous peoples and settlers their lives, and the government $20 million each year.[41] Following the American Civil War, the administration of Ulysses S. Grant put forward a new policy under the direction of the Commission of Indian Affairs, headed by Ely S. Parker (Seneca). The resultant "peace policy" negotiated land cession treaties; placed Indigenous people on reservations where they would be instructed in farming, domestic management, Christianity, and American values; and appointed Indian agents to oversee them. The American government also chose to delegate much of its services to Indigenous people to the Christian churches, and, as often as not in this period, Indian agents were missionaries. The emergent system was rife with corruption, and by 1871, Congress declared an end to treaty making, the end of the peace policy, and the movement of control from the Indian Office to the government-appointed Board of Indian Commissioners. Reservations, Indian agents (now government employees, not missionaries), and a host of

---

40 There were others, of course, set in other British settler colonies, but these offered more in the way of variation rather than alternative choices. For example, the British colonial office negotiated the Treaty of Waitangi (1840) with the Maori in advance of settlement.

41 J. R. Miller, *Compact, Contract, Covenant: Aboriginal Treaty-Making in Canada* (Toronto: University of Toronto, 2009), 156.

other personnel whose job it was to encourage assimilation were left in place.[42] The precedent of British imperial policy, linked to the lessons of American Indian policy, shaped Canadian initiatives.

But there were other factors closer to home. The collapse of the buffalo economy on the plains at once encouraged Indigenous people to sign treaties in the 1870s and burdened the federal government with significant responsibility to provide for the people now left without means of support. At the same time, a global economic downturn further fuelled the fears of the frugal Liberal government under Alexander Mackenzie.[43] As reluctant as the federal government was in assuming that responsibility in the long term, it nonetheless needed an administrative infrastructure on the ground, and fast. The Indian Act and the Department of Indian Affairs did just that. Once this infrastructure was in place, the promise of services, and of relief, and the withholding of those services then gave Canada phenomenal powers of persuasion in the field, forcing Cree leaders, for example, from lands they chose for their reserve to other, less desirable land of the government's choosing.[44] Needs and opportunities then acted also as causal factors. Thinking about causation further helps historians to understand the direct and sometimes indirect connections between events, people, circumstances, and actions.

Contingency

The fourth C—contingency—brings the interconnectedness of people and of actions into focus and sometimes offers us an opportunity to imagine different outcomes. Although this concept is perhaps the most difficult to understand, we have poignant examples to draw on when we consider the Indian Act and its effects. Take Indian schools, for example. During the treaty talks of the 1870s, Indigenous leaders repeatedly sought schooling for their children. They wanted their children to be able to read and write, to be able to negotiate with government officials without translators or mediators, to be able to manage their funds, and to interact on an equal basis with the settlers they knew were coming. Canada's first post-Confederation treaty, aptly named Treaty 1, included the promise of a school for each reserve where such was desired. By Treaty 6 and Treaty 7 (negotiated in 1876 and 1877, respectively), the promise had shifted from one of schools to one of teachers. While Indigenous parents asked for schools in their communities, the government now pledged only to pay for teachers. The intentions of government and the aspirations of Indigenous parents had begun to diverge.

---

42 Francis Paul Prucha, *American Indian Policy in Crisis: Christian Reformers and the Indian, 1865–1900* (Norman: University of Oklahoma Press, 1975); Roxanne Dunbar Ortiz, *An Indigenous History of the United States* (Boston: Beacon Press, 2014), 142; Thomas King, *The Inconvenient Indian,* 220.

43 Miller, *Compact, Contract, Covenant,* 175–81.

44 James Daschuk, *Clearing the Plains: Disease, Politics of Starvation, and the Loss of Aboriginal Life* (Regina: University of Regina Press, 2013), 122.

As early as the 1840s, the government of Canada was reviewing the work of religious organizations, such as the Methodist Church, in building and operating schools in Indigenous communities. By the end of the 1870s, the federal government was looking south of the border for examples of the kinds of schools that might produce assimilated graduates.[45] In 1879, Nicholas Davin submitted his report recommending residential schooling. As the TRC has proven, residential schooling was an attack on Indigenous children, their families, their nations, their languages, cultures, and spirituality.[46] This was not the kind of education that Indigenous treaty signatories expected. Not surprisingly, parents were reluctant to send their children to these schools. It appeared that residential schooling was a failure.

Deputy Superintendent General Hayter Reed did not see the failure as lying with the schools but rather with the parents and sought legislative means to force them to send their children to residential schools. In 1894, new regulations came in as an amendment of the Indian Act that proclaimed attendance compulsory, but only for those children who had been involuntarily committed to the schools. In 1920, the Indian Act was amended to include all students between the ages of 7 and 15.[47] Such an amendment would never have been required had the schools established for Indigenous people met their clearly stated needs. As with other amendments to the Indian Act, this amendment shows not so much the success of Indian policy but rather its failure. As we consider the history of compulsory residential schooling, we can take the chance to ask important "what if" questions. What if Indigenous people had been able to build the schools they wanted, to get the kind of education they desired? How might a more appropriate education system have changed Canada's relationships with Indigenous people? What if the Indian Act amendment that forced attendance in residential schools had never been necessary? Or if it had never been passed? Understanding how the actions of residential school principals and teachers, as well as of the Christian churches that hired them, resulted in changes to government policy highlights how each party's actions were *contingent* upon those of the other. Andrew Woolford, in his book *This Benevolent Experiment*, argues that the residential schools and the policies and practices that supported them were a kind of mesh in which Indigenous people were ensnared. Contingency helps us see the strands of that mesh.[48]

Contingency comes to the fore in another way. The archives we use to construct historical knowledge are themselves contingent.[49] Government archives keep records necessary for the work of government; church archives

---

45 Truth and Reconciliation Commission (TRC), *The Final Report*, 1: 72–82, 179–90.

46 TRC, *The Final Report*, 1: 162–67.

47 TRC, *The Final Report*, 1: 278.

48 Andrew Woolford, *This Benevolent Experiment: Indigenous Boarding Schools, Genocide, and Redress in Canada and the United States* (Winnipeg: University of Manitoba Press, 2015), 42.

49 Alice Te Punge Somerville, "'I Do Still Have a Letter': Our Sea of Archives," in *Sources and Methods in Indigenous Studies*, edited by Chris Andersen and Jean M. O'Brien (New York and London: Routledge, 2017), 121–28.

record the work of the church. For many years, scholars probed these archives, finding evidence of *some* of the violence of residential schooling: Kuper Island Residential School on Penelakut Island in British Columbia, for example, kept a "conduct book" that was, essentially, a log of punishments, including corporal punishment. But church and government records described mainly the day-to-day running of the schools.[50] Government and church archives were never meant to hold the history of the residential schools from the point of view of Indigenous people. It was only when scholars started listening to residential school survivors themselves that a more complex view of the schools emerged in mainstream history. The work of the TRC massively reoriented that history from one based on the records kept by the bodies that ran the schools to one based in the knowledge of those who endured them.

Complexity

All of this leads us, of course, to the fifth C—complexity. National myths—like the one that portrays Canada as a peaceable kingdom—have a tendency to shape more complex realities into a neat and compelling narrative. Until recently, Canadians were taught a history in which Canadians, as settlers, were the ones to decolonize, to win greater and greater sovereignty from Great Britain. Canadians have not perceived themselves to be colonizers. And yet the Indian Act shows that the Canadian government was very willing to make laws that would intervene in the lives of Indigenous peoples, even though those people could not vote for the governments that made these laws. Canada took control of the lands and resources of Indigenous peoples with or without treaties and then administered them without their consent. All of these practices are consistent with the methods of settler colonialism. As we recall Canada's colonial history, then, it behoves us to ensure that we include Indigenous histories in a more complicated narration of Canada's past.

At the same time, we must also remember that the categories of settler and Indigenous peoples that are at the heart of settler colonialism are themselves complicated and capacious. The Indian Act created the category Indian, status and non-status. It navigated around and ultimately rejected Métis as a subset of Indian, and, of course, it did not create the concept of "indigeneity," defined simply as being "indigenous" to a particular place place.[51] There were always families, relationships, and kin that exceeded the narrowing definitions put forward by the Indian Act. By building its identity politics on patriarchy, the Indian Act privileged the relationships of men as the way status was determined. Non-Indigenous women who married status Indian men gained status,

---

50 Kuper Island Industrial School fonds, "Conduct Book," 1891–1906, British Columbia Archives, MS-1267.38, volumes 38–9.

51 Alfred and Corntassel, "Being Indigenous"; Aileen Moreton-Robinson, "Introduction: Critical Indigenous Theory," *Cultural Studies Review* 15, no. 2 (2009): 11–12; Robert Warrior, "Native American Scholarship and the Transnational Turn," *Cultural Studies Review* 15, no. 2 (2009): 119–30.

making their children Indian as well. Indian Affairs officials did not necessarily like this result. Mid-nineteenth century and late twentieth century activist women became members of reserve communities, taking on their home communities concerns and ensuring that their children learned the culture and language of their fathers and their fathers' communities. Pauline Johnson is an example of one such child made Indian under the Indian Act who, embracing her Haudenosaunee heritage, became a prominent spokesperson on behalf of Indigenous peoples across the country. She used the Indian Act to talk back effectively to government.[52]

We also have an opportunity to see the complexity of the Indian Act's work, and to challenge that work, by adopting what critical race theorist Kimberle Crenshaw named as intersectional analysis. Such an analysis puts front and centre how systems of oppression, including sexism, racism, homophobia, and colonialism, work together.[53] We have already seen how deeply sexist the Indian Act is, but by virtue of recognizing only heterosexual marriage, it obscured lesbian, gay, bisexual, transgendered, queer, and two-spirited (LGBTQ2) identities and relations. This limited the reach of the Indian Act by refusing to police these relationships, but because the act also creates identities, it worked in tandem with the Christian churches to silence LGBTQ2 identities and relations within Indigenous communities.

A complex, intersectional analysis also allows us to see how individuals and communities might be oppressed and privileged at the same time. On the surface, Indigenous men would seem to benefit from the Indian Act, but a closer look shows us that they, too, have been profoundly and negatively affected by colonization and the heteronormative, patriarchal systems it introduced.[54] Critical Indigenous masculinity studies, moreover, trace how colonial cultures of schooling, sport, and violence overwrote Indigenous masculinities into forms dysfunctional for community life. Indigenous gender analysis asks that we be alert to non-binary and reciprocal gendered identities, both past and present, and to be aware of how policies such as the Indian Act shaped identities rooted in gender, socio-economic status, sexuality, and ability, as well as in racialization.[55] So as we examine the Indian Act and the historical documents that it generated, we need to be alert to complexity lest we, too, seek refuge in too-easy stories about the past.

---

52 Carole Gerson and Veronica Strong-Boag, *Paddling Her Own Canoe: The Times and Texts of E. Pauline Johnson-Tekahionwake* (Toronto: University of Toronto Press, 2000).

53 Kimberle Crenshaw, "Mapping the Margins: Intersectionality, Identity Politics, and Violence against Women of Color," *Stanford Law Review* 43, no. 6 (July 1991): 1241–99.

54 Robert Alexander Innis and Kim Anderson, *Indigenous Men and Masculinities: Legacies, Identities, Regeneration* (Winnipeg: University of Manitoba Press, 2015), 11.

55 Brendan Hokowhitu, "History and Masculinity," in *Sources and Methods in Indigenous Studies*, edited by Chris Andersen and Jean M. O'Brien (London and New York: Routledge, 2017), 194–204.

Indigenous Methodologies: Relationship, Responsibility, Respect, Reciprocity

Our historical methods, developed as they were in academic settings, are well suited to interpreting the Indian Act as a piece of settler colonial legislation. The Indian Act, meant as it is to separate Indigenous from settler people, acts as a gatekeeper between these two worlds. As such, it lives in both settler and Indigenous spheres. To use only historical methods to analyse the Indian Act would be to ignore this fact. Fortunately, Indigenous scholars have introduced their own methodologies to the academy in the last twenty years. Although Indigenous methodologies are principally meant to shape research done today, to decolonize Western methodologies so that research can challenge (or talk back to) the colonizing relationships in which we live, scholars are also profitably using them to analyse archival documents as well.[56] Indigenous methodologies offer up four touchstones to help shape the questions we ask our sources: relationship, responsibility, respect, and reciprocity—the 4 Rs.[57]

Relationship

As Lakota scholar Vine Deloria, Jr., famously wrote,

> "We are all relatives" when taken as a methodological tool for obtaining knowledge means that we observe the natural world by looking for relationships between various things in it. That is to say, everything in the natural world has relationships with every other thing and the total set of relationships makes up the natural world as we experience it. This concept is simply the relativity concept as applied to a universe that people experience as alive and not as dead or inert.[58]

Indigenous scholars from around the world emphasize that relationships— recognizing them, renewing them, honouring them—are central to Indigenous

---

56 Heidi Stark, "Respect, Responsibility, and Renewal: The Foundations of Anishinaabe Treaty Making with the United States and Canada," *American Indian Culture and Research Journal* 34, no. 2 (January 1, 2010): 145–64; Aileen Moreton-Robinson, "Relationality: A Key Presupposition of an Indigenous Social Research Paradigm," in *Sources and Methods in Indigenous Studies*, edited by Chris Andersen and Jean M. O'Brien (London and New York: Routledge, 2017), 69–77, see page 69.

57 Linda Tuhiwai Smith, *Decolonizing Methodologies: Research and Indigenous Peoples*. 2nd ed. (London and New York: Zed Books, 2012); Margaret Kovach, *Indigenous Methodologies: Characteristics, Conversations, and Contexts* (Toronto: University of Toronto Press, 2009); Bagele Chilisa, *Indigenous Research Methodologies* (London: Sage, 2012); Shawn Wilson, *Research Is Ceremony: Indigenous Research Methods* (Halifax and Winnipeg: Fernwood, 2008); Paulette Regan, *Unsettling the Settler Within: Indian Residential Schools, Truth Telling and Reconciliation in Canada* (Vancouver: UBC Press, 2011).

58 Vine Deloria, Jr., "Relativity, Relatedness, and Reality," in *Spirit and Reason: The Vine Deloria, Jr., Reader*, edited by B. Deloria, K. Foehner, and S. Scinta (Golden, Colorado: Fulcrum Publishing, 1999), 32–39, see page 34.

ways of knowing, ways of being, and ways of making ethical decisions.[59] Historical documents can seem detached from such relationships, but understanding how they and the people who created them were enmeshed in relationships offers important insights to historians.

Relationship with the land is foundational for Indigenous people, and acquiring land was the key goal of settler colonialism, so conflict was inevitable. The Indian Act was meant to mediate that conflict, but always with a view to making more land available for individual allotment within reserve communities and for settlement beyond reserve boundaries.[60] Settler colonial policy, and the Indian Act in particular, did not acknowledge that for Indigenous people, land was not a commodity to be bought and sold but an entity with which they were in a sacred trust relationship. As the Treaty Elders of Manitoba tell us, the belief in the "sacred special relationship with the land," is second only in importance to the belief in the Creator.[61] Relationships with the land extend as well to the animals and spirit beings that reside on lands and in waters, in the sacred places within Indigenous territories. Without an awareness of such beliefs and values, we cannot fully understand Indigenous protest over allotment and alienation. At the same time, the Indian Act offered some protection of the reserve land base by prohibiting sales of land without band council approval or the inheritance of land by non-band members. As such, it offered some protection of those important relationships to the land. Partly for these reasons, Indigenous leadership stopped the Pierre Trudeau government from abolishing the Indian Act when it proposed to do so with the 1969 White Paper. As the Indian Chiefs of Alberta began their response to the White Paper, "To us who are Treaty Indians there is nothing more important than our Treaties, our lands and the well being of our future generation."[62] Relationship to the land, relationship to future generations—this is what motivated their reaction to the White Paper.

---

59 Moreton-Robinson, "Relationality," 69, 71, 73; K. Tsianina Lomawaima, "Mind, Heart, Hands: Thinking, Feeling, and Doing in Indigenous History Methodology," in *Sources and Methods in Indigenous Studies*, 60–68; Kovach, *Indigenous Methodologies*; Kim Tallbear, "Standing with and Speaking as Faith: A Feminist-Indigenous Approach to Inquiry," in *Sources and Methods in Indigenous Studies*, 78–85; Wilson, *Research Is Ceremony*, 7, 15.

60 Daniel Rueck, "Commons, Enclosure, and Resistance in Kahnawá:ke Mohawk Territory, 1850–1900," *Canadian Historical Review* 95, no. 3 (September 2015): 352–81.

61 Doris Pratt, Harry Bone, and the Treaty and Dakota Elders of Manitoba with the contributions by the AMC Council of Elders, *Untuwe Pi Kin He—Who We Are: Treaty Elders' Teachings*, vol. 1 (Winnipeg: Treaty Relations Commission of Manitoba and the Assembly of Manitoba Chiefs, 2014), 83. The classic text in land-based history is Keith H. Basso, *Wisdom Sits in Places: Landscape and Language Among the Western Apache* (Albuquerque: University of New Mexico Press, 1996). Lisa Brooks, *The Common Pot: The Recovery of Native Space in the Northeast* (Minneapolis: University of Minnesota Press, 2008) also delves deeply into land-based knowledge and the human relationships to place, as does Julie Cruikshank's *Do Glaciers Listen? Local Knowledge, Colonial Encounters, & Social Imagination* (Vancouver: UBC Press, 2005); See also Moreton-Robinson, "Relationality," 71.

62 Indian Chiefs of Alberta, *Citizens Plus* (Edmonton: University of Alberta, 1970), 1.

Human relationships also suffered under the Indian Act, and so we must bear this in mind as we review the various documents that were generated in application of or in response to the act. Sometimes the documents reveal the emotions associated with the broken relationships caused by the act and sometimes not.[63] Dakelh parents from Saik'uz (Stoney Creek) banded together to demand a North-West Mounted Police investigation of the beating death of a child from their community, Melanie Quaw, at Lejac Indian Residential School in 1924, four years after the Indian Act made residential schooling compulsory. Their grief and outrage are palpable in the letters they wrote, as is the horror of the investigating constable Arthur Acland.[64] On the other hand, the form (enclosed in this volume) used to remit the future treaty annuities of Rosalie Ermineskin Howse is bureaucratic and dry, yet we can imagine what Rosalie's father, the chief of the Ermineskin band, felt as he made his mark on the document that would seal her fate as a non-status Indian because of her marriage to Adam Howse, whom the form describes as a half-breed. Heather Devine's *The People Who Own Themselves: Aboriginal Ethnogenesis in a Canadian Family* draws out the complicated relationship webs that entwined Cree and Métis families for generations before and after the Indian Act proclaimed Rosalie to no longer be a status Indian.[65] When viewed from the perspective of Indigenous law, the Indian Act's breaking of relationships and communities is even more troubling. Susan Hill writes that under Haudenosaunee law, for example, only very bad behaviour could wrest citizenship rights from individuals.[66] That women could lose their Indigenous rights through their choice of marriage partner must have been unfathomable. When we read the sometimes perfunctory band council minutes asking the Indian agent to reinstate the membership of a widow who had lost her status through marriage, it helps to recall that these councillors are speaking of their sisters, their cousins, and other kin. As we read the documents that follow, we can consider what relationships they represent.

Relationships shape the documents we use as well, and we will have trouble interpreting them accurately without thinking about whether the people who made the document had enough of a relationship with the people described to be accurate in their observations. In oral histories, for example, the relationship between the teller and the listener can affect what is told, what is heard, and what is recorded. Oral historian Wendy Wickwire has probed the relationships that underpinned the ethnographic writing of Orkneyman James Teit. She concludes that his relationships to Nlaka'pamux women, particularly his wives,

---

63   Tsianina Lomawaima, "Mind, Heart, Hands," 60–68.
64   North-West Mounted Police constable, A. E. Acland to Headquarters, June 8, 1924, Library and Archives Canada, Department of Indian Affairs fonds, RG 10 v6443 f88101 pt. 1.
65   Heather Devine, *The People Who Own Themselves: Aboriginal Ethnogenesis in a Canadian Family* (Calgary: University of Calgary Press, 2004), 232.
66   Susan M. Hill, *The Clay We Are Made Of: Haudenosaunee Land Tenure on the Grand River* (Winnipeg: University of Manitoba Press, 2017), 198.

helped to ensure that his observations were accurate.[67] Not all such ethnographers had such enduring relationships with their communities, so scholars approach their work with caution.

Responsibility

Relationships bring responsibility. The Indian Chiefs of Alberta responded to the White Paper in 1969 by affirming their responsibility to the land and to "the well being of our future generation."[68] The National Indian Brotherhood responded in the same way, acknowledging their commitment to grandchildren who would be affected by their decisions.[69] Women who agitated for the removal of the sex discrimination of the Indian Act framed their work as an obligation to themselves, their children, and their grandchildren, and as an action in honour of the strong women who came before them.[70] Repeatedly in the history of the Indian Act, Indigenous leaders have met to study it, have prepared detailed discussions of it, and have offered their views and their amendments because they believed they were responsible for doing so.[71]

Elected band councils, created through the Indian Act, knew that they were accountable not just to those who elected them but also to the wider community and particularly to traditional leaders. When they could, they delayed decision making until they could consult more widely. John Borrows writes of his great-grandfather, a descendent in a long line of chiefs, who was forced to submit to the Indian Act's provisions of elected band councils in order to be recognized as a chief by the Canadian government. His primary role, as he saw it, was to work to meet his community's needs.[72]

At the same time, the Indian Act brought a host of individuals into Indigenous communities as Indian agents, field matrons, schoolteachers, farm instructors, doctors, and nurses. These people were responsible to government or the Christian churches and *not* to the communities within which they lived or worked—*not* to Indigenous people. The documents they produced reflect that responsibility; they were never meant for Indigenous eyes. This responsibility influenced how they wrote about Indigenous people, and we need to bear this in mind as we read these documents; if they had anticipated an Indigenous readership, would that have changed what they said? Sometimes such authors were clear that what they said was limited by their fears that local Indigenous people would hear it. Residential school teacher and nurse Margaret Butcher wrote cryptically about Haisla spiritual beliefs to her readers in Vancouver,

---

67 Wendy Wickwire and James A. Teit, "Women in Ethnography: The Research of James A. Teit," *Ethnohistory* 40, no. 4 (1993): 539–62.
68 Indian Chiefs of Alberta, *Citizens Plus*, 1.
69 National Indian Brotherhood, "Statement on the Proposed New 'Indian Policy,'" June 27, 1969, in Keith Smith, ed., *Strange Visitors*, 307.
70 "Understanding the Impact of the Indian Act: Time to Connect—a Conversation between Lizabeth Hall and Sandra Gray," *Kinesis* (December 1999/January 2000): 11–13.
71 Chandra Murdock, "Reactions to Enactment," 11–18.
72 Borrows, *Drawing Out Law*, 21–22.

eastern Canada, and Great Britain, letting them know that she would offer a more complete account of what she had observed when they met in person, fearing, as she did, that her letters and what they contained would "filter back to the [Kitamaat] Village."[73] Most non-Indigenous writers, however, felt no such constraint. We need to consider this as we draw our own conclusions from sources penned by those who felt little responsibility to those they observed.

As students of history, we have a responsibility to the people we study. As tempting as it may be to judge the actions of our ancestors—whether these were people who crafted or who endured the Indian Act—our task as historians is to understand, not judge, the past. Being responsible to the communities whose past we study can help lead us to more nuanced and fair views. For example, scholars have sometimes judged harshly those Indigenous people who cooperated with the Indian Act's implementation. Community historians have come to contest these views, to show how Indigenous people could sometimes use the Indian Act to protect the vulnerable in their communities or to preserve their land base.[74] As we become accountable to the communities, we ensure that we interpret the documents we discover in culturally and historically appropriate ways.[75] More and deeper knowledge is revealed in the process.

Respect

As we consider all the factors that shaped Indigenous and colonial texts, we find that we are able to treat the knowledge they bring to us with respect. Although government agents often viewed Indigenous petitions or delegations as mere annoyances or complaints, we can see them as representative of relationships, as expressions of responsibility and of knowledge that was based in community and the land. We can take them, then, as teaching tools, documents that reveal Indigenous knowledge, how it is acquired, held, and used.

Respect is a theme that runs through Indigenous texts that speak of important relationships. Among the Nisga'a, there is the story of the volcanic eruption that wiped out upriver Nass villages. The lava flowed to punish the Nisga'a for not respecting the oolichan whose run on the Nass River marked the beginning of spring and whose bounty saved the Nisga'a from starvation year after

73 Mary-Ellen Kelm, ed., *The Letters of Margaret Butcher: Missionary-Imperialism on the North Pacific Coast* (Calgary: University of Calgary Press, 2006), 233.

74 See, for example, how the work of Jane Cook was misunderstood by scholars and how it has been reinterpreted by community historians. See Robin Brownlie and Mary-Ellen Kelm, "Desperately Seeking Absolution: Native Agency as Colonialist Alibi?" *Canadian Historical Review* 75, no. 4 (1994): 543–56; and Leslie A. Robertson with the Kwagu'l Gixsam Clan, *Standing Up with Ga'axsta'las: Jane Constance Cook and the Politics of Memory, Church and Custom* (Vancouver: UBC Press, 2012), who correct the limited interpretation of Brownlie and Kelm. See also the contrast between (1) how Peter Schmalz understood the work of individuals who reviewed the early versions of the Indian Act, and (2) the views of Susan Hill, writing on the Haudenosaunee's implementation of the Indian Act in the late nineteenth century. Peter S. Schmalz, *The Ojibwa of Southern Ontario* (Toronto: University of Toronto Press, 1991), 196; Hill, *The Clay We Are Made Of*, 199.

75 Kovach, *Indigenous Methodologies*, 97.

year. Among the Anishinaabe, there is the story of the treaty with Hoof Nation. In this treaty, the Hoof Clan agreed to be taken for food if their bodies were honoured and if no more than was needed by the people was taken. Gradually, the Anishinaabe took the Hoof Clan for granted, so the Hoof beings stayed away. Only when the people heard their grievances and negotiated a way to restore their relationship did the Hoof Clan return to the people.[76] Legal historian Heidi Kiiwetinepinesiik Stark argues that Indigenous people would have understood their relationships with settlers from within the context of such stories. They would have expected relationships built upon and maintained in a spirit of mutual respect.[77] In contrast, the Indian Act created relationships between Indigenous people and the Canadian state that were based in dependency and dominance. It is not surprising, then, that from 1876 onwards, Indigenous leadership demanded changes to the act that would be in accordance with a more mutually respectful relationship.

The archive generated by the Indian Act also offers us an opportunity to consider how respect is asserted through documentary sources. Authors both on the government side and among Indigenous people asserted their authority and demanded the right to be heard. The Indian Act's architects did so through a belief in their superiority as white Christian men. But they also used certain ways of speaking and of writing to convey that their views were well vetted and correct. As we will see in a minute, doing so sometimes meant government leaders indicating that their legislation had the support of Indigenous leaders and of politicians from other political parties.

Indigenous leaders, too, expected to be treated with respect, and they patiently explained to settler observers how their authority was derived. The Grand General Indian Council, which included Anishinaabe and Haudenosaunee leaders for much of the nineteenth century, began its meetings with a reading of wampum belts that reiterated the responsibilities of the Crown to Indigenous nations and indicated the authority of the group to negotiate with the Crown. Council members ran parliamentary-style elections for leadership and administrative positions, and in the process made their authority legible to their House of Commons' counterparts. They came to decisions through consensus, thus ensuring that any motions that went forward from the group fully represented its will. Finally, they printed and distributed their minutes informing government, their own people, and interested settlers of the results of their deliberations. Small town newspapers, such as the *Wiarton Echo*, printed their proceedings in full. Such proceedings were meant to indicate that Indigenous leadership deserved respect and should be treated by government accordingly. Thinking about respect allows us to remain humble in our interpretation of historical texts, as well as alert to the mechanisms through which the creators of such texts demanded to be treated with respect.

---

76 Heidi Kiiwetinepinesiik Stark, "Stories as Law: A Method to Live by," in *Sources and Methods in Indigenous Studies*, 249–56.

77 Stark, "Respect, Responsibility, and Renewal."

Reciprocity

Indigenous scholars studying the way that Indigenous people negotiated relationships with settlers and their governments have discovered that they often did so with the expectation of reciprocity. Treaties, they thought, were to share the land, to be of mutual benefit to all signatories and their kin, to be renewed and rethought as the needs of the communities involved changed over time.[78] In our brief history of the Indian Act above, we have emphasized the expectations of government officials for the Indian Act. We have much to learn about the expectations of those Indigenous people who talked back to it. As we saw when Pierre Trudeau wished to abolish the Indian Act, not all Indigenous people saw the Indian Act as a bad thing. What we see repeatedly, however, is a demand for balance, a demand for reciprocity. Indigenous leaders did not, for example, wholly reject enfranchisement. What they did not want was forcible enfranchisement, whereby the government could remove Indian status from a person without that person's consent. Band councils did not reject their right to make by-laws governing reserve lands, but they did reject the interference of Indian agents in the enforcement of these by-laws. They did not reject Canadian laws, but they wanted the recognition of their own systems of governance and law.[79]

Reciprocity was a value that was meant to order relationships within communities as well as between communities. Scholars who study Indigenous gendered relationships emphasize reciprocity between genders, *not* hierarchy, as well as the acceptance of multiple gendered identities beyond the binary of man and woman. Yet the Indian Act imposed both gender binaries and hierarchies by creating policy that affected men and women differently. It made hierarchy by prohibiting women from voting in band elections and from preventing them from holding positions of authority within Indian Act–approved governance. Women retained power within clan systems across the country, but the Indian Act's ability to remove women who married non-status men made their positions tenuous in their own communities.

From Thinking to Doing: Using Historical and Indigenous Methods to Read Historical Sources

The questions historians ask form their interpretations of the sources they use. Guided by historical thinking that prompts us to consider context, change over time, causality, contingency, and complexity, we will be able to see documents as more than static sources that can be mined for information. Recalling the touchstones of Indigenous methodologies—relationship, responsibility, respect, and reciprocity—we work to resituate sources in Indigenous ways of being and knowing. This is a critical step, not just for Indigenous sources but

---

78 J. R. Miller, *Compact, Contract, Covenant.*
79 Hill, *The Clay We Are Made Of,* 193–211.

Figure 0.1: Basket (the 5 Cs and 4 Rs). Historical and Indigenous understandings can be woven together as we interpret historical documents with the 5 Cs and 4 Rs in mind.

for all historical sources that were generated to span settler and Indigenous worlds—just as the Indian Act was and just as the many sources it generated did. Taken together, historical thinking and Indigenous methodologies generate questions with which we can probe our historical sources as we seek new and better ways to understand our past. We can think of Indigenous and historical methods as nested practices that, together, help us understand the world of the past better.

Here is a table listing questions that might help you analyse the documents and other sources that follow in this textbook.

Table 0.1: Questions and Concepts for Historical Analysis

QUESTION	CONCEPT
Who created the source?	Context
Who was its intended audience?	Context, Relationship
How do the authors represent or explain their ability to speak on the subject of the sources? What is their authority on the subject?	Respect
How might the authors' social position affect how they depict events or how they understood them?	Contingency, Complexity, Relationship, Responsibility, Respect
What was going on in the family/community/nation/region/world at the time this source was created that may have affected it?	Context, Causality, Relationship, Contingency
Was this source describing immediate events or those more distant by time and place? How might these factors have affected the authors' ability to represent events?	Context, Contingency, Relationship, Responsibility
What prompted the authors to create this source at this time?	Context, Contingency, Causality, Responsibility, Relationship
Do the authors acknowledge or describe changing events, attitudes, or policy?	Change over Time
Do the authors reveal or conceal emotion? How?	Contingency, Relationship, Respect
Do the authors depict or refer to power inequalities?	Contingency, Relationship, Responsibility, Respect, Reciprocity
Is there an argument expressed (or implied) in the source? Is the other side of the argument inherently expressed as well?	Context, Causality, Relationship, Respect, Reciprocity
Why was this source preserved?	Contingency, Responsibility, Respect
Does the type of source affect how it would have been received at the time? Or how we read it now?	Contingency, Complexity, Change over Time, Respect
What is not said? Who is silenced? What is absent?	Complexity, Contingency, Relationship, Respect
How might the audience have received this document differently than the authors intended it to be received? Do we receive it differently today?	Contingency, Change over Time, Relationship, Responsibility

Now let's practise by applying some of these questions to a short historical text: the report presented to Parliament by David Mills, minister of the interior in the Liberal government of Alexander Mackenzie, on the passing of the Indian Act in 1876:

THE INDIAN ACT, 1876.
During the last session of Parliament an Act, with the above short title, was passed, amending and consolidating the laws respecting Indians. The bill, I am informed, was very carefully prepared by the then Superintendent General, the Hon. Mr. Laird, who was at pains to obtain the views of many of the most intelligent Indian Chiefs in Ontario respecting its provisions, and the bill was, in some particulars, modified to meet their wishes. Referring, in his report last year, to this measure, Mr. Laird observes:

> "Our Indian legislation generally rests on the principle that the aborigines are to be kept in a condition of tutelage and treated as wards or children of the State. The soundness of the principle I cannot admit. On the contrary, I am firmly persuaded that true interests of the aborigines and of the State alike require that every effort should be made to aid the Red man in lifting himself out of his condition of tutelage and dependence, and that is clearly our wisdom and our duty, through education and every other means, to prepare him for a higher civilization by encouraging him to assume the privileges and responsibilities of full citizenship.
>
> "In this spirit and with this object the enfranchisement clauses in the proposed Indian Bill have been framed."

It is satisfactory to be able to report that the Act as passed has met with very general acceptance among the Indians of Ontario. At a general Indian Council, held in Saugeen in the month of July last, an almost unanimous vote was passed approving of its provisions.

In this short report, David Mills introduced his audience—the governor general of Canada, the House of Commons, the press, and the reading public—to the Indian Act. He wanted his audience to see the Indian Act as a shift in government policy, one that would enable Indigenous people to become full citizens. He wished his audience to see this policy as a kind and noble gesture. His unstated assumption, of course, was that full citizenship was inherently desirable and that Indigenous people were not ready for full citizenship until they had been exposed to education and "every other means."

As we look closely at this source, we see that David Mills does not rely solely on his position as cabinet minister to validate his views; rather he gestures to the authority of two other entities: David Laird, former minister of the interior and superintendent general of Indian Affairs, and "the most intelligent Indian Chiefs," including an Indian council held at Saugeen, Ontario. These two points are intriguing, and they demand that we use our historical thinking to consider context and our Indigenous methodologies as we think about relationships and the respect inherent in these two references. First, who was David Laird, and why was he an authority? David Laird was a Liberal politician from Prince Edward Island who was appointed the minister of the interior and superintendent general of Indian Affairs in November 1873. As minister, he proved his worth to the government of the day by negotiating Treaty 4 and Treaty 5. He was not a particularly strong parliamentarian, however, and the Indian Act was his greatest legislative accomplishment as minister. He was rewarded, much to his own chagrin, by being appointed lieutenant governor of the North-West Territories in 1876, where he negotiated Treaty 7 with the Siksika, Kainai, Tsuu T'ina, Piikani, and Nakoda First Nations. Laird's biographer writes that Mills did not particularly like Laird, but his accomplishments, however modest, meant that it was Laird, not Mills, who was the authority to recommend the Indian Act to the report's readers.[80]

Laird is not the only authority that Mills cited. He also says that "the most intelligent Indian Chiefs" also supported it. Who were these people? Here again, we can do some more investigation. We have included in this reader the document that records the minutes of the meeting of the Grand Ojibway Council to which Mills refers. It is likely that this council was a subset of the larger and more established political entity, the Grand General Indian Council of Ontario and Quebec. The minutes of this meeting seem to indicate profound support for the Indian Act, particularly its provisions for enfranchisement, the process by which an Indian, as defined under the act, could cease to be an Indian to gain voting rights and private property and hence, ostensibly, integration into Canada. The motion in support of the Indian Act, it is recorded, was made by Chief J. Henry and seconded by Chief J. Fisher. The minutes are signed by H. P. Chase and J. Jacobs and list those in attendance and the communities they represent, indicating the people to whom they were responsible. We can ask, as we did above, what relationships did these people (we can assume men but the document is not clear on the gender of participants) have with one another or with others that may have influenced their views? Indigenous methodologies and studies of treaty making at this time indicate that Indigenous people expected reciprocity in their relationships. They expected relationships to be nurtured and renewed. As historians, we can use this document respectfully to try to understand what led these leaders to make this decision. So let's step back to get some better sense of the context.

Secondary sources tell us that in the years leading up to the Indian Act of 1876, government officials and Indigenous leadership met repeatedly on matters

---

80 Andrew Robb, "Laird, David," in *Dictionary of Canadian Biography*, vol. 14, University of Toronto/Université Laval, 2003, http://www.biographi.ca/en/bio/laird_david_14E.html (accessed August 9, 2016); Peter Oliver, "Meredith, Edmund Allen," in *Dictionary of Canadian Biography*, vol. 12, University of Toronto/Université Laval, 2003, http://www.biographi.ca/en/bio/meredith_edmund_allen_12E.html (accessed August 15, 2016).

relating to the definition of "Indian" and the protection of reserve lands. In 1872, Mohawk leader Oronhyatekha visited Joseph Howe, then superintendent of Indian Affairs, to protest the way the 1869 act treated women. The Grand General Indian Council passed motions that made similar protests in 1874. In 1871, Simcoe Kerr, a prominent leader of the Six Nations, and Henry P. Chase, a Mississauga Methodist missionary, drafted their own Indian Act.[81] Peter Schmalz's *The Ojibwa of Southern Ontario* tells us that William Wawanosh from Sarnia, Chief John Henry from New Credit, and the Rev. Allen Salt, missionary at Christian Island, were all invited to Ottawa in February 1876 to discuss the new Indian Act.[82] It may be that when they represented it to the Grand Council in July of that year, they brought with them a sense of responsibility to government to bring the support of their people to the act. The evidence seems clear that Indigenous leadership from across Ontario had strongly expressed their views to the government, and perhaps they believed that this act was the best result possible at that time.[83] Given the importance of consultation with Indigenous leadership today (mandated most recently by the Supreme Court decision in *Tsilhqot'in Nation v. British Columbia* [SRC 257]), we may be surprised that consulting with and gaining the approval of Indigenous leadership for the Indian Act was considered important in 1876 and important enough that Mills mentioned it in his short report. This suggests that the government, and indeed the reading public, accepted that Indigenous people could be intelligent critics of Indian policy.

Henry P. Chase and the other Anishinaabe leaders of the Grand Council were part of a generation who sought to build relationships between Indigenous people and settler governments. Chase, William Wawanosh, and others were advocates of education for their people. The same year that Chase voted in favour of the Indian Act, he travelled to Britain at the behest of the Lord Bishop of Huron to raise money for the establishment of the University of Western Ontario, a school that William Wawanosh's sons attended.[84] While in Britain, Chase also met with the lord mayor of London and the Prince of Wales to press the needs of Anishinaabe people. Chase, at the confluence of a complex set of relationships, clearly believed that he could use these relationships to advance Anishinaabe interests—he expected reciprocity. His expressed views, however, also suggest that he did not accept the Indian Act's reconfiguration of Indigenous governance. He spoke as if the Grand Council continued to be responsible to its people and that its members had direct relationships to the British Crown. In short, he spoke as if the Indian Act of 1876 did not exist.[85]

---

81 Ted Binnema, "Protecting Indian Lands by Defining Indian: 1850–76," *Journal of Canadian Studies/Revue D'études Canadiennes* 48, no. 2 (2014): 28.

82 Schmalz, *The Ojibwa*, 295, n 24.

83 Leslie and Maguire, *The Historical Development of the Indian Act*, 69.

84 Schmalz, *The Ojibwa*, 195–96; Donald B. Smith, "Chase, Henry Pahtahquahong," in *Dictionary of Canadian Biography*, vol. 12, University of Toronto/Université Laval, 2003, http://www.biographi.ca/en/bio/chase_henry_pahtahquahong_12E.html (accessed October 15, 2016); Schmalz, *The Ojibwa*, 295, n 24.

85 Schmalz, *The Ojibwa*, 196.

Nonetheless, the view that Chase and other Anishinaabe leaders did not relinquish their autonomy is supported in the minutes of subsequent meetings of the council and by Anishinaabe legal scholar John Borrows. Band council decisions, he writes of the later nineteenth and early twentieth century, continued to be "community generated."[86]

Finally, we see hints of conflict, causality, and change over time. Mills quotes Laird as saying, "Our Indian legislation generally rests on the principle that the aborigines are to be kept in a condition of tutelage and treated as wards or children of the State. The soundness of the principle I cannot admit." In this passage, Laird and Mills are doing two things. First, they are engaging in partisan conflict, rejecting the policies of Conservative governments, first of the United Colony of Canada under John A. Macdonald and George-Etienne Cartier, and then the post-Confederation Conservative government of Macdonald. Second, Mills is calling out the perceived failure of previous acts to encourage enfranchisement—a failure that made a new act necessary.

Mills is also indicating some fundamental changes over time. When Mills quotes Laird as saying that the old legislation endeavoured to keep Indigenous people in a state of tutelage, he is rejecting decades of previous Indian policy. From 1763 onwards, the position of the British Crown was that Indigenous people and their lands should be protected against settler intrusion. Early nineteenth century reform elements in Britain and eventually in Upper and Lower Canada demanded that Indigenous people be integrated into colonial society through education, through a shared commitment to agricultural settlement, and through the ability to govern themselves according to British traditions. Until that time, however, reformers contended that reserves should remain protected spaces, self-governing communities for Indigenous people. This vision is what Laird was so roundly denouncing and what the Indian Act of 1876 fundamentally disregarded. In this brief document, Mills and Laird ensure that readers understand that change had occurred. As the Royal Commission on Aboriginal People concluded in 1996, through the Indian Act of 1876, "The transition from tribal nation in the tripartite imperial system to legal incompetent in the bilateral federal/provincial system was now complete."[87] Historians John Milloy and John Tobias both have argued that the Indian Act of 1876 and its subsequent amendments shifted the emphasis from preserving Indigenous communities to eradicating them as distinct entities.[88]

---

86 John J. Borrows, "A Genealogy of Law: Inherent Sovereignty and First Nations Self-Government," *Osgood Hall Law Journal* 30, no. 2 (1992): 291–353.

87 RCAP, vol. 1, chapter 9, section 8, paragraph 5, http://www.collectionscanada.gc.ca/webarchives/20071211051055/http://www.ainc-inac.gc.ca/ch/rcap/sg/sg24_e.html#79 (accessed August 15, 2016).

88 John L. Tobias, "Protection, Civilization, Assimilation: An Outline History of Canada's Indian Policy," in *Sweet Promises: A Reader on Indian-White Relations in Canada*, edited by J. R. Miller (Toronto: University of Toronto Press, 1991), 127–44; John Milloy, "The Early Indian Acts: Developmental Strategy and Constitutional Change," in *Sweet Promises: A Reader on Indian-White Relations in Canada* (Toronto: University of Toronto Press, 1991), 145–56.

But we can also ask some more probing questions, those that we might say read against the grain, against or through the intentions of the author. Here we test what the author is telling us. As we look more closely at the Indian Act itself, we can question Mills's statement that the act is designed to lift Indigenous people out of dependence. What sort of dependence is Mills speaking of? Recall that, even as the House of Commons was debating this act, the government of Canada was entering new relationships with First Nations across the west through the signing of treaties. Each of these treaties symbolized to the First Nations an ongoing relationship in which the government declared that it would assist First Nations to adapt to the new circumstances. First Nations did not conceive of these new relationships as ones of dependency but rather as ones of sharing and exchange, yet the government of the day was wary of the promises made to First Nations. What would they cost? How long were they to be honoured? Nor did that government accept that the sovereignty of First Nations would continue beyond the signing of the treaties—this in sharp contrast to the understanding of First Nations. Laird, having been part of these negotiations, would have understood these expectations well. The Indian Act, as many scholars have argued, is a direct repudiation of the treaties that were being made at exactly the same time. The treaties are not mentioned in Mills's report on the Indian Act, nor is the complexity of the relations into which the federal government had entered with Indigenous peoples across Canada. This silence is telling. And it hints at the complexity with which the Indian Act and the governments who supported it will contend over its entire lifespan.

We can also wonder at some of the silences within this short section. Did the Indigenous leaders that Mills cited view their current relationship with the fledgling Canadian government as one of dependence? We can also wonder at the views of other Indigenous leaders, as expressed through the minutes of meetings included in this reader, that indicate that they saw themselves in a nation-to-nation relationship with the Crown. These views were excluded, and given the willingness of local newspapers to print the minutes of Indigenous organizations, they would not have been unknown to local settler communities. We can assume that such views were held by those beyond what Mills described as the "most intelligent Indian Chiefs," but despite his attempts to discredit them, Mills's use of language admits their presence even if not their words. Other silences haunt the document. Women, children, clan leaders not represented among the newly educated Indigenous elites who attended the meetings of the Grand General Council have no voice in these documents. Sometimes, the men spoke for those not present. They certainly expressed their responsibility for them, but the views of more common or traditional Indigenous people are hushed in these documents.

We might also ask some questions about contingency. Why was this an act of Parliament? Was this the most appropriate form for a new relationship between Indigenous people and Canada? Given that only settlers (white men) could vote in federal elections, Parliament did not represent Indigenous people. We can ask how Mills's statement of relationship might have been different if it had come as part of a treaty? As the Indian Act is an act of Parliament, its form also makes clear that it was never intended to reflect the views of all parties engaged in the relationship. It was only ever meant to be the view of a government elected by settler Canadians. Not all settler Canadians had the right to vote, and because they had little representation in the halls of Parliament, their views might not have been captured. Certainly, there was not unanimity among settler Canadians about how Indigenous people should be integrated (or not) into Canadian society. The view of the government dominates our records because it is to government archives that historians so often turn; in this way, our sources themselves are contingent on the views of the bodies that generated them.

The Indian Act, Settler Colonialism, and Documentary Analysis

As you can see, the Indian Act and the archive of documents it has produced over its long, 140-year history makes it fertile ground for teaching historical and Indigenous methodologies. The chapters that follow are arranged according to some of the key areas in which the act intervened: governance, enfranchisement, gender, and land. In each section, we have included applicable sections of the Indian Act and related amendments. Documents that help explain the intentions of those who lobbied for, crafted, and passed the act and its amendments are included next. Then we turn our attention to sources that indicate or speak to the act's impacts—how it was implemented and what that meant in the lives of Indigenous people. Finally, we include Indigenous responses to the act that might take account of how people tried to work within this legislation, how they opposed it, or how they circumvented it. All these sources can be read both with and against the grain, and the questions of historical and Indigenous methodologies apply. We will introduce each document to offer context and to help stimulate questions that you may wish to ask. In the process, you will be learning not just to read documents but to "talk back" to them, building your own analysis of the Indian Act as you do so.

Chapter 1 begins with the Indian Act of 1876 itself and highlights its definitions. Parliamentarians of the day debated the Indian Act and, in so doing, expressed their intentions, as well as their dissatisfaction with previous acts and their concerns about this one. You will see the record of these debates here. We have included the minutes of the Grand Council of the Ojibway both at the time they accepted the act and later, acting as the Grand General Indian Council, as its members increasingly voiced their dissatisfaction with the act. A group representing the "Chiefs and Warriors of the Six Nation Indians" expressed their opposition to the act and their own view of the appropriate relationship between themselves and Canada in a letter to John A. Macdonald in 1879, and that is in this chapter as well.

Chapter 2 examines the Indian Act's role in trying to disrupt traditional leadership, in thwarting self-government, and in enforcing elected band council governance under the domination of the Indian agent. We begin with the section in the 1876 act that dealt with councils and chiefs, as well as amendments and subsequent, related acts that increasingly restricted the role of hereditary chiefs and defined and later enforced the elected system. Subsequent documents in this section demonstrate how the act was enforced, particularly in terms of imposing the Indian agent as arbiter of a chief's authority. We see this imposition both in the documents concerning the declaration of Crop Eared Wolf as chief of the Kainai and in those related to the agent's efforts to depose him eight years later. So far, most of our records have been internal records—private conversations, if you will, between government and Indigenous people. Our next two sources in this section reflect moments when Indigenous people spoke publicly to Canadians. In 1925, Deskaheh, a Cayuga chief speaking for the Six Nations Council, addressed Canadians over the radio, explaining how the Indian Act was being used to undermine their centuries-old longhouse government. You will find, in this text, a clear example of Indigenous leadership talking back to the Indian Act. Finally, we have included the opening sections of the "Governance" chapter of the Royal Commission on Aboriginal People (1995) because these include a discussion of sovereignty that incorporates many quotations from Indigenous leaders and scholars expressing what that term means to them.

Chapter 3 deals with enfranchisement, the process by which Indigenous people lost Indian status in exchange for Canadian citizenship. In the process, they lost access to reserve lands and were removed from their communities. We begin with the 1876 Indian Act and include here as well subsequent amendments and acts that enfranchised, voluntarily and forcibly, Indigenous men (the process that did the same to Indigenous women and their children is dealt with in the following chapter). Subsequent documents reveal the intentions of government agents over time, making clear their frustration with previous attempts to encourage voluntary enfranchisement. The next set of documents indicates how different First Nations viewed the possibilities of enfranchisement and how they reacted to the Indian Act.

Chapter 4 looks specifically at the gender discrimination of the Indian Act, particularly as it affected the membership of women and children in bands and their status as Indians. The relevant sections of the 1876 Indian Act are included, as well as amendments made in 1951 and 1985. We follow these with an archival document recording the commutation of annuity of one woman who found herself excluded from her community by this section of the act. We hear from Tobique elder Mavis Goeres about how women were affected by these provisions and why they agitated for change. The Manitoba Public Inquiry into the Administration of Justice and Aboriginal People discusses the impact that the 1985 amendment (most commonly referred to as Bill C-31) had on women and children. The role of the courts in this matter is revealed through the last two documents: the first is *McIvor v. The Registrar, Indian and Northern Affairs Canada* (2007 BCSC 827), heard before the British Columbia Supreme Court, and the second is a position paper of the Indigenous Bar Association of Canada on Bill C-3.

Chapter 5 examines how the Indian Act affected the land base of reserves in Canada. You will likely be struck by the increasingly draconian measures implemented by the Canadian government in order to release land reserved to First Nations into private ownership. The 1876 Indian Act's land provisions will be followed by those passed in 1905, 1906, and 1911. The case of the Songhees (Lekwungen) is an interesting one because it required its own statute and led the way to the 1911 amendment that affected many First Nations across the country. We have included three documents relating to this case: the statute itself, "An Act Respecting the Songhees Reserve," newspaper reportage of the case introducing a number of perspectives on the issue, and the view of government officials on the precedent this act has created. The Six Nations Council was among the many First Nations who protested these amendments, and we have included their letter and the response of the Department of Indian Affairs to the arguments outlined in that letter. Finally, we have included Lee Maracle's compelling short story about the effects of the eradication of Snauq. Snauq was a Squamish village removed by the City of Vancouver through an illegal land sale that, though based on the reasoning of the 1911 amendment, was ultimately found by the courts to have violated the Indian Act.

Critical reading is an essential skill for any student of history. This text has been designed to help you develop this skill. In the process, you will learn about the Indian Act and its place in Canada's history of settler colonialism. This history is not past. The Indian Act is still in force. Canada has a long way to go in order to live up to the promises of a nation-to-nation relationship with Indigenous people in this country. We all have plenty of opportunities to examine what we hear and what we learn about Indigenous people, and about Canada as a nation. We expect, then, that you will carry these methods—both historical thinking and Indigenous methodologies—with you as you confront our media-saturated world, and in so doing, become a critically engaged global citizen.

Chapter One

The 1876 Indian Act

On the March 2, 1876, the Hon. David Laird rose in the House of Commons to introduce the new "Act respecting the Indians of Canada." It was meant to consolidate the eight previous acts passed since 1850 to deal with questions of who was an Indian under the law, how Indian lands would be administered, and how Indian communities would be governed. Many of the previous acts had been passed by the Canadian legislature (made up of Canada West and Canada East, formerly Upper and Lower Canada, and known today as Ontario and Quebec), but this new Indian Act was to be administered across the new Dominion of Canada. An 1871 estimate set the Indigenous population of Canada at just over 102,000.[89] The documents in this section reveal aspects of the 1876 Indian Act itself, how it was debated in the House of Commons, how Indigenous organizations in Ontario responded to it, and how it affected people living in Western Canada years later. As you read and analyse these documents, we want you to keep in mind the 5 Cs of historical thinking (change over time, context, causality, contingency, and complexity) and the 4 Rs of Indigenous methodologies (relationship, responsibility, respect, and reciprocity).

Let's begin with the first document that sets out sections 1 to 3 of the 1876 Indian Act, in which the terms used in the act are defined. Here, the legislators introduce us to a vocabulary of administration, of governance, and of categorization—a vocabulary that exists to this day. In the rest of this book, you will see repeatedly the terms "reserve," "band," and "agent," particularly "Indian agent." As you examine these sections, have a look at the language used. Think about relationships: what type of relationship is being established through this act between Canada and the people it defines as Indian? Is it a reciprocal

---

89 Canada, *Census of Canada 1871—Reprint of Censuses of Canada: 1665 to 1871* (Ottawa, 1876).

relationship? Can Indigenous people involved expect respect and reciprocity? Why or why not?

Among the most important parts of section 3 is the definition of "Indian" itself, the most detailed definition to be found in legislation up to this point. There had been other definitions, at least four between 1850 and 1869, each one narrowing in scope. As you examine the definitions, ask questions. What do the definitions tell you about the kinds of family relations that legislators envisioned? What did they not envision? There is an obvious gender bias— what is it? And where do you think it comes from?

Scholars have noted that Indian Affairs officials were particularly concerned about white men who might come to settle on reserves and what they would do with the land they acquired through marriage. Indigenous leadership too debated the place of such families, sometimes arguing that Indian women who married non-Indians should no longer have any claim on the lands or financial benefits of their home communities, while others protested that any legislation that would exclude such women was unjust and immoral, that "Indian women [should] have the privilege to marry when and to whom they please."[90] Might there be other reasons that government officials were wary of non-Indian men becoming part of Indigenous communities; why were they less concerned about non-Indian women doing so? These definitions ask us to consider intersectional questions about gendered norms but also about gendered access to power and influence, both within Indigenous communities and within Canada as a whole at this time.

As we turn to the debates, we can carry on the discussion of relationships. The *Dictionary of Canadian Biography* (www.biographi.ca) is a great resource for finding out who these debaters were and what relationships were behind the rhetoric of the House of Commons debates. What were their party affiliations? What ridings did they represent? To whom are they responsible? Are there some speakers who seem to have had relationships with Indigenous communities and hence might have been asking questions they thought they might have to answer when they next encountered people from those communities? We also see hints of context and change over time. What are the broader contextual matters that are referred to in the discussion? As Hector Langevin was the architect of the 1869 Graduate Enfranchisement Act, what do you make of his criticism of the current act, or of the criticisms levelled against Langevin's legislation by the drafters of the 1876 Indian Act? How have ideas, practices, and circumstances changed over time, and how is this change reflected in the debates? Is there any sense that Indigenous knowledge and experience are respected? Why or why not?

The next three documents are minutes from meetings of Indigenous leaders as they debate the 1876 act. Again, using the *DCB*, try to understand why Henry

---

90 Oronhyatekha, Letter to the Minister of the Interior, June 16, 1872, Library and Archives Canada, Department of Indian Affairs fonds, RG 10 vol 1394, file 3541.

P. Chase is an advocate for the 1876 legislation. Why do the members of the Grand Indian Council of the Province of Ontario have more reservations about the Indian Act by 1879? What is the nature of their concerns? Why do some still support it? How is the discussion infused with a sense of the relationship each has with the others and of their responsibility for the good of the whole community? How is their discussion of the exclusion of women gendered? Are you surprised by the local settler interest in events at the Grand Indian Council? Were there any visitors to the meetings, and if so what role did they play?

Next, turn to the petition of the Six Nations chiefs. What kind of relationship are they wishing to maintain? What are their fears for themselves and for their communities? Do they feel respected by this new legislation?

Finally, we turn to excerpts from the oral history interviews of Indigenous men done in the 1970s and 1980s for a project documenting Indigenous history in Canada. Consider first Vern Harper's interview. Do you think the concerns of the Six Nations chiefs were realized at least on the reserves Vern Harper visited? What was the nature of the relationships between Indian agents and the people? What Indigenous values (relationship, responsibility, respect, and reciprocity) were trampled in this relationship? Then turn to the interview with Adam Solway. What long-term effects do you see of the assimilationist policies of the Indian Act on communities and families? How are these effects gendered (with respect to both masculinity and femininity)?

Documents

1.1 An Act to Amend and Consolidate the Laws Respecting Indians [Indian Act of 1876], sections 1 to 3

The Indian Act sets the relationship between Canada and Indigenous people. In the opening sections of the 1876 act, these definitions make clear the nature of the relationship that the Canadian government envisioned with Indigenous people. A cabinet minister, the minister of the interior, gained control over all land, money, and property of the people defined here as Indians. By legislative act, the Canadian government made all Indians legally children and wards of the state. It made itself their guardian, their legal parent.[91]

The Indian Act denied Indigenous sovereignty over lands and resources. Later in the Indian Act, the Canadian government prohibited Indigenous people, as individuals, from homesteading on Crown land (section 70), a restriction that applied in the province of British Columbia as well. In this way, Indigenous people were denied both collective and individual property rights unless

---

91 Miller, *Compact, Contract, Covenant*, 190.

they gained those through enfranchisement and, in becoming enfranchised, obtained a location ticket from within reserve lands set aside for their community (see Chapters 3 and 5).[92]

The other definitions in this section related to who is and who is not an Indian under this act. This overall definition, too, is a denial of the fundamental rights of sovereign nations and of rights now enshrined under Canada's Constitution Act (1982) and articulated by the *United Nations Declaration on the Rights of Indigenous Peoples (UNDRIP)*. In Chapter 4, we will deepen our discussion of the gendered dynamics of the Indian Act.[93]

Source: Canada, An Act to Amend and Consolidate the Laws
Respecting Indians, *Statutes of Canada* 39 Vic. (1876) c.18.

CHAP. 18.
An Act to amend and consolidate the laws respecting Indians.

[Assented to 12th April, 1876.]

Preamble.	WHEREAS it is expedient to amend and consolidate the laws respecting Indians: Therefore Her Majesty, by and with the advice and consent of the Senate and the House of Commons of Canada, enact as follows:—
Short title and extent of Act.	1. This Act shall be know and may be cited as "*The Indian Act, 1876;*" and shall apply to all the Provinces, and to the North West Territories, including the Territory of Keewatin.
Superintendent General.	2. The Minister of the Interior shall be the Superintendent-General of Indian Affairs, and shall be governed in the supervision of the said affairs, and in the control and management of the reserves, lands, moneys and property of Indians in Canada by the provisions of this Act.

TERMS

Meanings assigned to terms in this Act.	3. The following terms contained in this Act shall be held to have the meaning hereinafter assigned to them, unless such meaning be repugnant to the subject or inconsistent with the context:—

92 See An Act to Amend and Consolidate the Laws Respecting Indians, section 70 (1876) in Chapter 3 of this book; *An Ordinance to Amend and Consolidate the Laws Affecting Crown Lands in British Columbia* SBC (1870) c.18. Daniel Rueck provides a useful case study of erosion of Kahnewá:ke collective land rights in his article, "Commons, Enclosure and Resistance."

93 Indigenous Bar Association of Canada, "Position Paper on Bill C-3 – Gender Equity in Indian Registration Act." Submitted to the Senate Committee on Human Rights, December 6, 2010.

Band.	1.	The term "band" means any tribe, band or body of Indians who own or are interested in a reserve or in Indian lands in common, of which the legal title is vested in the Crown, or who share alike in the distribution of any annuities or interest moneys for which the Government of Canada is responsible; the term "the band" means that band to which the context relates; and the term "band," when action is being taken by the band as such, means the band in council.
Irregular Band.	2.	The term "irregular band" means any tribe, band or body of persons of Indian blood who own no interest in any reserve or lands of which the legal title is vested in the Crown, who possess no common fund managed by the Government of Canada, or who have not had any treaty relations with the Crown.
Indians.	3.	The term "Indian" means:

First. Any male person of Indian blood reputed to belong to a particular band;

Secondly. Any child of such person;

Thirdly. Any woman who is or was lawfully married to such person.

As to illegitimates.	(a)	Provided that any illegitimate child, unless having shared with the consent of the band in the distribution moneys of such band for a period exceeding two years, may, at any time, be excluded from the membership thereof by the band, if such proceeding be sanctioned by the Superintendent-General:
Absentees.	(b)	Provided that any Indian having for five years continuously resided in a foreign country shall with the sanction of the Superintendent-General, cease to be a member thereof and shall not be permitted to become again member thereof, or of any other band, unless the consent of the band with the approval of the Superintendent-General or his agent, be first had and obtained; but this provision shall not apply to any professional man, mechanic, missionary, teacher or interpreter, while discharging his or her duty as such:

Woman marrying other than an Indian.

(c) Provided that any Indian woman marrying any other than an Indian or a non-treaty Indian shall cease to be an Indian in any respect within the meaning of this Act, except that she shall be entitled to share equally with the members of the band to which she formerly belonged, in the annual or semi-annual distribution of their annuities, interest moneys and rents; but this income may be commuted to her at any time at ten years' purchase with the consent of the band:

Marrying non-treaty Indians.

(d) Provided that any Indian woman marrying an Indian of any other band, or a non-treaty Indian shall cease to be a member of the band to which she formerly belonged, and become a member of the band or irregular band of which her husband is a member:

As to half-breeds.

(e) Provided also that no half-breed in Manitoba who has shared in the distribution of half-breed lands shall be accounted an Indian; and that no half-breed head of a family (except the widow of an Indian, or a half-breed who has already been admitted into a treaty), shall, unless under very special circumstances, to be determined by the Superintendent-General or his agent, be accounted an Indian, or entitled to be admitted into any Indian treaty.

1.2 Selections of House of Commons Debates on the Indian Act, March 2 to April 4, 1876

Over a period of several weeks in the spring of 1876, Canada's members of Parliament debated a piece of proposed legislation that came to be known as the Indian Act. In the selections from this debate reproduced below, partisan differences are clear enough, but so too are shared understandings, especially related to the assimilation of Indigenous people and the utility of the policy of enfranchisement in facilitating that assimilation. There are differences of opinion about the policy, to be sure, but these can be seen as primarily tactical rather than strategic. While assimilation was a central plank in Canada's policy toward Indigenous people across successive administrations, enfranchisement, which is relatively voluntary here, becomes much more coercive over time. This point can be investigated through later chapters of this book. The discussions in the House of Commons below also indicate shared sympathies about several interrelated themes: the role that women would play in the assimilative process, what it is that constitutes indigeneity, to whom the act's provisions would apply initially, and how land would be held by Indigenous communities. On this latter issue, land and the nature of consent required to alienate it, there is consensus that the Indigenous communities should and would be protected, even if what constitutes a majority was regularly flouted by ambitious Indian Affairs officials intent on removing reserve land from Indigenous control.[94] A final point to keep in mind is the demographics of Parliament in 1876. There were, for example, no women and no one with Indian status.

Source: Canada, House of Commons, *Debates*, 2 March 1876, pp. 342–43; 21 March 1876, p. 753; 28 March 1876, p. 869; 30 March 1876, p. 928–29; 4 April 1876, pp. 1037–40.

[March 2, 1876]

THE INDIANS

Hon. Mr. LAIRD introduced a Bill entituled [sic] "An Act respecting the Indians of Canada." He said: The principal object of this Bill is to consolidate the several laws relating to Indians now on the statute books of the Dominion and the old Provinces of Upper and Lower Canada. We find that there are three different statutes on the Dominion law books, as well as portions of several Acts that were in operation under the laws of Old Canada, and which are still in operation. It is advisable to have these consolidated in the interests of the Indian population throughout the Dominion, and have it applied to all the Provinces. Several amendments of various kinds are introduced. The principal amendment relates to the enfranchisement of Indians. Under the present law an Indian who becomes enfranchised only obtains a life interest in the land set apart for him, and his children have no control over it after his death. The present Act proposes that his children can control the land after his death by will from him. The operation of this it is considered will be an inducement for the Indians to ask for enfranchisement. Hitherto the inducement has been so small that very few of the Indians have asked for the privilege. This Bill proposes to go further; any Indian who is sober and industrious can go to one of the agents appointed for the purpose, to see whether he is qualified for the franchise or not; if qualified he receives a ticket for land, and after three years he is entitled to receive a patent for it which will give him absolute control of the portion allotted to him for his own use during his lifetime, and after that it will be controlled by whoever it is willed to. It is thought that this will encourage them to improve their land, and have a tendency to train them for a more civilized life. It is also intended that after they have obtained the patent for their land, if they wish to go on further and get possession of their share

---

94 See for example Peggy Martin-McGuire, *First Nation Land Surrenders on the Prairies 1896–1911* (Ottawa: Indian Claims Commission, 1998).

of the invested funds of the land, they can make application accordingly, and after three years further they will be entitled to a distribution of the funds; thus after six years of good behaviour they will receive their land and their share of the moneys in the hands of the Government, and will cease in every respect to be Indians according to the acceptation of the laws of Canada relating to Indians. We will then have nothing more to do with their affairs, except as ordinary subjects of Her Majesty.

Sir JOHN A. MACDONALD—The Bill is a very important one. It affects the interests of the Indians who are especially under the guardianship of the Crown and of Parliament. From the statement of the hon. Gentleman, I have a great deal of doubt whether it would be well to give every Indian, when he becomes 21 years of age, the right of absolute disposal of his lands. I am afraid it would introduce into this country a system by which land-sharks could get hold of their estates. However, we will have a better opportunity of discussing the question on the second reading.

. . .

[March 21, 1876]

THE LAWS RESPECTING INDIANS

. . .

Mr. MCGREGOR thought that the Bill was a step in the right direction, as Indians should have it within their power to obtain the full privileges of the white men. The Leader of the Opposition had had the honour of attending at a banquet given to an Indian residing in the County of Peel. The latter's brother, if in the House, would hardly be supposed to be an Indian, and indeed, many hon. members would sooner be so considered than this person.

The Minister of the Interior had visited his county last year, and settled a dispute, which had long existed there between the whites and Indians, the males being allotted 100 and the females 50 acres of the land, the balance being sold. They occupied about 8,000 acres. He regretted that the term of probation was not shorter, as three-quarters of the Indians in his county might very properly be enfranchised at once.

Mr. SNIDER had had a great deal to do with Indian Reserves and with Indians, who he knew were very grateful to the Minister of the Interior for the interest the hon. gentleman had taken in their welfare. He had with great pleasure shown educated Indians around the Parliament Buildings, and these he could say would do the House no discredit if they occupied seats on this floor, being more intelligent than the great majority of white men. This was a great improvement on former similar Bills, and the Indians were perfectly satisfied with its provisions. He did not think that Indians could be so easily tempted with bribes as whites; and he hoped that the Bill would be made as perfect as possible.

Mr. FLEMIMNG [sic] contended that the policy to be pursued with regard to the Indians, must be either one of preservation or one of absorption and amalgation

[sic]. Legislation during the past twenty years had a tendency in the former direction. In 1857 he believed the first Bill having relation to the enfranchisement of Indians had been introduced by the right hon. member for Kingston, who explained that the object was to raise them to the position of white men. If it had failed this was to be ascribed to the fact that the machinery provided had not been sufficient for the purpose. Indians should be placed precisely on the same footing with whites; and they should be made more self-reliant and self-dependent. He was greatly gratified on account of the introduction of the Bill; and he would have been better pleased had it gone still further, offering them greater inducements for self-advancement.

...

[March 28, 1876]

INDIAN LEGISLATION

Hon. Mr. LAIRD moved the House in to Committee of the Whole on the Bill to amend and consolidate the laws respecting Indians.

The first and second clauses were adopted without amendment.

On clause 3,

Mr. PATERSON suggested that the word "male" be struck out.

Hon. Mr. LAIRD said it made no difference, because when an Indian man married a white woman she became a member of the band, but when an Indian woman married a white man, her children did not share in the lands.

Mr. PATERSON doubted if it was wise to impose a penalty on an Indian woman for marrying a white man. He contended it would be a benefit to the country to encourage such intermarriages.

Hon. Mr. Laird said there was a great deal of force in the remarks of the hon. member, and an endeavour was made in another sub-section to meet the objection. It was proposed to allow an Indian woman who married a white man to retain her annuity moneys during her life time, and if she wished to receive the capital sum, she could do so by drawing ten years' purchase of annuity money. Of course she and her husband would then cease to have any connection with the band, and their children would not be considered.

The sub-section was passed.

...

[March 30, 1876]

THE INDIAN LAWS

...

Hon. Mr. LANGEVIN, with reference to Section 26th which provides for the release or surrender of Reserves, held that the majority of the band should be required to be present when this was in consideration.

Hon. Mr. MACKENZIE remarked that an officer of the Government would be present on such occasions, preventing any chance of a mistake.

Hon. Mr. LAIRD was of the opinion that the section gave more protection than when simply the presence of the majority of the Chiefs was required.

Hon. Mr. LANGEVIN—At all events the majority of the band should be present.

Hon. Mr. MACKENZIE—It will never be done without the assistance of the majority.

Mr. SCHULTZ entirely agreed with this hon. friend from Charlevoix [Langevin] in this relation. It was perfectly well known that some of the recent difficulties with Indians in the States has arisn [sic] from the fact that such assent was not obtained.

Hon. Mr. LAIRD—The provision confers quite sufficient protection; an officer of the Government will be in attendance, and if any serious complaint is made attention can be given to it.

Hon. Mr. MACKENZIE—That is substantially provided for in another part of the Bill.

Hon. Mr. LANGEVIN—In what part?

Hon. Mr. MACKENZIE—In the 61st section.

Hon. Mr. LANGEVIN—I cannot prevent the clause from passing but I say once more that the protection is not sufficient. When I was at the head of the Department, complaints were preferred against our officers. They were very jealous—and properly so—of their rights.

Hon. Mr. MACKENIZE [sic]—Is the hon. gentleman satisfied with a majority?

Hon. Mr. LANGEVIN—The majority of the band should be present.

Hon. Mr. MACKENZIE—That is is [sic] required in the 61st Section.

The section was passed.

. . .

[April 4, 1876]

THE INDIAN LAWS

[On section 86, the enfranchisement provisions of the Act]

Hon. Mr. LANGEVIN stated, that after three years of probation, if he remembered right, the Indian would obtain under this Act full title to his property; consequently he might sell it at any time, and white men purchasing might intrude on the reserves. He knew that this had been the objection to the law as it now stood and which was enacted in 1869. The consent of the band to enfranchisement would be obtained for this reason: it would introduce whites on the reserves, and bring about all the evils which followed the mingling of the two races. Great difficulty, at least, would be experienced in obtaining the assent of a band to the enfranchisement of one of their number fitted to enjoy this privilege. He was aware of the delicate nature of this question, but it nevertheless must be settled. They should have in view the gradual enfranchisement of all the Indians living amongst us. He thought that the intention of the government was good, but he did not consider that the result would meet the views of the Minister of the Interior. He drew attention to these matters, because this clause of course contained the principle of this section of the Bill.

Hon. Mr. LAIRD agreed with a great portion of the remarks of the hon [sic] member for Charlevoix; but in the first place the Government thought that it would be very undesirable to frame any scheme for enfranchisement which would not be acceptable to the Indians. If this were done regardless of the consent of the band, confusion, want of harmony, and dissatisfaction would be produced. They knew from experience, and from the deliberations of the Council held the other year at Sarnia, that the Indians generally in these Provinces, were willing to accord enfranchisement to intelligent members of these Bands. By the 88th clause of the Bill, while the enfranchisement enabled them to hold their lands in fee simple, they also had the right to sit in Council and draw their annuities; and this was precisely what the Indians desired. The hon. member remarked that white men might settle on the reserves if these provisions were enforced; but if the great privilege in question was not accorded they would run counter to the whole policy of the Government regarding the surrenders which had existed for years. It was our boast that we did not take an acre of land from the Indians without their consent; and if this privilege were denied them, they would have a right to complain. This Act was in entire harmony with the surrender principle; and he did not think that much trouble would be met in carrying it into effect. The Six Nation Indians did not seem quite prepared for it, but when they saw other Bands accept it, they would soon follow their example. As regarded the North-West Territories, Manitoba and British Columbia, they did not expect that these provisions would be applicable to the Indians living in these regions for some years to come. This was the best they could do under the circumstances; and while they could offer counsel and advice to the Indians at all times, he thought that they should not attempt to act in any way contrary to the views of the Indians, at least as far as their rights to property were concerned. This was the policy of the Administration.

Mr. PATERSON remarked that in 1857 the right hon. member for Kingston had introduced a Bill, in which this feature of enfranchisement was recognised. This law was amended by the hon. member for Charlevoix in 1869, and though the principle was recognised, the law had remained inoperative—in fact a dead letter in this respect. Only one Indian he believed had sought to obtain this privilege under it, but when he had secured it, no land was allotted to him. The Minister of the Interior dwelt upon this subject in his report in language full of eloquence and of truth, stating that he was firmly persuaded that the true interests of the aborigines and the State alike require that every effort should be made to aid the red man in lifting himself out of his condition of tutelage and dependence. It was the duty of the Government then to consider whether every aid was given the Indian seeking enfranchisement. He feared that in some of the tribes the consent of the majority of the Band required by the Acts would not be given, and thus the desire of the Indian seeking enfranchisement be denied.

He would suggest that it should be so amended that when the majority of the tribe refused to allow one of their number the right of enfranchisement, he could have the right of appeal to the General Superintendent; without such a remedy the Bill would, he feared, be defective.

Hon. Mr. Laird said this Bill was found to meet the wishes of the Indians themselves, and consequently they expected it to be more effective than the Bill of 1857. If it was found after a year or two that the suggestion of the hon. gentlemen would be any improvement the law would be easily amended.

Mr. FLEMING said the Indians of the Six Nations were too shrewd and intelligent to accept of the enfranchisement offered under the Acts of 1857 and 1869. If we would enfranchise the Indians we must offer them such inducement as would make it worth their while to ask for. They should first be located on their reserves; first decide what land they should have, and let them feel that this land was theirs forever, but do not give them the power to alienate it to white men, and as soon as they knew exactly what they possessed then they would look for enfranchisement; but the most intelligent Indians were debarred from it by this clause, which would put them in a worse position than they now occupied.

Mr. SCHULTZ said that as the discussion on this Bill had already occupied much time, he would content himself with making some observations generally on the clauses under the heading of enfranchisement. The clauses under this head, he thought objectionable for the following reasons:—They are merely a repetition in a modified form of existing rules which have been found to be utterly inapplicable and are so complicated and cumbersome that it would be next to impossible for an Indian, however well qualified otherwise, to become enfranchised under them; and this is proven by the fact that although the law has been long in existence, no Indian, as far as he knew, has ever availed or attempted to avail himself of its provisions. Again, these clauses would make enfranchisement contingent, not only on the breaking up of the reserves into separate freehold allotments, but also on the Indians ceasing to be Indians under the meaning of the Statutes. It would therefore follow that Indians, no matter how wealthy, intelligent or well-educated, must continue to be without civil rights, unless they comply with rules which, even if they could be complied with, would have the effect of breaking up the whole system of Indian management, thus depriving the Indians of the protection they have hitherto enjoyed, and it is well known, or at least, generally supposed that these rules were adopted in the first instance, with a view to breaking up the tribal system and enabling the white man to get possession of the lands of the Indians.

Again—these causes being, as proved by practical experience of similar ones, inapplicable, will continue to be inoperative, in fact a dead letter, except in so far as that they will, as heretofore, deprive a large number of very deserving people in Ontario at least, of civil rights, and a well-to-do Indian will still have the mortification of seeing his white labourers voting at elections, while he, the son of the soil, finds himself in an inferior position, branded in fact as an outlaw, and unfit to share in the common privileges of a white man. The Act will thus have the very opposite effect to that which was no doubt intended. Instead of imbuing the Indian with a sense of self-respect, and leading them to feel that when they have advanced in civilization they are to stand on an equal footing with the white man, it will have a tendency to degrade them in their own eyes and in the estimation of those around them. The Indians are everywhere so attached to their tribal system that they will not abandon it, and some way should be found of leading them to civilization and independence without trenching on this, their most cherished institution. In Ontario the Indians have, in many cases, passed the probationary period and are in a position to exercise the franchise as judiciously as the majority of white men.

The interpretation of the word "enfranchisement," section 3, subsection 5, does not make the matter any better, but the clause might be relieved to some extent of its objectionable features by using the words "freehold" and "freeholder" for "enfranchised" and "enfranchisement;" and it should be left entirely to the Provinces to say who shall, or who shall not vote at elections, which is the spirit at least, of the present election law.

Hon. Mr. LAIRD said that the term "enfranchised" was defined in the Bill, and in view of hls [sic] hon. friend's representations he proposed introducing an amendment.

Mr. SCHULTZ said he was aware of it, but the definition did not relieve the objectionable features of these clauses. However, he was glad to learn that, in view of the different condition of the Indians of the North-West as compared with those of the older Provinces, the hon. Minister intended to make an amendment to the Bill and as he (Mr. Schultz) had before explained the different circumstances of the Indians of the North-West, he hoped the amendment would be of such a character as would render the Bill applicable to both.

Hon. Mr. LANGEVIN said the Minister of Interior would agree with him it would not be wise to give the Superintendent General the power to enfranchise Indians who had been refused that privilege by the band. It would be better to fix a time—say a period of fifteen years—at the expiration of which all the members of a band should be enfranchised.

Hon. Mr. LAIRD—They would not all be fit.

Hon. Mr. LANGEVIN said there were many white men who were not fit for enfranchisement, yet they enjoyed all the rights of freemen. By being educated all the members of a band would become fit for taking their places in Society. The object of this Bill was to keep the Indians, with the exception of a few, in a state of tutelage. Looking to the future of the race, he believed the true policy should be to do away with that system, by the gradual emancipation of all the Indians who lived in villages and were settled on lands.

Hon. Mr. LAIRD said that would offer no inducement to them to become fit for enfranchisement. Under this Bill they were given some aim to better themselves, and he believed that was the true policy.

Mr. PATERSON said at the same time it struck a blow at the very root of the tribal relation. The very fact of an Indian seeking enfranchisement implied that he no longer wished to be recognized as an Indian.

Hon. Mr. LAIRD—An Indian is not cut off from his band by enfranchisement. He belongs to the tribe as much as ever he did.

Mr. PATERSON said it was impossible at the same time to preserve the tribal relations and facilitate the enfranchisement of the Indians. If the Government were prepared to take the position that the tribal relations must continue for all time to come, then it was a mistake to do any thing in the way of enfranchisement at all. It was evident the proposition of the hon. member for Charlevoix would have to be adopted ere long—a time must be fixed when all Indians living in the midst of civilized communities and refusing to move to the North West, must be enfranchised. Take the Brant reserve for instance. The Indians there are increasing rapidly, and something must be done to meet their case. They would not remove to a larger reserve, and there remained only the alternative of enfranchising the whole band at a certain time.

The clause passed.

. . .

1.3 Report of Proceedings Relative to and Comprising a Resolution Passed by the Chippewa or Ojibway Grand Council Approving of the New Indian Act, 1876

The Indian Act received royal assent in April 1876. In July, a meeting of the Grand Council of the Ojibway met to discuss the Indian Act. Anishinaabe had a long tradition of summertime meetings that brought together people from autonomous settlements for political, social, and cultural work. Formal councils of Anishinaabe political leaders had been meeting to discuss the legislative work of colonial governments since at least the 1850s, and a council was convened to review the 1857 "Act to Encourage the Gradual Civilization of the Indian Tribes." In 1870, the Grand River Haudenosaunee invited Anishinaabe, Munsee, and Moravian delegates to join them in a meeting to discuss relations with Canada and the successive acts passed by colonial legislature, and the Grand General Indian Council of Ontario and Quebec—or the Grand Council—was formed.[95] Over the 1860s and 1870s, several Anishinaabe and Haudenosaunee leaders travelled to Ottawa to meet with government officials and maintained active correspondence on matters relating to Indigenous lands, rights, and governance. In 1870, a lengthy meeting of the Grand Council rejected many of clauses of the 1869 Gradual Enfranchisement Act. The Grand Council remained, however, willing to work with the government and offered its own proposed amendments and revisions to the 1869 act. Councillors conferred with government officials on the drafting of the 1876 legislation. In the 1876 Indian Act, they recognized some of their own suggestions, in particular their view that bands should retain control over who could be enfranchised and what land could be allotted to them. In this way, communities retained sovereignty over membership and over land allocation, at least as far as enfranchisement was

---

95 Norman Shields, "Anishinabek Political Alliance in the Post-Confederation Period: The Grand General Indian Council of Ontario, 1870–1936" (master's thesis, Queens University, 2001), 39.

concerned. The fact that Anishinaabe leaders had been successful in shaping some portion of the Indian Act is likely the reason they supported the act in this vote. It should be noted, however, that the minutes here are of the "Grand Ojibway Council" not the Grand Council that included Anishinaabe, Munsee, Moravian, and Six Nations members.[96]

Source: Department of the Interior, Indian Branch, "Headquarters—Report of Proceedings of the Chippewa Grand Council Approving of the New Indian Act," LAC, RG 10, vol. 1994, file 6829, online MIKAN no. 2079430.

Southampton, Saugeen, Grand Ojibway Council, July 12th 1876

Grand Council opened at 9 am. Seventeen Bands or Reservations being represented, viz. Rama, Saugeen, Walpole Island, Kettle Point, Sauble, Snake Island, Georgina Island, Scugog, Garden River, Muncytown, Cape Croker, New Credit, Alnwick, Rice Lake, Sarnia, Christian Island & Shawanaga—Total 17.

The President & Vice President read and explained the various sections of [the] whole of the new Indian Act of 1876, after which a lengthy & interesting discussion ensued, in which, the following took part, Chief J. Henry, Puhgwujenine, Wm. Wawanosh, Lamorandrer, Waucaush, J. T. Kirby, Revd H. P. Chase, Revd J. Jacobs, J. B. Nanigishkung, Andrew Jacobs, D. Sawyer, Sumner, Mahjegeshig, Kabaosa, Wahbemama, Menace, J. Fisher, Paudaush, etc, etc.

After which the following resolution was moved by Chief Chief [sic] J. Henry & seconded Chief J. Fisher and resolved—"That this Grand Council hereby direct their President & Secretary to notify the Hon. D. Laird, Supt. Genl. of Indian affairs for Canada, that this Grand Council accepts the Indian Act of 1876, passed by the Dominion Parliament at their last session, carried."

Sixty six delegates voted in favour of the resolution, & one against it. Great cheering ensued at the passing of this resolution by such an overwhelming Majority, or almost unanimous vote.

Moved by Chief Wm. Wawanosh, Vice Prest and seconded by the Revd J. Jacobs, Grand Secretary, "That this Grand Council assembled at Saugeen, desire to express its gratitude to the Hon. D. Laird, S.G.I.A. and to the other members of the present Dominion Government for the Indian Act of 1876, passed at their last session, and hope to see the Indians of Canada elevated & benefitted by the enfranchisement therein permitted, and have not doubt that many of our people will avail themselves of its advantages," Carried unanimously.

Signed,
H. P. Chase.
J. Jacobs, Grand Secretary
Grand Ojibway Council Room, Saugeen Indian Village, July 12, 1876

---

96 Shields, "Anishinabek Political Alliance," 57.

1.4 Grand Indian Council of the Province of Ontario, Held at Sarnia, June 27, 1879

These minutes were reproduced in a local settler newspaper, the *Wiarton Echo*, which indicates significant interest in Indigenous politics among local settler communities. Many of the individual people named here were well known locally. They were ordained ministers in the Anglican Church (then known either as the Episcopalian Church [American usage] or the Church of England). Especially well known were Rev. Henry P. Chase and Rev. John Jacobs. Abel Waucaush remained in a leadership position into the 1890s. William Wawanosh was elected chief of Aamjiwnaang (in this document referred to as Sarnia) in 1874 and then again in 1899. The Six Nations had, in 1878, withdrawn from the Grand Council. Although the minutes were taken by the secretary and reproduced in English, delegates spoke in their own Indigenous languages and with translators working tirelessly to ensure that all understood the proceedings.[97]

Source: *Wiarton Echo,* August 15, August 29, September 5, September 12, September 19, October 17, 1879.

Grand Indian Council of the Province of Ontario

Held at Sarnia, June 27th, 1879.

Inquiries having been made, as to what has been done at the Grand Indian Councils held from time to time in different parts of the Province of Ontario, we have decided to publish the entire proceedings of the last Grand Council, held at Sarnia of 187[9] for the benefit of our readers who are interested.

First Days Session.

Sarnia, June 27th 1879.

At 11 am the Chiefs and delegates to the Grand Council of the Province of Ontario, formed themselves into a procession and marched to the Council House in the following order:

New Credit Brass Band
Delegates
Chiefs

---

97   Shields, "Anishinabek Political Alliance," 60–61; Murdoch, "Reactions to Enactment."

Grand Secretary
Vice-President
The President.

When assembled, the president, Rev. H. P. Chase, gave out the first hymn, which was sung in the native tongue. The Grand Secretary, Rev. J. Jacobs, then called the roll of delegates, when 85 chiefs and delegates answered to their names.

The Bands represented at present number 13, viz: 1. New Credit, Georgina and Snake Island; 2. Six Nations, of Grand River; 3. Walpole Island; 4. Lower Muncey; 5. Chippewas of Munceytown; 6. Rama; 7. Cape Croker; 8. Alnick; 9. Saugeen; 10. Garden River; 11. Sarnia; 12. Kettle Point and Sauble.[98]

. . .

The President [Chief John Henry] then rose and made a short but very impressive address . . . and declared the Council open for transaction of business and in doing so, would say that there were several sections in the Act of 1876 that he would like to bring under the notice of the Grand Council, a state of which he would lay before them viz: Sections 16, 12, Sub. 12, 79, 16, 88, 91, 83 and Sub. 3.

. . .

Before the business of the council was resumed, Senator Vidal made a short and happy address, referring to the part he had taken in the Upper House to pass the temperance part of the Indian Act of 1876 stating that also the Government was protecting the rights of the Indians to the jealousy of the whites. . . .

Abel Waucaush said that the Indian Act for 1876 did not give sufficient protection. They could not prosecute and get convictions for trespass on their reserve. He would therefore move, seconded by [John] French, that Section 16 be rejected or altered to suit the requirements for which it was intended. Chief G. H. M. Johnson said—before the motion was put he wished to make a few remarks. He found no difficulty in enforcing the law and had, under its provision made several convictions. He was satisfied with it. The white people alone who were made to suffer under it, thought it was too stringent. John French said that he was very much surprised to hear the last speaker say that the law did not want any alteration. They had been unable to obtain satisfaction. They had to get advice from the Superintendent-General, and the delay thereby incurred was the means of the getting away out of reach of trespassers.

. . .

Rev. John Jacobs[99] now came forward and referred to the steps he had taken to avail himself of the franchise, (Sec. 86, Sub-sec.1) but had received official letters

---

98 The discrepancy in number may result from Kettle Point and Sauble sometimes being considered one community and sometimes two separate "bands."

99 For more information on John Jacobs, see "Finding Syncretism in John Jacob's Hymnbook," *Confronting Colonialism: Land, Literacies & Learning*, Huron University College Research Paper, http://www.huronresearch.ca/confrontingcolonialism/finding-syncretism-in-john-jacobs-hymnbook/ and David A. Nock, "Wilson, Edward Francis," in *Dictionary of Canadian Biography*, vol. 14, University of Toronto/Université Laval, 2003, http://www.biographi.ca/en/bio/wilson_edward_francis_14E.html (both accessed June 29, 2018).

to say that professional men had no further claim amongst their own people, and therefore laid the matter before the Grand Council. President John Henry said that the law depriving ministers of their rights was a hardship, and the clause ought to be laid aside. Moved by Andrew Jacobs, seconded by Joseph Wawanosh, that Subsection 1, under Section 86, be annulled.

. . .

Josiah Hill . . . went on to say that at Grand River[100] they did not wish to exclude their professional men unless they went away of their own accord. The Act ought to have two years more of trial. He considered it the best law ever made for the Indians, and the Grand Council would commit an act of folly to ask for its repeal.

Chief Summer [sic] said that the Chippewas ought to be careful how they considered the Act, as it was not all good. All they had to do was to ask for alterations where they saw [sic] objections.

William Wawanosh[101] wished to point out that if Mr. Jacobs was very anxious to make his exit as the law stood, give him free liberty to do so; but at the same time he objected to the law, and thought it very wrong. Under it no one would try to attain high positions.

Josiah Hill again urged in sustaining the whole Act.

Abel Waucaush spoke in favor of protecting educated Indians in their laudable efforts to attain high situations. He did not want to take away what belonged to them from their births, and otherwise made a good argument, sustaining his address.

The motion was then put and carried by a large majority.

. . .

Fred Wahbezee said at Saugeen cases had occurred where two women had lost their annuities in marrying outside their own Band. He thought it a great hardship when the law deprived them of their birthright, and it should be changed. They had tried to get the men admitted into their Band, but failed.

Joseph Wawanosh said he being a Treaty Indian, he liked the law as it stood. He said there was [sic] plenty of instances here where strange and outside Indians had married into the Band, and of course had been admitted to share all the privileges enjoyed by themselves. Those persons had invariably proved to be drunkards and disturbers of the peace, which gave the local Indian a very bad name. He would fight against the motion.

The mover said he did not wish to press his motion, but would merely say that if left as it is, it will do a great injustice. Stated cases of the kind taking place in his own reserve.

David Sawyer said he saw no harm the law could do if left as it is.

John Nicholas said he was in favour of holding the law as it stood. It was

---

100 Josiah Hill served as secretary to the Grand River Council for forty years until his death in 1915. Grand River is the largest Haudenosaunee reserve in Ontario. Hill, *The Clay We Are Made Of*, 211.

101 For more information on the reserve at Sarnia, Aamjiwnaang, see "History," Aamjiwnaang, http://www.aamjiwnaang.ca/history/.

expected that a man was able to support his wife, and did not marry for the sake of money, and was bound to take his wife to his own home and act like a man. (Great laughter).

1.5 Memorial from about 300 Chiefs and Warriors of the Six Nations to the Right Honourable Sir John A. Macdonald against the [Indian] Act of 1876, Ohsweken Council House, January 8, 1879

The Great Law of Peace established the Haudenosaunee Confederacy by uniting the Mohawks, Oneidas, Onondagas, Cayugas, and Senecas long before the arrival of Europeans. Later, the Tuscarora joined to make the Six Nations Confederacy. As a complex and united political entity, the Haudenosaunee Confederacy made its own alliances and treaties with the Dutch, English, and French colonial authorities. In particular, the "Covenant Chain" and the two-row wampum signify nation-to-nation relationships between European powers and the Haudenosaunee. For this reason, the Haudenosaunee have always considered themselves beyond the authority of the Canadian settler state.[102] This document is a clear statement of their position and their view of the Indian Act.

Source: "Six Nations Reserve—Petition form Several Indians Protesting the Indian Act of 1876," LAC, RG 10, vol. 2077, file 11,432, MIKAN no. 2063084

To the

Right Hon. Sir John A. McDonald [sic]

Premier and

Superintendent of Indian Affairs

We the undersigned Chiefs and warriors of the Six Nations Indians residing on the Grand River Reservation desire to say a few words concerning our affairs touching the welfare of our people, the Six Nations Indians.

1st We find the Indian Act of 1876 are [sic] not calculated to promote our welfare if we accept it because it empowers the Superintendent General of Indian affairs to manage, govern, and control our lands, moneys, and properties without first

---

102 Hill, *The Clay We Are Made Of.*

obtaining the consent of the chiefs of the Six Nations, as in section 2nd of the Act, is contrary to the will of the Six Nations.

2nd Moreover, the Dominion parliament can pass a special Act under the said Act and carry out the same without first obtaining the consent or the approval of the Chiefs in Council, as it has been done already before we have legally accepted the said Act.

3rd We believe that the Act in question will in time deprive us of our liberties, rights, and privileges which we now enjoy under the Treaty between Great Britain and the Six Nations Indians, and we have no wish other than faithfully adhering to the Treaty with pleasure so great the words of our brother the Earl of Dufferin when he visited us in 1874 saying the people of Canada and the people of Great Britain will not cease to recognise these obligations which have been impressed upon them by the hand of Providence towards their Indian fellow subjects, and never shall a word of Britain once pledged be broken. This we are well aware and have every confidence in the government of our Great Mother, Queen Victoria, that she will never overlook these high and important obligations which have entered into but will respect it and continue till the end of time.

Therefore we wish you to take this into your serious consideration and cause the Governor in Council may be please to exempt us from the operation of this Act. But rather have us frame our own laws, rules and regulations suitable for our advancement as well as our welfare and have the Governor in Council confirm the same for our deed is given by King George the 3rd through General Haldimand with the seal of Great Britain . . . declares that the Mohawks and others of the Six Nations enjoy the land it covers, they and their heirs for ever.

Council House, Ohsweken, 8th January 1879.

1.6 Vern Harper, Interview Transcript, Indian History Film Project, Interviewed by Alex Cywink at the Toronto Native Friendship Centre, June 23, 1983

Between 1982 and 1985, interviewers Christine Welsh, Tony Snowsill, and their colleagues recorded conversations with Indigenous people from Manitoba, Saskatchewan, and Alberta in preparation for a film series for television. The film series was to depict Canadian history from Indigenous perspectives. It was never produced.[103]

Vern Harper. Cree/Métis, was born in Toronto on June 17, 1936. In this interview, Mr. Harper talks about life in a foster home and the suppression of life on reserves in the 1950s. He then goes on to discuss traditional values, philosophy, and ceremony, which he encountered on his grandmother's reserve at Sandy Lake. The excerpt begins as he returns to Canada during a cross-country

---

103 Indian History Film Project, fonds description, Oral History Centre, http://www.
oralhistorycentre.ca/fonds/indian-history-film-project (accessed July 31, 2017). Reprinted by
permission of the University of Regina Press.

trip from Toronto to his family's home at Mistawasis reserve and Sandy Lake reserve, the home of his grandmother.

Source: Vern Harper, Interview conducted by Alex Cywink, June 23, 1983, tape number IH-OT.23, transcript disc 115, Indian History Film Project, Canadian Plains Research Centre, University of Regina, http://ourspace.uregina.ca/handle/10294/26 (accessed July 31, 2017). Reprinted by permission of The University of Regina Press.

And coming into Canada I got excited, because, you know, I hadn't seen my relatives and at that time—that was in the '50s, early, almost middle '50s, no early '50s I guess, '53, '54—and that time reservations, reserves as we call them in Canada—were very tight. They had Indian Agents, farmer instructors [. . .] they had power. The chiefs and councillors really had no say, no nothing. That had been taken away from them. And they had . . . it was very difficult because the Indian agent associated with the non-natives, he wouldn't associate with other Indian people—only on the business. And most of the time these farmer instructors and Indian Agents were ex-RCMP, are ex-provosts. They were Canadian army—they have a military policy, are called provosts. So they came from military background and they were usually men who had been in service [. . .] and so they gave them jobs too. So they were very materialistic, and very military-oriented, and they ruled . . . I remember the Mistawasis Reserve, and I go to my grandma's reserve, Sandy Lake, Star Blanket Reserve and another one, and it was very, they were like concentration camps in the thick sense of—where the Indian agent had total control. And they had health nurses there, and the health nurses were white, the missionaries were white, the Indian agent was white and they all kept to themselves. And they were very paternalistic towards the native people there. I know the style, I know the style. It was pretty, pretty, it took quite adjusting to . . . [. . .]

I remember some times the door being kicked open by this farmer instructor and Indian Agent. And then they used to like travelling around with the RCMP for . . . sometimes with children who weren't going to school . . . just for minor things, or someone didn't pay a fine, they would kick the person's door down and drag them out. That was the early '50s where none of the people on the reserve had any control of their lives or anything. [. . .]

1.7 Adam Solway, Interview Transcript, Indian History Film Project, Interviewed by Christine Welsh and Tony Snowsill, on the Blackfoot Reserve, Alberta, January 29, 1983

This interview is another one collected as part of the Indian History Film Project. In this interview, Chief and Councillor Adam Solway reflects on his life on the Blackfoot (Siksika) reserve, where he came to live after being orphaned at eight years old. He speaks about his time in residential school; his first paid employment on the reserve, burying the dead, including those left unburied following a smallpox epidemic in the 1860s; and then on the various political battles fought on the Blackfoot reserve, including a land surrender in 1908. As a political leader within the Blackfoot, he was among those who protested the White Paper in 1969, and participated in the negotiations around the place of Aboriginal rights in the repatriated Canadian constitution.[104] He had just stepped down from his position of band councillor at the time of this interview. Here he reflects specifically on the impact of the social services placement of children in non-Indigenous homes, known as the "sixties scoop," on the effects of assimilation on Indigenous governance, and on the impact of enfranchisement on Indigenous women.

Source: Adam Solway, Interview 1, conducted by Christine Welsh and Tony Snowsill, on the Blackfoot Reserve, Alberta, January 29, 1983, tape number IH-010, transcript disc 4, Indian History Film Project, Canadian Plains Research Centre, University of Regina, http://ourspace.uregina.ca/handle/10294/2152 (accessed July 31, 2017). Reprinted by permission of the University of Regina Press.

Some of our leaders today, they have been placed in homes, in non-Indian homes by social services. Naturally these people are living like the white man outside until such age when they reach 21 years then they will have a say. Because they never had no say while from birth up to 21. And that is the age limit they allow, when they are 21 years old make up your mind, you want to go back to your tribe or be franchised. Naturally, a lot of them go back to their tribes. And the poor old stupid Indian comes around, "Oh look at that guy, he is educated. Look at the English he is using, look at all of the big words. He must be educated." And he is the guy that was brought up outside, never had any insight of his own people, how they were living from day to day, how they went about their religious doctrines, how they went by with their Indian government, no idea whatsoever with their education as an Indian student. Poor Indian says, "Okay I'll elect or nominate this guy that was brought up outside." And the poor bugger he gets elected and he gets himself into a bind. He wants to brainwash the rest of his tribe to live the way he was brought up. In which it is a real, real hard thing to do. You can't change a Chinaman into an Indian. Sure, he might know the slang or the language that they use but you can't, by the nature things, that is your problem. You can remain an Indian, you were born an Indian, he'll die as an Indian. But how in the heck are you going to get that brown stain off of your skin? That is

---

104 In 1969, the federal government introduced the "Statement of the Government of Canada on Indian Policy, 1969," which sought to remove distinct legal status from Indians under the law. It was roundly rejected by Indigenous political entities. Forceful lobbying on the part of Indigenous political groups forced the government to include them in constitutional discussions. J. R. Miller, *Skyscrapers Hide the Heavens: A History of Indian-White Relations in Canada*, 3rd ed. (Toronto: University of Toronto Press, 2000), 331–57.

what they are trying to do here, that is why they are integrating. So, what we do here, we respect these things, sure he is educated, but there is limitations on his knowledge. There is limitations in his religious belief. . . .

. . . my daughter is married to a non-Indian and I told her, I said, "My girl, you got special status, you got a treaty right, aboriginal right, and you got your rights of culture. If you do franchise and marry this guy by law, you are franchised automatically. You are no more Indian. You have no more benefits for education, health, or economic development." "Oh," she says, "I am going to marry a guy that is rich. He has a store, he has an elevator, he has a bus, and he is a big farmer." "Oh by gosh, by all means, if he is that rich, go ahead, but I still say you are richer than him. If he fails in these operations, where does he go? You go down to welfare or skid row." Exactly what I told them. This fellow couldn't run that elevator, he couldn't run the store, couldn't run the bus, fired here and there. Where is she? She is trying to make a U-turn, come back on the reserve. And that is the biggest problem we have in politics today. . . .

Chapter Two

Governance

In the last chapter, we emphasized the first three categories of analysis drawn from historical and Indigenous methodologies: change over time, relationship, and context. These concepts continue to be foundational. In this set of documents, you can observe change over time, as the Indian Act amendments shifted and shaped the nature of reserve community governance. We want you to consider consulting the reports of the Department of Indian Affairs found in the *Sessional Papers* of Canada's Parliament; these will give you important context.[105] You may also wish to consult the sources referred to in the footnotes for further information. Crop Eared Wolf and Deskaheh both have entries in the *Dictionary of Canadian Biography*, and so we ask that you consider both the author and the audience of the documents about or by these Indigenous men. Relationships permeate these documents, as the Indian Act seeks to determine who governs and how, and the subsequent documents reveal the effects of the Indian Act on relationships within Indigenous communities and between them and settler communities and government.

In this chapter, we are going to ask you to build on these foundational concepts and add two more: responsibility, adapted from Indigenous methodologies, and causality, from the five Cs of historical thinking.

Indigenous methods ask us to consider responsibility—to whom are the actors in our texts responsible? Who gives them authority to act on their behalf, and how do leaders respond to and express that responsibility? The Department of Indian Affairs used a form to capture the moment when an Indigenous person became chief of his reserve community. What do we learn about the nature of the chief's responsibility from this form? How does the

---

105 These reports are available online and are keyword searchable. They can be found here: https://www.bac-lac.gc.ca/eng/discover/aboriginal-heritage/first-nations/indian-affairs-annual-reports/Pages/introduction.aspx.

form itself constrain events? What rules does it express? How might there be slippage between the form and the event?

As we examine the letter from R. N. Wilson to the Indian Commission, we can read with the grain and ask how R. N. Wilson seeks to describe Crop Eared Wolf as irresponsible? What language does he use? Have a look at the "Questions of Content" section of "Appendix A: Reading Historically" to think more deeply about how Wilson makes his case against Crop Eared Wolf. Do you find his argument convincing? At what point in his argument are you more inclined to agree, and are there points when he loses you?

Reading against the grain, we can also discern instances and practices whereby Crop Eared Wolf indicates to whom he feels responsible and how he expresses that responsibility. To whose authority does Crop Eared Wolf appeal? Whom does he consult? How does he act upon his convictions as a leader? Is there unity within the community? Is unity a realistic expectation of Crop Eared Wolf's chieftainship? Why or why not? What does this tell us about Indigenous leadership? Has the Indian Act revised the way leaders act in this Kainai community; in what ways is leadership different and in what ways is it not?

Turning to the text *New Story of the Iroquois* by Chief Deskaheh, we can add questions of causality to those of responsibility, relationship, context, and change over time. To whom is Deskaheh speaking? And over what medium? Are you surprised by this? What has caused him to give this speech at this time and in this way? What specific factors have led him to take this action? What actions taken by the Canadian government did he wish to expose? How do these factors shape not only the medium and timing of this speech but also its tone and the language he uses? Again, review the "Questions of Content" in Appendix A and look closely at Deskaheh's language and argument. How does he describe change over time, and how does this shape the way he addresses his audience? What aspects of Haudenosaunee history did he feel warranted the respect of Canadians and Americans?

As you examine the text and the context of it, ask how responsibility and the importance of relationship are expressed. To whom was Deskaheh responsible? What relationships gave him authority, and how did the Indian Act seek to destroy those relationships? How did he view Haudenosaunee relationships with the Crown, with the Canadian and American people? How does he seek to build relationship with his audience, so its members will understand his message?

Now turn your attention to the selections from the final report of the Royal Commission on Aboriginal Peoples (RCAP) on governance. The tone of this document is very different from that of the ones discussed previously. How is its tone meant to convey authority? The commission itself discusses its context in the first volume of its report, found here: https://www.aadnc-aandc. gc.ca/eng/1100100014597/1100100014637#chp1.

What caused the Canadian government to undertake this commission at the time it did? How might the tone and content of its report be a response to these circumstances? Look at the footnotes. Where did the bulk of the commission's information originate? How and why is this significant? To whom were the report's writers responsible?

As you read the selections we have chosen from the RCAP, consider how responsibility is expressed through leadership and decision making. Having read this document, read back over the letter from R. N. Wilson and the address by Deskaheh. Does the report of the Royal Commission on Aboriginal Peoples add to your understanding of these documents? Do you have more information that would allow you to read against the grain to see beyond the intended message of either Wilson or Deskaheh? Is there anything, particularly in R. N. Wilson's letter, that now strikes you as questionable?

These are the kinds of questions that historians use to query sources, to pull out as much meaning from the written text as we possibly can. Are there questions that you used on these documents that you think might be useful to consider when you read or hear about Indigenous governance today?

Documents

2.1 An Act to Amend and Consolidate the Laws Respecting Indians [Indian Act of 1876], sections 61 to 63, Council and Chiefs

This section of the Indian Act defined who could participate in government at the local level. The intent of this section is clear: to encourage Indigenous peoples to abandon their traditional forms of governance and to take up a limited form of democracy. In line with the Canadian franchise, only men over the age of 21 were permitted to vote. Officially, then, women, who had often played quite powerful roles in traditional forms of Indigenous governance, were now shut out of the political process.

Indian agent surveillance constrained local autonomy. The Indian agent oversaw elections, determined if the men elected were fit to serve, and removed those deemed unfit. Despite these intrusions, Indigenous people never relinquished political sovereignty at the local level. Indigenous leaders took the list of local responsibilities ascribed to "Chiefs and Councils" by this section of the Indian Act as evidence that the government recognized their ability to administer their own communities, but their powers of enforcement were scarce. Subsequent iterations of and amendments to the Indian Act only further constrained Indigenous self-government. Indigenous leadership and organizations such as the Grand Council persistently lobbied for legislative changes that would allow them greater sovereignty.[106]

---

106 Murdoch, "Reactions to Enactment."

Source: Canada, An Act to Amend and Consolidate the Laws
Respecting Indians, *Statutes of Canada* 39 Vic. (1876) c.18.

_____

CHAP. 18.
An Act to amend and consolidate the laws respecting Indians.

[*Assented to 12th April, 1876.*]

COUNCILS AND CHIEFS

Votes at election of chiefs.

61. At the election of chief or chiefs, or the granting of any ordinary consent required of a band of Indians under this Act, those entitled to vote at the council or meeting thereof shall be the male members of the band of the full age of twenty-one years; and the vote of a majority of such members at a council or meeting of the band summoned according to their rules, and held in the presence of the Superintendent-General, or an agent acting under his instructions, shall be sufficient to determine such election, or grant such consent; *In ordinary cases.* Provided that in the case of any band having a council of chiefs or councillors, any ordinary consent required of the band may be granted by a vote of a majority of such chiefs or councillors at a council summoned according to their rules, and held in the presence of the Superintendent-General or his agent.

Periods of election how fixed: and term of office.

Number of chiefs.

Proviso: as to life chief.

62. The Governor in Council may order that the chiefs of any band of Indians shall be elected, as hereinbefore provided, at such time and place, as the Superintendent-General may direct, and they shall in such case be elected for a period of three years, unless deposed by the Governor for dishonesty, intemperance, immorality, or incompetency; and they may be in the proportion of one head chief and two second chiefs or councillors for every two hundred Indians; but any such band composed of thirty Indians may have one chief: Provided always, that all life chiefs now living shall continue as such until death or resignation, or until their removal by the Governor for dishonesty, intemperance, immorality, or incompetency.

Chiefs to make regulations for certain purposes.

63. The chief or chiefs of any band in council may frame, subject to confirmation by the Governor in Council, rules and regulations for the following subjects, viz.:
   1. The care of the public health;
   2. The observance of order and decorum at assemblies of the Indians in general council, or on other occasions;
   3. The repression of intemperance and profligacy;
   4. The prevention of trespass by cattle;

5. The maintenance or roads, bridges, ditches and fences;
6. The construction and repair of school houses, council houses and other Indian public buildings;
7. The establishments of pounds and the appointment of pound-keepers;
8. The locating of the land in their reserves, and the establishment of a register of such locations.

...

2.2 An Act to Amend and Consolidate the Laws Respecting Indians, S.C. 1880, chapter 28, section 72

Within four years, legislators were already working to amend the Indian Act (1876). This amendment, which achieved royal assent in May 1880, now stated that elected chiefs could displace the authority of life chiefs. Elsewhere in the act, further powers were given to elected band councils, including input into the selection school teachers, weed control, and the addition of mechanisms for enforcing band council by-laws, so long as this enforcement was overseen by a justice of the peace, often the Indian agent.[107]

Source: Canada, An Act to Amend and Consolidate the Laws
Respecting Indians, *Statutes of Canada* 43 Vic. (1880) c.18.

_____

CHAP. 28.
An Act to amend and consolidate the laws respecting Indians.

[Assented to 7th May, 1880.]

Governor in Council may provide for election of Chiefs. 72. Whenever the Governor in Council deems it advisable for the good government of a band to introduce the election system of chiefs, he may by Order in Council provide that the chiefs of any band of Indians shall be elected, as hereinafter provided, at such time and place as the Superintendent-General may direct; and they shall, in such case, be elected for a period of three years, unless deposed by the Governor for dishonesty, intemperance, immorality or incompetency;

_____

107 Shields, "Anishinabek Political Alliance," 65; Murdock, "Reactions to Enactment"; Leslie and Maguire, *The Historical Development of the Indian Act*, 78.

Proviso: as to number.	and they may be in the proportion of one head chief and two second chiefs or councillors for every two hundred Indians: Provided, that no band shall have more than six head chiefs and twelve second chiefs, but any band composed of thirty Indians may have one chief:
Proviso: as to present life chiefs.	Provided always, that all life chiefs now living shall continue to hold the rank of chief until death or resignation, or until their removal by the Governor for dishonesty, intemperance, immorality or incompetency:
Further proviso as them.	Provided also, that in the event of His Excellency ordering that the chiefs of a band shall be elected, then and in such case the life chiefs shall not exercise the powers of chiefs unless elected under such order to the exercise of such powers.

2.3 An Act for Conferring Certain Privileges on the More Advanced Bands of the Indians of Canada, with the View of Training Them for the Exercise of Municipal Powers [Indian Advancement Act], 1884

This act, also known as the Indian Advancement Act, was passed in order to promote municipal-style government for Indigenous peoples in Quebec, Ontario, New Brunswick, and Nova Scotia.[108] In addition to regular council elections and set terms of office, the act allowed for tax collection and by-law enforcement.[109] Although some appreciated the expanding jurisdiction of the band councils, others recognized that the act was designed to undermine traditional governance. The Haudenosaunee Confederacy Council, for example, was quick to denounce the act.[110] The intent of these measures was made even clearer when set in the context of Parliament's larger legislative agenda for Indigenous peoples. Also in 1884, the Indian Act was amended in response to resistance in western Canada to make it illegal to sell or give fixed ammunition or ball cartridges to Indians of Manitoba and the North-West Territories (now Alberta and Saskatchewan). The same amendment also criminalized the ceremonies by which leadership among Indigenous people of the north Pacific Coast was confirmed—known by the word used for them in the Chinook trading jargon: potlatch. These acts and amendments were clearly designed to encourage

---

108 John F. Leslie, "The Indian Act: An Historical Perspective," *Canadian Parliamentary Review* 25, no. 2 (n.d.): 25.

109 John Leslie and Ron Maguire, *The Historical Development of the Indian Act*, 85.

110 Susan M. Hill, *The Clay We Are Made Of*, 192.

Euro-Canadian-style governance under the direction of the Indian agent and to undermine Indigenous sovereignty.[111]

Source: Canada, Indian Advancement Act, *Statutes of Canada* 47 Vic. (1884) c.28.

CHAP. 28.
An Act for conferring certain privileges on the more advanced Bands of the Indians of Canada, with the view of training them for the exercise of municipal powers.

[Assented to 19th April, 1884.]

Meetings of the Council: agent or deputy to preside, his powers and duties.

9. The council shall meet for the despatch of business, at such place on the reserve, and at such times as the agent for the reserve shall appoint, not being less than four nor more than twelve times in the year for which it is elected, and due notice of the time and place of each meeting shall be given to each councillor by the agent; at such meeting the agent for the reserve or his deputy, to be appointed for the purpose with the consent of the Superintendent General or his deputy, shall preside and record the proceedings, and shall have full power to control and regulate all matters of procedure and form, and to adjourn the meeting to a time named or sine die, and to report and certify all by-laws and other acts and proceedings of the council to the Superintendent General; and full faith and credence shall be given to his certificate thereof in all courts and places whatsoever: he shall address the council and explain and advise them upon their powers and duties, and any matter requiring their consideration, but shall have no vote on any question to be decided by the council ; but each councillor present shall have a vote thereon, and it shall be decided by the majority of votes, the chief voting as a councillor and having also a casting vote in case the votes would otherwise be equal; four councillors shall be a quorum for the despatch of any business.

---

111 Leslie and Maguire, *The Historical Development of the Indian Act*, 81; Hill, *The Clay We Are Made Of*; Tobias, "Protection, Civilization, Assimilation," 134.

Illustration 2.1: Crop Eared Wolf, circa 1900–1913.

Source: Glenbow Archives (NB-3-9)

2.4 Declaration of Crop Eared Wolf as Chief, October 17, 1900

The Indian Act necessitated an enormous bureaucracy in order to administer
its provisions. The Department of Indian Affairs had personnel in Ottawa and
in communities across Canada. Forms such as this one were meant to stan-
dardize the interactions between staff and Indigenous leaders, and to ensure
that agreements made between staff and Indigenous people conformed to
the Indian Act. In this form, we see that Crop Eared Wolf has signed with an
X. This may indicate that he was not literate. If this is the case, then we have
no way of knowing whether he knew precisely to what he was agreeing when
he affixed his X to this form.

Source: Declaration of Crop Eared Wolf as Chief, October 17, 1900, Department of Indian Affairs fonds, LAC, RG 10, vol. 3939, file 121698 3, image 9/76.

DECLARATION OF CHIEF OR COUNCILLOR.　　　　204979

DOMINION OF CANADA.　)
　　　　　　　　　　　　)
DISTRICT OF *Alberta,*　)
　　　　　　　　　　　　)
Blood Indian Agency.　)　I, Crop Ear Wolf do solemnly
declare that I will well and truly serve our Sovereign Lady the Queen in the Office of *Head Chief* of the *Upper----------* band of Indians, without favour or affection, malice, or ill-will; that I will strictly obey all the laws and regulations of our Sovereign Lady the Queen; that I will to the best of my ability endeavor to prevent all contraventions of the said laws and regulations by any member of my band; that I will report all infractions of the laws and regulations by any member of my band; that I will report all infractions of the laws and regulations at the earliest opportunity to the Indian Agent over me; and that I will strive to advance the interests of all the Indians of my band morally and financially, both by precept and example, and generally fulfil all the duties of the office to which I have been elected for an indefinite term, to the best of my skill and knowledge.

That this declaration has been read through to me and explained to me ~~both~~[112] in the *Blackfoot* languages, and I understand the nature of the said declaration.

Declared before me at *Blood Agency,*　　　　　*His*
In the District of *Alberta*　　　　　　　　*Crop Ear Wolf* X
This *17th* day of *October*　　　　　　　　*Mark.*
A.D. 1900, this declaration ~~having been~~
~~first read through to me by the department~~
~~Blackfoot~~
~~in the English language which he [?] appeared~~
~~to clearly understand,~~
　　(having been interpreted to him in
　　(
　　(my presence in the *Blackfoot* language
　　(
　　(which he understood.
　　　　Jas. Wilson
　　　　Indian agent
　　Witness + Interpreter J. English

112　Strike-throughs in this document are in the original.

Illustration 2.2: Kainai Chiefs, 1905. L-R back row: Joe Healy, interpreter; Running Crane. L-R front row: Blackfoot Old Woman, Day Chief, Crop Eared Wolf.

Source: Glenbow Archives (NA-201-1)

2.5 Letter from Department of Indian Affairs Agent R. N. Wilson to Indian Commissioner David Laird, June 29, 1908

Indigenous leaders who were elected chiefs by Indian Act provisions still had to be endorsed by the Indian agent. As you saw in the previous document, the chief's declaration included an injunction that the chief would strive to "advance the interests of all Indians" in the band "morally and financially, both by precept and example," to uphold the laws and regulations of the Canadian government, and to report any infractions of those laws by his own people to the Indian agent "over" the chief. The Indian agent, therefore, tended to affirm the election of chiefs who would support the assimilationist goals of the department, and this could include the surrender of some of their land base if the agent thought this prudent or profitable.

In 1907, local settlers pressured the Department of Indian Affairs to force the Kainai of the Blood Reserve to sell 2,400 acres of their land. Crop Eared Wolf (Makoyi-Opistoki) personally opposed this sale and encouraged a vote against the land cession. Indian Affairs inspector J. A. Markle wrote the Department of Indian Affairs suggesting that a threatening letter from Ottawa promising to replace Crop Eared Wolf with a leader "who would more quickly take up advanced ideas and be a help to the Department instead of a hindrance," might encourage Crop Eared Wolf to cease his opposition. The department refused to write such a letter but reminded Markle that leaders living an intemperate life could be deposed. Markle's attempts to enlist the North–West Mounted Police to investigate Crop Eared Wolf were unsuccessful; NWMP superintendent Primrose responded to the request by saying that "if the Indian Dept., wish to do any work of this nature, I think they had better do it themselves. Speaking of Crop Eared Wolf as I know him I should be very sorry to see him deposed from office."[113]

In 1908, Indian Agent R. N. Wilson picked up the cause of deposing Crop Eared Wolf, as you see here. Crop Eared Wolf filed a complaint of harassment directly to Indian Commissioner David Laird, who had first recommended him for the position of chief. Instead of surrendering the land, the Kainai turned to cultivating it, harvesting 24,000 bushels of wheat in 1909.[114] Crop Eared Wolf retained his position.

Source: Department of Indian Affairs Agent R. N. Wilson to Indian Commissioner, June 29, 1908, LAC, Department of Indian Affairs fonds, RG 10, vol. 3939, file 121698-3, images 37–41, online MIKAN no. 2058251.

(Copy)
Blood Agency, Macleod,
The Indian Commissioner,
Winnipeg, Man.[115]

June 28, 1908.

Sir,

I have the honor to request that one of the chiefs of this reservation named Crop-eared-wolf be deposed for incompetency.

Since I placed this Indian on the self-support list four years ago he has opposed and endeavored to block every move made by me for the advancement of these

---

113 Smith, *Liberalism, Surveillance and Resistance*, 125–26.

114 Hugh A. Dempsey, "Makoyi-Opistoki," in *Canadian Dictionary of Biography*, vol. 14, University of Toronto/Université Laval, 2003, http://www.biographi.ca/en/bio/makoyi_opistoki_14E. html (accessed July 31, 2017).

115 In the original document, these two lines of address ("The Indian Commissioner" and "Winnipeg, Man.") were at the bottom of the first page of the letter. They have been moved here for the convenience of the modern reader, and so as not to confuse.

people. At the inauguration of the self-support movement in 1904 the only serious difficulty encountered was the violent opposition of Crop-eared-wolf who tried to get the other Indians affected by that policy to revolt against it but was unsuccessful except with one other individual as reported at the time. When I then informed him that he would lose his chiefship if he persisted in his opposition he subsided to some extent so far as the subject of "self-support" was concerned but from that time to this he has been a chronic kicker and general michief [sic] maker.

In connection with the farming operations he has been particularly objectionable. Two years ago when extensive farming at this point was decided upon by the Department I naturally took an early opportunity of explaining the plans to Crop-eared-wolf but as soon as he had heard enough to see that a serious attempt to cultivate a portion of the reserve was intended he abruptly terminated the discussion by refusing to hear any more of the subject and peremptorily ordering me to drop it. He said that he would have no farming done on this reservation other than what the Indians cared to do in their own way, which as I pointed out to him, after 25 years of reserve life then amounted to "nil." He at once enlisted the support of the late Thunder Chief and two or three others of the older chiefs who with a dozen or so of the worthless element among the Indians set themselves up as an opposition and endeavored to persuade the other Indians to refuse to farm. After that I ignored these men entirely and confined my attention to the working element with the result that the applications from the working Indians for the broken land soon aggregated more acreage than the steam plow could break in two years, which is practically the situation yet though twenty-three farms have been supplied to date. After the work was well under way last year and the first large block of farms issued to 15 lower Indians the recipients were subjected to all sorts of annoyance through the efforts of Crop-eared-wolf and his adherents to induce them to abandon the work. Three of them backslided but others took their places and the ground was duly prepared by the Indians and seeded by them in good and proper time. Yesterday a Mormon farmer drove through these Indian farms and declared that they are the best crops that he has seen this year.

Finding his tactics unsuccessful with the lower Indians Crop-eared-wolf then tried to get the farming confined to the lower end of the reserve and passed word around that no farming was to be done up the river. No attention, however, was paid to him and the machinery was this spring moved up the river and put to work on the location selected for a block of farms for the use of the central or Farm 3 Indians. These farms eight in number (which are several short of the applications at that point) being nearly finished I selected for the third location a fine piece of land directly south of Chief Running Crane's place near the river and above the mouth of Bull-horn Coulee. This block will be issued to Chief Running Crane, his son, his son-in-law and other immediate neighbours. On Thursday last the 25th, instant I was from earlymorning [sic] engaged in laying out these farms with the assistance of Stockman Hillier, Assistant Stockman Thomas Spotted Bull, Chief Running Crane, and Black Plume his son-in-law. By two o'clock in the afternoon we had located and partially marked with posts seven farms of eighty acres each and then went off for lunch. During our absence Mr. Crop-eared-wolf came along and pulled up all of the posts, put them in his wagon, drove to Chief Running Crane's and threw them inside of Running Crane's fence. As most of the eleven posts had been set in post holes, and at least three miles of travelling would have to be covered in getting to them all, the chief went to some little trouble in order to undo what we had accomplished. After finishing this task Crop-eared-wolf went on to the Stockman's house where I was at lunch and told me that he had called to tell me to stop marking out those farms as he wanted no farming done up there. He said nothing about having removed the landmarks. I explained to him that no plowing would be done on his land or for himself or children until they requested me to do it for them, but that the farms then being laid out were for men living alongside of them like Running Crane and his son who wanted the farms and that it is my intention to plow land for every Indian who asks for it and has the horses necessary to work it. I also told him that if he could not as chief assist me in my work he might at least abstain from interference with it. To this he replied that he was chief of this reserve and that nothing should be done on it that he disapproved of.

When returning to work I was informed of what Crop-eared-wolf had done with the posts and presently he came driving along when I asked him why he had molested the landmarks, he replied "I told you that I do not want any farming done on this reserve and I pulled up those posts for the same reason." In reply to my remark that his property was two or three miles further up the river and that he had no right to interfere with work being done for Running Crane and these other Indians, he said, "The whole reserve belongs to me. The Government made me chief over it all and no Indian or white man has a right to do anything that I tell him not to do," with which comprehensive statement the discussion closed.

I did not replace the posts as he would only have removed them again. When the plow begins work up there within a few days I can re-stake the land one line at a time and have the plow follow thus running a furrow along the lines that will make them permanent without the posts.

You will doubtless concur in my opinion that it is imperative in the interests of the Blood Indians and of our work on their behalf that Crop-eared-wolf be removed from his position of chief as promptly as the Department can act in the matter. While he confined himself to talk he was bad enough and for his excesses in that line should have been deposed long ago. Now, however, that he has resorted to physical force in order to prevent me carrying on work of great importance, and claims a right to do so by virtue of his insane idea of his authority as chief, nothing remains but for the Department to depose him as incompetent and appoint in his stead a normally constituted Indian who will be competent to perform his duties. There are Indians on this reservation, and many of them, who have ever since the establishment of the agency honestly and intelligently followed the lines laid down for them by the Department. Several of the Bloods of this better class I have had the pleasure of recommending for chiefs in the past and a man of the same industrious element should wear the head chief's medal at present held by Crop-eared-wolf.

Please note that Crop-eared-wolf is not the spokesman of a portion of the tribe in this obstruction but is presenting his own views only. Also, there is no property dispute involved in his last action as his house and fields and those of his children are located two or three miles beyond the premises of Running Crane whose near neighbors as well as himself merely desire to farm the land in their immediate vicinity.

Your obedient servant,
(sd.) R. N. Wilson
Indian Agent.

2.6 *The New Story of the Iroquois* by Chief Des-ka-heh, A Radio Address, March 10, 1925

Cayuga Hoyaneh Levi General (Deskaheh)[116] was the speaker of the Haudenosaunee Confederacy Council in the 1920s when the Canadian government sought greater and greater control over the internal affairs of the Grand River reserve through the abolition of Haudenosaunee traditional longhouse governance. In 1922, the council asked Deskaheh to take its case to the British government in London and then to the League of Nations in Geneva. He argued that the Haudenosaunee had a nation-to-nation treaty relationship with Great Britain, having served as her military allies, and that the people of his nation had never yielded their sovereignty to Canada nor had they ever been conquered. In September 1924, Prime Minister Mackenzie King and Governor General Byng signed an order in council abolishing the Haudenosaunee Council. In December, acting on that order, the RCMP raided the Ohsweken Council House and the homes of wampum keepers, confiscating documents and sacred wampum belts. That same year, the Canadian government denied entry to Deskaheh as he tried to return home from Europe. In 1925, he died, a political refugee living in the home of Tuscarora Chief Clinton Rickard on the Tuscarora Indian Reservation in New York State.[117]

---

116 Many Indigenous groups, nations, and leaders spell their own names in various ways. Chief Deskaheh (or Des-ka-heh) was no exception. This book uses the most common current spelling when discussing sources, but it stays true to the actual spellings used in the sources themselves, even when these are inconsistent.

117 Susan M. Hill, *The Clay We Are Made Of*, 230; Deskaheh, *The Red Man's Appeal for Justice* (London: Kealeys Limited, 1923); Smith, *Strange Visitors*, 143.

Illustration 2.3: Deskaheh (in headdress) speaking to an unidentified man with spectators in the background, Scarborough, Ontario.

Source: Copyright American Philosophical Society

Source: Des-ka-heh, *The New Story of the Iroquois, aka "The Last Speech of Des-ka-heh"* (Brantford: Ontario, 1925), LAC, Department of Indian Affairs fonds, RG 10, vol. 2286, file 57, 169-1, pt. 5, MIKAN no. 2083362, images 111–15.

The New Story of the Iroquois.

By CHIEF DES-KA-HEH

Told over W—H—A—M at
Rochester, N.Y.
March 10th, 1925.

Brantford, Ontario
1925

PREFACE

The purpose of this booklet is to let the public read the last speech made by the late CHIEF DESKAHEH, at Rochester, N.Y., Radio Station, on the night of March 10, 1925. Next morning he was ordered by the doctor to the hospital, as he had a serious attack of pleurisy and pneumonia. He was under treatment at the Homeopathic Hospital for eight weeks, then the doctors giving him up, he was removed to the Tuscarora Indian Reservation along the banks of the Niagara River where he died on June 27th, 1925.

Chief Deskaheh was born on the Grand River Lands in the year 1872. He became a chief of his Young Bear Clan of the Cayuga Nation on July 4th, 1917. In the year 1921, he was appointed a Speaker of the Six Nations Council, the same year he crossed to England, to carry the news to King George V, of the aggressiveness of his Majesty's Colony, in spite of the Treaty of 1874 [1784] in existence between the British Crown and his people of the Six Nations of the Grand River Lands, known as the Haldimand Treaty.

He returned home in the Autumn of the same year, without much assurance from the British Authorities.

A large majority of his people insisted on him appealing to the highest court in the world for justice to Redmen, this he did. On account of his determination to seek justice he had to leave his home to escape from the clutches of the invaders on some trumped up charge, on February 21st, 1923, to seek asylum south of the Great Lakes, until his people could find the necessary money. He left on July 12th, 1923, arriving in Geneva, Switzerland, during the latter part of August, where he awaited the action of the League of Nations on his appeal for justice for the Redmen. As no action was taken by the League, he returned to America, arriving in Rochester, N.Y., January 18th, 1925.

This is what he had reference to in his last speech. The result of his mission to the League of Nations, on behalf of his people of the Grand River Lands.

THE NEW STORY OF THE IROQUOIS

Nearly every one who is listening to me is a pale face I suppose. I am not. My skin is not red but that is what my people are called by others. My skin is brown, light brown, but our cheeks have a little flush and that is why we are called red-skins. We don't mind that. There is no difference between us, under our skins, that any expert with a carving knife has ever discovered.

My home is on the Grand River. Until we sold off a large part, our country extended down to Lake Erie, where, 140 winters ago, we had a little sea-shore of our own and a birch-bark navy. You would call it Canada. We do not. We call the little ten miles square we have left the "Grand River Country." We have the right to do that. It is ours. We have the written pledge of George III that we should have it forever as against him or his successors and he promised to protect us in it. We didn't think we would ever live long enough to find that a British promise was not good. An enemy's foot is on our country and George V knows it for I told him so but he will not lift his finger to protect us nor will any of his ministers. One who would take away our rights is of course, our enemy. Do you think that any government should stop to consider whether any selfish end is to be gained or lost in the keeping of its word?

In some respects, we are just like you. We like to tell our troubles. You do that. You told us you were in great trouble a few winters ago because a great big giant with a big stick was after you. We helped you whip him. Many of our young men volunteered and many gave their lives for you. You were very willing to let them fight in the front ranks in France. Now we want to tell our troubles to you—I do not mean that we are calling on your governments. We are tired of calling on the governments of pale-faced peoples in America and in Europe. We have tried that and found it was no use. They deal only in fine words—We want something more than that—We want justice from now on. After all that has happened to us, that is not much for us to ask. You got half of your territory here by warfare upon red-men, usually unprovoked, and you got about a quarter of it by bribing their chiefs, and not over a quarter of it did you get openly and fairly. You might have gotten a good share of it by fair means if you had tried. You young people of the United States may not believe what I am saying. Do not take my word but read your history. A good deal of true history about that has got into print now. We have a little territory left—just enough to live and die on. Don't you think your governments ought to be ashamed to take that away from us by pretending it is part of theirs? You ought to be ashamed if you let them. Before it is all gone, we mean to let you know what your governments are doing. If you are a free people you can have your own way. The governments at Washington and at Ottawa have a silent partnership of policy. It is aimed to break up every tribe of red-men so as to dominate every acre of their territory. Your high officials are the nomads to-day—not the Red people. Your officials won't stay at home. Over in Ottawa they call that policy "Indian Advancement." Over in Washington, they call it "Assimilation." We, who would be the helpless victims, say it is tyranny. If this must go on to the bitter end, we would rather that you come with your guns and poison gases and get rid of us that way. Do it openly and above board. Do away with the pretense that you have the right to subjugate us to your will. Your governments do that by enforcing your alien laws upon us. That is an underhanded way. They can subjugate us if they will through the use of your law courts. But how would you like to be dragged down to Mexico, to be tried by Mexicans and jailed under Mexican law for what you do at home?

We want none of your laws and customs that we have not willingly adopted for ourselves. We have adopted many. You have adopted some of ours—votes for women, for instance—We are as well behaved as you and you would think so if you knew us better. We would be happier to-day, if left alone, than you who call yourselves Canadians and Americans. We have no jails and do not need them. You have many jails, but do they hold all the criminals you convict? And do you convict or prosecute all your violators of the thousands of laws you have?

Your governments have lately resorted to new practices in their Indian policies. In the old days they often bribed our chiefs to sign treaties to get our lands. Now they know that our remaining territory can easily be gotten away from us by first taking our political rights away in forcing us into your citizenship, so they give jobs in their Indian Offices to the bright young people among us who will take them and who, to earn their pay, say that our people wish to become citizens with you and that we are ready to have our tribal life destroyed and want your government to do it. But that is not true. Your governments of to-day learned that method from the British. The British have long practiced it on weaker peoples in carrying out their policy of subjugating the world, if they can, to British Imperialism. Under cover of it, your law-makers now assume to govern other peoples to [sic] weak to resist your courts. There are no three mile limits or twelve mile limits to strong government who wish to do that. About three winters ago the Canadian government set out to take mortgages on farms of our returned soldiers to secure loans made to them intending to use Canadian courts to enforce those mortgages in the name of Canadian authority within our country. When Ottawa tried that our people resented it. We knew that would mean the end of our own government. Because we did so the Canadian government began to enforce all sorts of Dominion and Provincial laws over us and quartered armed men among us to enforce Canadian laws and customs upon us. We appealed to Ottawa in the name of our right as a separate people and by right of our treaties and the door was closed in our faces. We then went to London with our treaty and asked for the protection it promised and got no attention. Then we went to the League of Nations at Geneva with its covenant to protect little peoples and to enforce respect of treaties by its members and we spent a whole year patiently waiting but got no hearing.

To punish us for trying to preserve our rights, the Canadian government has now pretended to abolish our government by Royal Proclamation and has pretended to set up a Canadian-made government over us composed of the few traitors among us who are willing to accept pay from Ottawa and do its bidding. Finally Ottawa officials, under pretense of a friendly visit, asked to inspect our precious wampum belts, made by our fathers centuries ago as records of our history, and when shown to them those false-faced officials seized and carried away those belts as bandits take your precious belongings. The only difference was that our aged wampum-keeper did not put up his hands. Our hands go up only when we address the Great Spirit. Yours go up, I hear, only when some one of you is going through the pockets of his own white brother. According to your newspapers they are up now a good deal of the time. The Ottawa Government thought that with no wampum belts to read in the opening of our Six Nations councils, we would give up our home rule and self-government, the victims of supersticion [sic] Any superstition of which the Grand River people have been victims was not in reverence for wampum belts but in their trust in the honor of governments who boast of a higher civilization.

We entrusted the British, long ago, with large sums of our money to care for when we ceded back parts of our territory. They took $140,000.00 of that money seventy-five winters ago to use for their own selfish ends and we have never been able to get it back.

Your government of the United States, I hear, has just decided to take away the political liberties of all the red-men you promised protect forever, by passing such a law through your congress in defiance of the treaties made by George Washington. That law, of course, would mean the breaking up of the tribes if enforced. Our people would rather be deprived of their money than their political liberties. So would you.

I suppose some of you never heard of my people before and that many of you, if you ever did, supposed that we were all long gone to our happy hunting grounds. NO! There are as many of us as there were a thousand winters ago. There are more of you than there used to be and that makes a great difference in the respect we get from your governments.

I ask you a question or two. Do not hurry with your answers. Do you believe— really believe—that all peoples are entitled to equal protection of international law now that you are so strong: Do you believe—really believe—that treaty pledges should be kept? Think these questions over and answer them to yourselves.

We are not as dependent in some ways as we were in the early days. We do not need interpreters now. We know your language and can understand your words for ourselves and we have learned to decide for ourselves what is good for us. It is bad for any people to take the advice of an alien people as to that.

You mothers, I hear, have a good deal to say now about your government. Our mothers have always had a hand in ours. Maybe you can do something to help us now. If you white mothers are hard-hearted and will not, perhaps you boys and girls who are listening and who have loved to read stories about our people—the true ones I mean—will help us when you grow up if there are any of us left then to be helped. If you are bound to treat us as though we were citizens under your government then those of your people who are land hungry will get our farms

TALKING BACK TO THE INDIAN ACT

away from us by hooks and crooks under your property laws and in your courts that we do not understand and do not wish to learn. We would then be homeless and have to drift into your big cities to work for wages to buy bread and have to pay rent, as you call it, to live on this earth and to live in little rooms in which we would suffocate. We would then be scattered and lost to each other and lost among so many of you. Our boys and girls would then have to intermarry with you or not at all. If consumption took us off or if we brought no children into the world or children mixed with the ocean of your blood then there would be no Iroquois left.[118] So boys and girls if you grow up and claim the right to live together and govern yourselves and you ought to and if you do not concede the same right to other peoples (and you will be strong enough to have your own way) you will be tyrants won't you. If you do not like that word use a better one if you can find one, but don't deceive yourselves by the word you use.

Boys—you respect your fathers because they are members of a free people and have a voice in the government over them and because they helped to make it and made it for themselves and will hand it down to you. If you knew that your fathers had nothing to do with the government they are under and were mere subjects of other men's wills, you could not look up to them and they could not look you in the face. They would not be real men then. Neither would we. The fathers among our people have been real men. They cry out now against the injustice of being treated as something else and being called incompetents who must be governed by another people—which means the people who think that way about them. Boys—think this over. Do it before your minds lose the power to grasp the idea that there are other peoples in this world beside your own and with an equal right to be here. You see that a people as strong as yours is a great danger to other peoples near you. Already your will comes pretty near being law in this world where no one can whip you, think then what it will mean if you grow up with a will to be unjust to other peoples to believe that whatever your government does to other peoples is no crime however wicked. I hope the Irish-Americans hear that and will think about it—they used to when that shoe pinched their foot.

This is the story of the Mohawks, the story of the Oneidas, of the Cayugas—I am a Cayuga—of the Onondagas, the Senecas and the Tuscaroras. They are the Iroquois. Tell it to those who have not been listening. Maybe I will be stopped from telling it. But if I am prevented from telling it over, as I hope to do, the story will not be lost. I have already told it to thousands of listeners in Europe—it has gone into the records where your children can find it when I may be dead or be in jail for daring to tell the truth—I have told this story in Switzerland. They have free

---

118 Consumption was a common term for the disease tuberculosis, which was a major health concern for Indigenous people in this time. There were many causes of this health crisis including the poor conditions of residential schools where the disease spread rapidly. For more information see Christian W. McMillan, *Discovering Tuberculosis: A Global History 1900 to the present* (New Haven: Yale University Press, 2015); Maureen Lux, *Separate Beds: A History of Indian Hospitals in Canada, 1920s to 1980s* (Toronto: University of Toronto Press, 2016).

speech in little Switzerland. One can tell the truth over there in public even if it is uncomfortable for some great people.

This story come [sic] straight from Des-ka-heh, one of the chiefs of the Cayugas. I am the Speaker of the Council of the Six Nations, the oldest League of Nations now existing. It was founded by Hi-a-wa-tha. It is a League which is still alive and intends, as best it can, to defend the rights of the Iroquois to live under their own laws in their own little countries now left to them; to worship their Great Spirit in their own way and to enjoy the rights which are as surely theirs as the white man's rights are his own.

If you think the Iroquois are being wronged, write letters from Canada to your Members of Parliament and from the United States to your Congressmen and tell them so. They will listen to you for you elect them. If they are against us, ask them to tell you when and how they got the right to govern people who have no part in your government and do not live in your country but live in their own. They can't tell you that.

One word more so that you will be sure to remember our people. If it had not been for them, you would not be here. If, one hundred and sixty-six winters ago, our warriors had not helped the British at Quebec, Quebec would not have fallen to the British. The French would then have driven your English-speaking fore-fathers out of this land, bag and baggage. Then it would have been a French-speaking people here to-day, not you. That part of your history can not be blotted out by the stealing of our wampum belts in which that is recorded.

I could tell you much more about our people and I may some other time—if you would like to have me.

2.7 *Report of the Royal Commission on Aboriginal Peoples, Volume 2: Restructuring the Relationship—Governance, 1996, Section 1, Aboriginal Perspectives*

The 1980s were years of intense lobbying, protests, and negotiations, as Indigenous peoples, at both the leadership and grassroots level, demanded profound change in their relationship with Canada. Indigenous leaders worked hard and appeared repeatedly at constitutional conferences held in 1983, 1984, 1985, and 1987 to argue in favour of self-determination. But little was accomplished. Indigenous communities from the Lubicon Cree of northern Alberta to the Teme-Augama Anishnabai of northern Ontario took provincial and federal governments to court over land rights and title, petitioning to be included in treaties and to be compensated for lands lost or habitat destroyed, but both ended in disappointing decisions by provincial justices. The same was true for the Gitxsan and Wet'suwet'en of central British Columbia, as Justice Allan McEachern rejected their oral histories, traditions, and legal systems in his 1991 decision. Just the year before, disputes over land led to violence as the Sûreté du Québec stormed the blockade erected by the Kanesatá:ke Mohawks when the town of Oka tried to expand a golf course over their cemetery grounds.

The government of Brian Mulroney sent in Canadian troops at the request of Quebec premier Robert Bourassa. When the Mohawks at nearby Kahnawá:ke blockaded the Mercier Bridge, a crucial commuter route into Montreal, local townsfolk at LaSalle stoned elders and pregnant women who sought medical attention beyond the blockade. The summer of 1990 was filled with footage of military standoffs between Canadian troops and Mohawk warriors that stunned many Canadians. At the same time, the horrors of residential schooling were gradually entering Canadian consciousness as residential school survivors took high-ranking church officials to court on charges of sexual assault.[119] Partly as a result of these events, the Mulroney government appointed a Royal Commission on Aboriginal Peoples. Chaired by the former national chief of the Assembly of First Nations, Georges Erasmus, and Quebec judge René Dussault, the four Indigenous commissioners (including Inuit, Métis, and Indian) and three non-Indigenous commissioners were tasked with answering one overriding question: "What are the foundations of a fair and honourable relationship between Aboriginal and non-Aboriginal people of Canada?" The commission generated a tremendous amount of research, holding 178 days of public hearings in 96 communities. It released its report in 1996. The historical components of the report are excellent—often the first time Indigenous historical perspectives were put front and centre in a government document. Critics noted, however, that the report was too focused on the past and future relationships between Canada and First Nations to deal adequately with contemporary problems, particularly those of urban Indigenous people, and that it did not address the residential schools clearly enough, recommending a further public inquiry into those institutions.[120]

Source: Canada, Royal Commission on Aboriginal Peoples, *Report of the Royal Commission on Aboriginal Peoples, volume 2, Restructuring the Relationship: Part One* (Ottawa: The Commission, 1996), chapter 3, "Governance," http://www.collectionscanada.gc.ca/ webarchives/20071124130703/http://www.ainc-inac.gc.ca/ch/rcap/sg/shm3_e.html (accessed August 23, 2017). Reprinted by permission of the Government of Canada, 2018.

---

119 For a summary of these times, see Miller, *Skyscrapers Hide the Heavens*, 364–85; the case *R. v. O'Connor* began in 1991 and was among the first to call attention to the widespread sexual violence within the schools. See the case summary at West Coast Leaf, http:// www.westcoastleaf.org/our-work/r-v-oconnor-1995/ (accessed August 23, 2017); for an institutional history of the Royal Commission on Aboriginal Peoples, see https://www.aadnc-aandc.gc.ca/eng/1307458586498/1307458751962 (accessed August 23, 2017).
120 Miller, *Skyscrapers Hide the Heavens*, 385.

3
Governance

IN THE TIME BEFORE *there were human beings on Earth, the Creator called a great meeting of the Animal People.*

During that period of the world's history, the Animal People lived harmoniously with one another and could speak to the Creator with one mind. They were very curious about the reason for the gathering. When they had all assembled together, the Creator spoke.

"I am sending a strange new creature to live among you," he told the Animal People. "He is to be called Man and he is to be your brother.

"But unlike you he will have no fur on his body, will walk on two legs and will not be able to speak with you. Because of this he will need your help in order to survive and become who I am creating him to be. You will need to be more than brothers and sisters, you will need to be his teachers.

"Man will not be like you. He will not come into the world like you. He will not be born knowing and understanding who and what he is. He will have to search for that. And it is in the search that he will find himself.

"He will also have a tremendous gift that you do not have. He will have the ability to dream. With this ability he will be able to invent great things and because of this he will move further and further away from you and will need your help even more when this happens.

"But to help him I am going to send him out into the world with one very special gift. I am going to give him the gift of the knowledge of Truth and Justice. But like his identity it must be a search, because if he finds this knowledge too easily he will take it for granted. So I am going to hide it and I need your help to find a good hiding-place. That is why I have called you here."

A great murmur ran through the crowd of Animal People. They were excited at the prospect of welcoming a new creature into the world and they were honoured by the Creator's request for their help. This was truly an important day.

One by one the Animal People came forward with suggestions of where the Creator should hide the gift of knowledge of Truth and Justice.

"Give it to me, my Creator," said the Buffalo, "and I will carry it on my hump to the very centre of the plains and bury it there."

"A good idea, my brother," the Creator said, "but it is destined that Man should cover most of the world and he would find it there too easily and take it for granted."

"Then give it to me," said the Salmon, "and I will carry it in my mouth to the deepest part of the ocean and I will hide it there."

"Another excellent idea," said the Creator, "but it is destined that with his power to dream, Man will invent a device that will carry him there and he would find it too easily and take it for granted."

"Then I will take it," said the Eagle, "and carry it in my talons and fly to the very face of the Moon and hide it there."

"No, my brother," said the Creator, "even there he would find it too easily because Man will one day travel there as well."

Animal after animal came forward with marvellous suggestions on where to hide this precious gift, and one by one the Creator turned down their ideas. Finally, just when discouragement was about to invade their circle, a tiny voice spoke from the back of the gathering. The Animal People were all surprised to find that the voice belonged to the Mole.

The Mole was a small creature who spent his life tunnelling through the earth and because of this had lost most of the use of his eyes. Yet because he was always in touch with Mother Earth, the Mole had developed true spiritual insight.

The Animal People listened respectfully when Mole began to speak.

"I know where to hide it, my Creator," he said. "I know where to hide the gift of the knowledge of Truth and Justice."

"Where then, my brother?" asked the Creator. "Where should I hide this gift?"

"Put it inside them," said the Mole. "Put it inside them because then only the wisest and purest of heart will have the courage to look there."

And that is where the Creator placed the gift of the knowledge of Truth and Justice.[121]

. . .

1. Aboriginal Perspectives

1.1 Basic Concepts

As our opening story suggests, human beings are born with the inherent freedom to discover who and what they are. For many Aboriginal people, this is perhaps the most basic definition of sovereignty—the right to know who and what you are. Sovereignty is the natural right of all human beings to define, sustain and perpetuate their identities as individuals, communities, and nations.

Many Aboriginal people see sovereignty as much as a human right as a political and legal one. Seen in this way, sovereignty is an inherent human attribute that cannot be surrendered or taken away.

> *What is sovereignty? Sovereignty is difficult to define because it is intangible, it cannot be seen or touched. It is very much inherent, an awesome power, a strong feeling or the belief of a people. What can be seen, however, is the exercise of Aboriginal powers. For our purposes, a working definition of sovereignty is the ultimate power from which all specific political powers are derived.*
>
> Roger Jones, Councillor and Elder
> Shawanaga First Nation
> Sudbury, Ontario, 1 June 1993

---

121 Based on a story by Phil Lane, Jr., Four Worlds Development. University of Lethbridge, Lethbridge, Alberta, as retold by Richard Wagamese [this note was in the source document].

As an inherent human quality, sovereignty finds its natural expression in the principle of self-determination. Self-determining peoples have the freedom to choose the pathways that best express their identity, their sense of themselves and the character of their relations with others. Self-determination is the power of choice in action.

Self-determination is looking at our desires and our aspirations of where we want to go and being given the chance to attain that . . . for life itself, for existence itself, for nationhood itself . . .

René Tenasco, Councillor
Kitigan Zibi Anishinabeg Council
Maniwaki, Quebec, 2 December 1992

. . .

1.2 Traditions of Governance

In most Aboriginal nations, political life has always been closely connected with the family, the land, and a strong sense of spirituality. In speaking to the commission of their governance traditions, many Aboriginal people emphasized the integrated nature of the spiritual, familial, economic, and political spheres. While some Canadians tend to see government as remote, divorced from the people and everyday life, Aboriginal people generally view government in a more holistic way, as inseparable from the totality of communal practices that make up a way of life.

This outlook is reflected in Aboriginal languages that express the concept of government in words meaning "our way of life" or "our life":

If you take the word bemodezewan, *you will find that it is a way of life . . . That is why it is difficult when you ask an Indian person to describe self-government. How do you describe a way of life and its total inclusion of religious rights, social rights, government rights, justice rights and the use of the family as a system by which we live? . . . We are not prepared at this time to separate those things. They are a way of life for our people.*

Leonard Nelson
Roseau River, Manitoba
8 December 1992

Most Aboriginal people continue to be guided, to some degree, by traditional outlooks in their approach to matters of governance. In some instances, Aboriginal communities have made traditional laws, practices and modes of leadership the basis of their contemporary governmental institutions. In other cases, however, traditional systems of governance have fallen into disuse or been replaced by new systems, such as those imposed by the Indian Act.

Faced with these changes, many Aboriginal people have called for a revitalization of traditional values and practices, and their reintegration into institutions of government. Aboriginal people see this process occurring in a variety of ways. A number of representations made to the Commission emphasized the need to root contemporary governmental initiatives in traditional attitudes and institutions:

> If self-government is to become the vehicle by which Native people resume their rightful place in North American society, it must grow, unaffected, out of a strong knowledge of the past. Only in this way, is it assured that the Anishinabek, and other traditional governing structures, will be resuscitated for future growth and development . . . Knowledge of pre-contact Native societies will serve as the proper base upon which we can carefully and slowly construct models of governance. These models will be founded in the past and developed to consider environmental changes and the realities of today.[122]

Nevertheless, in calling for governmental structures that are grounded in Aboriginal peoples' cultures and values, some interveners also spoke of the need to adopt certain features of mainstream Canadian governments.

> The Lheit-Lit'en solution was to recognize what had been lost, which is a traditional form of government. What had been lost was culture. What had been lost was any relationship between the community, the children, the adults and the elders as well as language. And that needed to be regained, the community decided.

> But at the same time, the community also felt that since we live in a contemporary non-Aboriginal world that it would be impossible to regain that out of context . . . As a consequence, the Lheit-Lit'en decided to combine traditional and contemporary methods of governments, contemporary as well as traditional methods of justice.

Erling Christensen
Prince George, British Columbia
1 June 1993

. . .

There is no uniform Aboriginal outlook on these topics, many of which are the focus of lively discussion and exchange among Aboriginal people. Nevertheless, the very fact that they are the object of such interest shows their continuing importance in the panoply of Indigenous approaches to governance.

---

122 Union of Ontario Indians, "Anishinabek Traditional Governing, A New Era for the Anishinabek: Understanding the Past for the Challenges of Tomorrow," brief submitted to RCAP (1993), 4–5 [this note was in the source document].

One point needs to be emphasized. For most Aboriginal people, 'tradition' does not consist of static practices and institutions that existed in the distant past. It is an evolving body of ways of life that adapts to changing situations and readily integrates new attitudes and practices. As a study of traditional Inuit governance explains:

> This . . . Inuit approach to 'traditions' and the 'traditional culture' moves 'traditional culture' away from its exoticized state depicted in books and displayed in museums and presents it instead in the everyday actions of northern individuals. This insider view grounds 'traditional culture' not in a time frame (the pre-contact period) but instead in a set of practices engaged in by Inuit of both the recent or distant past.[123]

Here, Aboriginal people are no more prisoners of the past than other Canadians are. They do not need to replicate the customs of bygone ages to stay in touch with their traditions, just as Parliament does not need to observe all the practices of eighteenth-century Westminster in order to honour the parliamentary tradition. Aboriginal people, like other contemporary people, are constantly reworking their institutions to cope with new circumstances and demands. In doing so, they freely borrow and adapt cultural traits that they find useful and appealing. It is not the heedless reproduction of outmoded practices that makes a vigorous tradition, but a strong connection with the living past.[124]

. . .

Leadership

In many Aboriginal societies, political power was structured by familial relationships and tempered by principles of individual autonomy and responsibility. As described in one brief, leaders were viewed as servants of the people and were expected to uphold the values inherent in the community. Accountability was not simply a goal or aim of the system, it was embedded in the very make-up of the system.[125]

---

123 Nancy Wachowich, "Women's Traditional Governance Research Project: Pond Inlet Inuit Contribution," research study prepared for RCAP (1994) [this note was in the source document].

124 In order to keep the length of the primary documents included in this reader manageable, we have had to excise significant discussion of the other principles that Indigenous people in Canada see as important to good governance. The RCAP reported that centrality of the land, individual autonomy and responsibility, the rule of law, the role of women, the role of elders, the role of family and clan, leadership, consensus in decision making, and the restoration of traditional institutions were all important themes in the testimony given by Indigenous people to the commission on the theme of governance. We have included only the sections entitled "leadership" and "consensus in decision making."

125 Union of Ontario Indians, "Anishinabek Traditional Governing," 39 [this note was in the source document].

Within families, clans, and nations, positions of leadership could be earned, learned, or inherited. Frequently, these methods operated in conjunction.

The selection of Chief was hereditary through a patriarchal line; the first born descendant would not automatically enter this position, it had to be earned. From a very young age the candidate for leadership would be trained and advised by his peers to ensure that he would be ready to assume his role.... The selection of leadership was a process that required much time and devotion. To become a leader was a great honour. The role of Chief was not one of power, rather it was a responsibility to fulfil the needs of the people.[126]

In many instances, elders were viewed as community leaders. They sat in their own councils, which were frequently composed of both men and women. Decisions made by the elders council were expected to be observed and implemented by other leaders in the community.

In some First Nations, leadership functions were dispersed among the holders of various positions:

> We do not follow the present day concept of chief and band council that was created by Indian Affairs. We have a traditional spiritual chief who is a medicine man; also we have four thinkers whose responsibility is for the welfare of the clan and to look into the future. Then we have our Tukalas whose responsibilities are for the protection and security of the clan.
>
> Dennis Thorne
> Edmonton, Alberta
> 11 June 1992

In other cases, leaders were expected to take on a variety of roles and had to possess a wide range of personal qualities. For example, a study of leadership among Dene identifies the functions of spokesperson, adviser, economic leader (as hunter and trapper), spiritual adviser, prophet and role model. Qualities associated with these functions include oratorical skill, wisdom, authority, economic proficiency, generosity, spiritual insight and respect.[127] Among certain Aboriginal people, one clan was vested with responsibility for leadership and its members were expected to cultivate the relevant skills.

---

126 Union of Ontario Indians, "Anishinabek Traditional Governing" [this note was in the source document].

127 Rene M. J. Lamothe, "'It was Only a Treaty': A Historical View of Treaty 11 According to the Dene of the Mackenzie Valley," research study prepared for RCAP (1993) [this note was in the source document].

If one was born into the Leadership Clan, then there would be the gift of speech, to be able to have the power to influence by using language. Again, they learned all those skills as they were growing up, and also to have a good understanding of what leadership meant in those days.

Chief Jeannie Naponse
Whitefish Lake
Toronto, Ontario, 18 November 1993

In other instances, clan mothers had the responsibility of choosing leaders from among the members of families holding leadership titles. The clan mothers also had the power to remove leaders who were derelict in the performance of their duties.[128] In such societies, children were identified as potential leaders by the women of the clan.

Within the Haudenosaunee Confederacy, positions of leadership were specialized. Each clan within the nation was represented at the Council of the Confederacy by *rotiianeson*, or hereditary chiefs. These offices were hereditary in the sense that eligibility to fill them was inherited by the individual. Pine tree chiefs, who were not from families holding hereditary titles but earned their titles through merit, sat with and advised the councils of their nations. War chiefs[,] as military leaders[,] had the responsibility of executing decisions made in council by the rotiianeson.[129]

Traditional Inuit societies exhibited a variety of patterns of leadership, as revealed in Marc Stevenson's study of traditional decision making in the Nunavut area. Among the Iglulingmiut of the Foxe Basin and north Baffin Island, the institution of leadership was well developed, with the eldest resident hunter in a band usually assuming the role of *isumataq*, the one who thinks. The authority of the isumataq often extended to socio-economic matters affecting the entire camp, including the sharing and distribution of game and other food. Iglulingmiut society placed great emphasis on the solidarity and hierarchical structure of the extended family, with a person's place in the hierarchy being determined by age, generation, sex and blood affiliation. The Iglulingmiut also recognized a broader tribal identity, beyond the extended family and the band.[130]

A second pattern of leadership is represented by the Netsilingmiut, who live on the Arctic coast west of Hudson Bay. Originally, most local Netsilingmiut groups were based on the relationship between men, ideally brothers. Although the eldest active hunter in the group was usually regarded as the leader, important

---

128 Paul Williams and Curtis Nelson, "Kaswentha," research study prepared for RCAP (1995). See also Kenneth Deer, RCAP transcripts, Kahnawake, Quebec, May 6, 1993 [this note was in the source document].

129 Williams and Nelson, "Kaswentha." See also Deer, RCAP transcripts [this note was in the source document].

130 Marc G. Stevenson, "Traditional Inuit Decision-Making Structures and the Administration of Nunavut," research study prepared for RCAP (1993) [this note was in the source document].

decisions affecting the community were generally made jointly by several adult males. In effect, leadership took second place to the maintenance of cooperative relations among the males in the group. Male dominance and solidarity were expressed in the separation of men and women at meal times, the close bonds of affection and humour between male cousins, and the high incidence of female infanticide, which was the man's prerogative. There was little sustained cooperation among local groups and much mutual suspicion and hostility. There seems to have been no recognition of an overall tribal identity.[131]

Another distinctive pattern is represented by the Copper Inuit, who lived on Banks and Victoria islands and the adjacent mainland in the central Arctic. The Copper Inuit were organized around the nuclear family, whose independence was absolute in all seasons of the year, whether during the summer when people were dispersed inland or during the winter when they assembled in large groups on the sea ice. In social structure and ideology, the Copper Inuit were highly individualistic and egalitarian, and in this respect differed notably from other Inuit of the Nunavut area. As Stevenson notes:

So great was the emphasis on egalitarianism that there were no positions or statuses demarcating certain individuals as standing above or apart from others outside the nuclear family . . . While a man because of his ability or character might attain a position of some influence, as his powers faded, so too did his prestige and authority . . . Even women outside the domestic sphere enjoyed equal status with that of men in decision making.[132]

The emphasis on individual autonomy made communal action very difficult, and there was no common council for decision making, no recognized leader to provide direction, and no special deference to the views of elders. As a result, murders and other transgressions against society often went unpunished.

Generally, however, traditional Inuit societies recognized two types of leadership. The first type is *angajuqqaaq*, a person to be listened to and obeyed, and the second is *isumataq*, one who thinks. Both types of leadership were earned. However, in the first case, leadership depended on a person having a certain position in an organized system, while in the second case leadership depended more on individual merit and the ability to attract and maintain a group of followers. Nevertheless, the distinction between the two types of leadership was not hard and fast, and most successful leaders combined the features of both. Such persons could not abuse their authority or neglect their other leadership role

131 Stevenson, "Traditional Inuit Decision-Making Structures" [this note was in the source document].
132 Stevenson, "Traditional Inuit Decision-Making Structures" [this note was in the source document].

without risking the loss of respect and ultimately an erosion of their influence and authority.[133]

In speaking of their traditions of governance, many Aboriginal people emphasize that their leaders were originally chosen and supported by the entire community. This was especially true in non-hierarchical societies where leaders were equal to all others and held little authority beyond that earned through respect. In such societies, support for leaders could be withdrawn by the community as a whole or by those (such as clan mothers) with specific responsibilities in the matter.

> Part of the principles under our traditional system of government was that the leader does not have a voice in his own right. He has to respect the wishes of the people. He cannot make statements that are at odds with what the people believe.
>
> Margaret King
> Saskatoon Urban Treaty Indians
> Saskatoon, Saskatchewan, 28 October 1992

Leadership was reflective of the people's faith and confidence in that particular individual's capabilities as a Chief. If for some reason these duties as leader were not fulfilled or met satisfactorily by the people then they could "quietly withdraw support."[134]

Many First Nations interveners spoke of how the Indian Act system of government had eroded traditional systems of accountability, fostered divisions within their communities, and encouraged what amounted to popularity contests. The first past the post system, whereby the greatest number of votes elected a candidate, was seen as especially problematic. It permitted large families to gain control of the council and shut other families out of the decision-making process.

A number of First Nations, such as the Teslin Tlingit, the Lheit-Lit'en, and the Gitksan and Wet'suwet'en, have taken steps to replace leaders elected under the system imposed by the Indian Act with traditional leaders.

> Our Clan leaders have always been alive and well and thriving in Teslin, but their duties were mainly confined to cultural activities . . . They were stripped of all the powers they traditionally held. They were consequently stripped of their respect.

---

133 Stevenson, "Traditional Inuit Decision-Making Structures" [this note was in the source document].
134 Union of Ontario Indians, "Anishinabek Traditional Governing" [this note was in the source document].

What the constitution does is it puts the Clan leaders and the Elders in their rightful spot in Tlingit society, and that is at the top of the totem pole.

Chief David Keenan
Teslin, Yukon
27 May 1992

In some cases, this objective is being achieved through a return to band custom, by means of a procedure laid down in the Indian Act. In other instances, as with the Teslin Tlingit, traditional systems are being revived through self-government agreements. Certain communities are in a transitional period, with band councils operating side by side with traditional leaders . . .

Consensus in decision making

The art of consensus decision making is dying. We are greatly concerned that Aboriginal people are increasingly equating 'democracy' with the act of voting. . . . [W]e are convinced that the practice of consensus decision making is essential to the culture of our peoples, as well as being the only tested and effective means of Aboriginal community self-government.[135]

Decision making took a variety of forms in traditional Aboriginal societies. For example, decentralized systems of government often relied on the family and its internal structures to make decisions. In such societies, the autonomy of family groups was a fundamental principle.[136] Societies with a more complex political organization made decisions not only at the level of the family but also through broader communal institutions. The potlatch, as practised among the peoples of the northwest coast, is an example of a communal institution serving multiple functions.

The potlatch was a gathering of people, often including people from surrounding nations. According to the Lheit-Lit'en Nation, the potlatch was usually a culmination of smaller earlier meetings where individual issues were dealt with. At this final gathering, all people were included so that everyone could participate in final discussions and be aware of the decisions and agreement reached. The gathering dealt with territorial and justice issues and was generally the main instrument of community control, community watch, defence of territory and any issues relating to the community.[137]

---

135 Council of Elders, "A Negotiations Process for Off-Reserve Aboriginal Peoples of Ontario," brief submitted to RCAP (1993), 5 [this note was in the source document].
136 Deh Cho Tribal Council, "Dene Decision Making," brief submitted to RCAP (1993), 21 [this note was in the source document].
137 BC Native Women's Society, "Self-Government: The Quest for Self-Determination and Self-Reliance of Aboriginal Peoples," brief submitted to RCAP (1993), 11 [this note was in the source document].

Whatever their system of government, many Aboriginal people have spoken of the principle of consensus as a fundamental part of their traditions. Under this principle, all community members should be involved in the process of reaching agreement on matters of common interest. Among some peoples, discussions generally begin at the level of the family. In this way, the views of women, children and all who are not spokespersons may help shape the view expressed by the family or clan. Discussions may then proceed at a broader level and involve all family spokespersons, clan leaders or chiefs. In certain cases, all members of the community meet in assembly. Through a prolonged process of formulation and reformulation, consensus gradually emerges, representing a blend of individual perspectives.

In describing how an Anishnabe nation with seven clans came to decisions through a consensus-seeking process, an intervener made these observations:

> Peter Ochise . . . said seven twice is eight . . . It's taken me some time to grasp what he meant. Seven perspectives blended, seven perspectives working in harmony together to truly define the problem, truly define the action that is needed makes for an eighth understanding. It's a tough lesson that we don't know all the answers, we don't know all the problems. We really own only one-seventh of the understanding of it and we only know one-seventh of what to do about it. We need each other in harmony to know how to do things . . . This process that we had was 100 per cent ownership of the problem.

Mark Douglas
Orillia, Ontario
14 May, 1993

In consensus-based political systems, the concept of 'the loyal opposition,' as in parliamentary systems, does not exist. As Williams and Nelson point out, decision making by consensus, often referred to as coming to one mind, is gradual, and the resolution of issues is built piece by piece, without confrontation.[138]

A study of Dene governance traditions notes that "consensus among the Dene is more a quality of life than a distinct process, structure or outcome."[139] It permeates all levels of decision making, from the extended family to local and regional communities and the nation as a whole. Nevertheless, the same study observes that certain conditions are necessary for consensus systems to operate properly. These include face-to-face contact among members and the opportunity for those affected by decisions to take part in them. Consensus systems also require a broad pool of shared knowledge, including recognition of the leadership qualities of particular individuals, their family, history, spiritual training and so on. These

---

138 Williams and Nelson, "Kaswentha" [this note was in the source document].
139 Deh Cho Tribal Council, "Dene Decision Making" [this note was in the source document].

conditions presuppose a basic political unit having strong continuing ties, such as those found in the extended family.

In many First Nations communities, the family-based consensus process has been displaced by majority-based electoral systems, which have altered the roles of women, elders and other members of the community. According to some interveners, these electoral systems have had the effect of splintering viewpoints, alienating the community from decision making, and breeding distrust of leaders and officials. Electoral systems have also been susceptible to domination by numerically powerful families in the community.

> When you look at elections in communities with the DIA elected system it's common knowledge that the ones with the bigger families are the ones that get elected in these positions today.

Jeanette Castello
Terrace, British Columbia
25 May 1993

As the submission of the Stó:lo Tribal Council observes, if a community has only five extended families, it is relatively easy under the plurality system for one large family or interest group to dominate council and monopolize power. Indeed, it has been reported that councillors representing minority families often feel so politically redundant that they stop attending meetings. For some interveners, such a system lacks legitimacy:

To the Stó:lo Elders, it is intellectually inconceivable that any government can be viewed as legitimate when a leader can be chosen, for example, from a list of three candidates and be declared winner despite up to 66% of the people voting against him.[140]

Numerous First Nations interveners called for their governments to revive traditional methods of decision making that incorporate broader and more balanced systems of accountability. In their view, to gain legitimacy and credibility, First Nations governments and leaders must reflect the entire group they represent. Decision-making processes must be accessible and responsive to the views of communities, families and individuals.

---

140 Keith T. Carlson for the Stó:lo Tribal Council, "Leadership Review: The Indian Act Election System, Traditional Sto:lo Socio-political Structures, and Recommendations for Change," brief submitted to RCAP (1993), 15 [this note was in the source document].
141 Union of Ontario Indians, "Anishinabek Traditional Governing," 39 [this note was in the source document].

The leadership must pursue a course of increased accountability to the people. This begins with returning authority and responsibility to the community. It means opening the lines of communication and providing a network of dialogue. This dialogue will be fundamental in building the bridge between the leaders and the Anishinabek people.[141]

Chapter Three

Enfranchisement

In exploring the documents provided in the first two chapters of this book, you were encouraged to bring to bear several key strategies drawn from Indigenous thought and historical methods of analysis. We would like you to continue to employ these tools as you move through the documents included in this chapter as well. We hope, for example, that you will continue to reflect on the ways in which the authors of the documents in this section express and confirm responsibilities to their various constituencies. Carry on too exploring how the Indian Act was adapted over time to meet Indigenous challenges to the fundamental settler understandings that led to its creation in the first place. When you read through the documents in this chapter, we would also like you to consider two additional categories of analysis: respect, from the four Rs of Indigenous methodology, and contingency, from the five Cs of historical thinking.

In the general introduction at the beginning of this text, we confirmed that settler representatives did not often afford respect to Indigenous delegations or Indigenous concerns. Nonetheless, of all the methodologies we explore here, respect is perhaps the easiest for us to understand. We all strive for respect for what we do and for how we choose to identify ourselves as individuals and as members of families and communities. It is difficult, in fact, to think of anything that is more central to the core of who we are than how we perceive ourselves and how we would like to be seen by others. Yet, as the result of a particularly severe lack for respect for Indigenous cultures, a central goal of Canada's policy was to transform those cultures and assimilate Indigenous people into Anglo-Canadian Christian society. Indeed, the multifaceted effort to reshape Indigenous identities is a consistent theme running through the textual historical record of Indigenous-settler relations in Canada. In chapter 1, for example, we examined how Canada, through the Indian Act, sought to further its assimilative agenda by taking upon itself the authority to determine who was and was not an Indian in Canadian law. In this present chapter, we follow this theme by providing documents that position attempts to reshape Indigenous identities as central concerns.

As we discuss much more fully in Chapter 4, the identity of Indigenous women was already circumscribed in the 1876 Indian Act by attaching their identity as Indians solely to the status of their fathers and then, if they marry, their husbands. For the most part, though, the 1876 legislation encouraged rather than compelled Indigenous people—men, at least—to enfranchise, or give up their identity as Indians under the law, in exchange for some of the apparent benefits of settler society, including the right to vote. As you read the documents in this chapter with the grain, think about the reasons presented in support of Canada's goal of enfranchisement and what these tell us about our country's respect for Indigenous ways of being. What aspects of Indigenous lifeways did Canada seem set on modifying or eradicating? What elements or intentions related to identity are initiated, reinforced, or augmented by the 1920 amendments to the Indian Act? What arguments are presented to discredit Indigenous resistance?

The issue of enfranchisement was often a central point of discussion at Indigenous political gatherings, such as at the meeting of the Grand Council of the Chippewas held at Sarnia in 1874. What reasons for opposition to enfranchisement are presented in the proceedings of the Grand Council, the *London Free Press* article, and the letter from Loft to Lougheed by those disinclined to accept either the original Indian Act provisions or those in the 1920 amendment? What differences in objectives and strategy do you see between the various Indigenous representatives and their communities? What level of respect is shown among Indigenous representatives for those with differing perspectives?

Next, read the 1920 amendment, the unsigned memo, and D. C. Scott's testimony against the grain. On what assumptions are the calls for enfranchisement based? What echoes or hints of Indigenous resistance to enfranchisement can you see? What elements of the policy of enfranchisement further Canada's larger objective of assimilation? How might enfranchisement alter relationships within Indigenous communities?

Unlike respect, contingency, one of the 5 Cs, is a much more difficult and disconcerting concept to grapple with. Once we begin to consider how our world and its relations of power are dependent on a complex web of earlier circumstances, conditions, and choices, at least some of which might have seemed relatively insignificant at the time, we begin to see how fragile the present is and how easily things could have been different. If you had decided to go to *that* university instead of the one you are at, if you had chosen to take another history course and not the one you are in, if you had chosen to sit at the back instead of the front, you may not have met your life partner, who was sitting in the row behind you on that first day. Less facetiously, if European powers had decided to develop respectful relationships with Indigenous nations of the Americas parallel to the way they dealt with other Europeans, there would perhaps be no need for a Truth and Reconciliation Commission.

According to Loft in his February 1921 letter to Lougheed, how might the choices made by Indian Affairs officials related to enfranchisement negatively affect Indigenous families? What does he see as the necessary requirements for bettering the conditions faced by Indigenous people? Why do you think Canada might be unwilling to make the choices necessary to achieve the goals that Loft seeks? Shifting to the proceedings of the Grand Council in 1874, ask these questions in particular: How are the proposals outlined parallel to what Loft is suggesting, and how do they differ? Turning to Scott's testimony before the Special Committee of the House of Commons and the unsigned memo, consider contingency. How is contingency masked or ignored by suggesting inevitability, predictability, or natural superiority and entitlement? Is there any indication of this in the 1876 act or the 1920 amendment?

Documents

3.1 An Act to Amend and Consolidate the Laws Respecting Indians [Indian Act of 1876], sections 86 to 94

The title of one of the first pieces of legislation related to Indigenous people that the new country of Canada introduced in 1869, the Gradual Enfranchisement Act,[142] signified the importance of enfranchisement and assimilation to Canadian parliamentarians and the settler society they represented. As the selection below illustrates, the 1876 Indian Act clarified, expanded, and collected together under a single heading the related provisions of Canada's 1869 act and earlier legislation passed by the parliament of the United Kingdom. This section also mentions reserves and how these collectively held lands would be broken up and allotted in fee simple title, eventually, to individual enfranchised Indians. Certainly, there is a degree of compulsion here for some, as section 86(1) indicates, but there is also a degree of individual choice and community authority in determining who would become enfranchised and who would remain Indians under Canadian law. This measure of consent and approval would disappear in later versions of the Indian Act.

Source: Canada, An Act to Amend and Consolidate the Laws
Respecting Indians, *Statutes of Canada* 39 Vic. (1876) c.18.

---

142 The full title of the 1869 legislation is "An Act for the Gradual Enfranchisement of Indians, the Better Management of Indian Affairs, and to Extend the Provisions of the Act 31st Victoria, Chapter 42."

CHAP. 18.
An Act to amend and consolidate the laws respecting Indians.

[Assented to April 12, 1876.]

ENFRANCHISEMENT

Report of Agent when Indian obtains consent of Band to be enfranchised.

86. Whenever any Indian man, or unmarried woman, of the full age of twenty-one years, obtains the consent of the band of which he or she is a member to become enfranchised, and whenever such Indian has been assigned by the band suitable allotment of land for that purpose, the local agent shall report such action of the band, and the name of the applicant to the Superintendent-General; whereupon the said Superintendent-General, if satisfied that the proposed allotment of land is equitable, shall authorize some competent person to report whether the applicant is an Indian who, from the degree of civilization to which he or she has attained, and the character for integrity, morality and sobriety which he or she bears, appears to be qualified to become a proprietor of land in fee simple; and upon the favorable report of such person, the Superintendent-General may grant such Indian a location ticket as a probationary Indian, for the land allotted to him or her by the band.

Inquiry thereupon.

Location ticket on favorable report.

Indians admitted to degrees in Universities, &c.

(1.) Any Indian who may be admitted to the degree of Doctor of Medicine, or to any other degree by any University of Learning, or who may be admitted in any Province of the Dominion to practice law either as an Advocate or as a Barrister or Counsellor or Solicitor or Attorney or to be a Notary Public, or who may enter Holy Orders or who may be licensed by any denomination of Christians as a Minister of the Gospel, shall ipso facto become and be enfranchised under this Act.

Patent after certain period of probation.

87. After the expiration of three years (or such longer period as the Superintendent-General may deem necessary in the event of such Indian's conduct not being satisfactory), the Governor may, on the report of the Superintendent-General, order the issue of letters patent, granting to such Indian in fee simple the land which had, with this object in view, been allotted to him or her by location ticket.

Indian to declare name chosen; and to be known by it.

Wife and minor children enfranchised.

Effect of such enfranchisement.

Proviso as to children attaining majority before their father's probation expires.

Proviso as to children found unqualified, or being married.

88. Every such Indian shall, before the issue of the letters patent mentioned in the next preceding section, declare to the Superintendent-General the name and surname by which he or she wishes to be enfranchised and thereafter known, and on his or her receiving such letters patent, in such name and surname, he or she shall be held to be also enfranchised, and he or she shall thereafter be known by such name or surname, and if such Indian be a married man his wife and minor unmarried children also shall be held to be enfranchised; and from the date of such letters patent the provisions of this Act and of any Act or law making any distinction between the legal rights, privileges, disabilities and liabilities of Indians and those of Her Majesty's other subjects shall cease to apply to any Indian, or to the wife or minor unmarried children of any Indian as aforesaid, so declared to be enfranchised, who shall no longer be deemed Indians within the meaning of the laws relating to Indians, except in so far as their right to participate in the annuities and interest moneys, and rents and councils of the band of Indians to which they belonged is concerned: Provided always that any children of a probationary Indian, who being minors and unmarried when the probationary ticket was granted to such Indian, arrive at the full age of twenty-one years before the letters patent are issued to such Indian, may, at the discretion of the Governor in Council, receive letters patent in their own names for their respective shares of the land allotted under the said ticket, at the same time that letters patent are granted to their parent: and provided, that if any Indian child having arrived at the full age of twenty-one years, during his or her parents' probationary period, be unqualified for enfranchisement, or if any child of such parent, having been a minor at the commencement of such period, be married during such period, then a quantity of land equal to the share of such child shall be deducted in such manner as may be directed by the Superintendent-General, from the allotment made to such Indian parent on receiving his probationary ticket.

Case of Indian dying before expiration of probation or failing to qualify.

89. If any probationary Indian should fail in qualifying to become enfranchised, or should die before the expiration of the required probation, his or her claim, or the claim of his or her heirs to the land, for which a probationary ticket was granted, or the claim of any unqualified Indian, or of any Indian who may marry during his or her parents' probationary period, to the land deducted under the operation of the next preceding section from his or her parents' probationary allotment, shall in all respects be the same as that conferred by an ordinary location ticket, as provided in the sixth, seventh, eighth and ninth sections of this Act.

As to children of widows probationary or enfranchised.

90. The children of any widow who becomes either a probationary or enfranchised Indian shall be entitled to the same privileges as those of a male head of a family in like circumstances.

Rules for allotting lands to probationary Indians.

91. In allotting land to probationary Indians, the quantity to be located to the head of a family shall be in proportion to the number of such family compared with the total quantity of land in the reserve, and the whole number of the band, but any band may determine what quantity shall be allotted to each member for enfranchisement purposes, provided each female of any age, and each male member under fourteen years of age receive not less than one-half the quantity allotted to each male member of fourteen years of age and over.

Proviso: as to power of Band in this behalf.

As to Indians not members of the Band, but permitted to reside on their reserve.

92. Any Indian, not a member of the band, or any non-treaty Indian, who, with the consent of the band and the approval of the Superintendent-General, has been permitted to reside upon the reserve, or obtain a location thereon, may, on being assigned a suitable allotment of land by the band for enfranchisement, become enfranchised on the same terms and condition as a member of the band; and such enfranchisement shall confer upon such Indian the same legal rights and privileges, and make such Indian subject to such disabilities and liabilities as affect Her Majesty's other subjects; but such enfranchisement shall not confer upon such Indian any right to participate in the annuities, interest moneys, rents and councils of the band.

Proviso.

Provision when Band decides that all its members may become enfranchised.

93. Whenever any band of Indians, at a council summoned for the purpose according to their rules, and held in the presence of the Superintendent-General or of any agent duly authorized by him to attend such council, decides to allow every member of the band who chooses, and who may be found qualified, to become enfranchised, and to receive his or her share of the principal moneys of the band, and sets apart for such member a suitable allotment of land for the purpose, any applicant of such band after such a decision may be dealt with as provided in the seven next preceding sections until his or her enfranchisement is attained; and whenever any member of the band, who

Or when Indian becomes qualified by exemplary conduct.

for the three years immediately succeeding the date on which he or she was granted letters patent, or for any longer period that the Superintendent-General may deem necessary, by his or her exemplary good conduct and management of property, proves that he or she is qualified to receive his or her share of such moneys, the Governor may, on the report of the Superintendent-General to that effect, order that the said Indian be paid his or her share of the capital funds at the credit of the band, or his or her share of the principal of the annuities of the band, estimated as yielding five per cent out of such moneys as

If such Indian be a married man or widow.

may be provided for the purpose by Parliament; and if such Indian be a married man then he shall also be paid his wife and minor unmarried children's share of such funds and other principal moneys, and if such Indian be a widow, she shall also be paid her minor unmarried children's share:

And as to unmarried children of such enfranchised married Indians.

and the unmarried children of such married Indians, who become of age during either the probationary period of enfranchisement or for payment of such moneys, if qualified by the character for integrity, morality and sobriety which they bear, shall receive their own share of such moneys when their parents are paid, and if not so qualified, before they can become enfranchised or receive payment of such moneys they must themselves pass through probationary periods; and all such Indians and their unmarried minor children who are paid their share of the principal moneys of their band as aforesaid, shall thenceforward cease in every respect to be Indians of any class within the meaning of this Act, or Indians within the meaning of any other Act or law.

Provision as to
Indians in British
Columbia, N.W.
Territories or
Keewatin.

94. Sections eighty-six to ninety-three, both inclusive, of this
Act, shall not apply to any band of Indians in the Province
of British Columbia, the Province of Manitoba, the North-
West Territories, or the Territory of Keewatin, save in so far
as the said sections may, by proclamation of the Governor-
General, be from time to time extended, as they may be,
to any band of Indians in any of the said provinces or
territories.

3.2 Minutes of the Grand General Council of the Chippewas, Munsees, Six Nations, etc., 1874

The Grand General Council was an early post-Confederation political organization of Indigenous communities in Ontario and Quebec with a membership
that extended beyond individual nations and cultural groupings. It was developed largely to consider—and, when necessary, confront—federal policy and
legislation and to offer proposals for modification. In the long term, differences between the Anishinaabe (Chippewa) and the Six Nations, especially,
and even internally within the Six Nations' leadership over whether or not the
Indian Act should even apply to them, made unified political action difficult.
There does, though, seem to have been a general will to collaborate where possible at the Grand General Council. The 1874 meeting included more than 120
delegates, and there was a general consensus among them about the need for
more community authority and less interference from Ottawa. The first issue
on the agenda, and a central concern of the 1874 meetings overall, was enfranchisement. The recommendations that came out of the meetings parallel, albeit
with augmentation, what was included two years later in the 1876 Indian Act.

Source: *The Grand General Council of the Chippewas, Munsees, Six Nations, &c., &c.,
Held on the Sarnia Reserve, June 25th to July 3rd, 1874* (Sarnia ON: Canadian Steam
Publishing Establishment, 1874), 8–10, 17–23. LAC, RG 10, vol. 1942, file 4103.

GENERAL COUNCIL, SARNIA RESERVE

Monday, June 29th, 1874.

. . .

At the request of the Council, Chief Wm. Wawanosh was called upon to
introduce the first topic of business.

Chief Wawanosh then introduced the subject of the enfranchisement of the
Indian. He thought it was high time that a certain number in each Reservation
should be placed on a level with the whites. On looking over the Dominion he

saw many of his race who, on account of their education, industry, integrity and general knowledge, were competent persons to be enfranchised. While thus he spoke so encouragingly of some of his people, there were others, and they formed the majority, who did not possess the qualification necessary for enfranchisement; and he feared they would still remain, as they have in the past, in the capacity of minors. To enfranchise the unqualified Indian in Canada, he believed, would bring upon him the same disastrous results as it had done in Michigan and Kansas. This, he thought, could be avoided in Canada by making certain rules and regulations, and he offered the following suggestions:— "That when an Indian wished for enfranchisement, his case should be considered in Council by his Tribe, or the Band to which he belongs, and if he is found to be a person possessing a fair education and general knowledge, industrious, and bearing a good moral character, then his Tribe may petition the Government to grant a Title Deed to the lot of land which has been apportioned by the Tribe to the enfranchised Indian. He is also to receive a portion of the principal money belonging to the Tribe; after which he is to be cut off entirely from any further privileges enjoyed by his Tribe."

Chief Wawanosh concluded a powerful address by urging the Council to open a door to those ready for enfranchisement.

Chief John Henry next addressed the Council somewhat as follows:— He stated that he spoke as the representative of the Chippewas of the River Thames. Foreigners hailing from all parts of the world, and coming into Canada were made citizens at once; and he could not see why the original owners of the soil were not elevated to this position. This, he thought, was one of the main reasons of the grand assemblage before him. He spoke of the Negro in the United States. As soon as he was emancipated, he began to fill important positions; and his voice was soon heard in the Legislative Assembly and in Congress. Chief Henry thought that we could never have peace until we opened a door to those yearning for enfranchisement. He coincided with the proposals offered by Chief Wawanosh, with the exception of cutting off the enfranchised Indian from any further participation in the annuities, &c. The annuity, he considered, was a birthright to the Indian and his family, whether he remained a minor or was elevated to the position of a citizen. Chief Henry also alluded to the great progress in civilization as having been made by the Indians in Canada during the last fifty years; for it was only since that time we emerged from Paganism into Christianity. No other nation, he thought, could have made such progress in such a short time. Why then are we not citizens yet! It is for us to work for this privilege. We are here representing every tribe and most of the Reservations in Canada, and surely we ought to accomplish something towards the elevation and improvement of the Indian. He suggested the retention of the annuity by the enfranchised Indian and his family, for this reason: That it would prove a kind of link between himself and the Reserve to which he formerly belonged. If afterwards he was elected to sit on the Municipal Council or County Council, or was even elected a member of the Parliament, he could thereby do a great deal for the good of his tribe. There were also many on the Reserves, especially the old people, who, after they were left or deserted by the enfranchised Indians, would not be able to manage their affairs, so the enfranchised Indian, if privileged still to participate in the annuity, would still be interested in his tribe, &c. If, however, the enfranchised Indian sold the portion of land for which he was deeded, he is not to look to the Reserve for another share; he is to be cut off entirely as far as land was concerned.

Council adjourned for dinner, until 1.30 p.m.

. . .

GENERAL COUNCIL, SARNIA RESERVE

Wednesday Evening, July 1st.

. . .

The debate on Enfranchisement *pro* and *con* was again resumed.

Chief Wm. Wawanosh reiterated his sentiments given to the Council on Monday last. He hoped that the first Indians to be enfranchised should so prosper, as to induce others to follow their example.

J. Henry thought it would be very uncharitable to cut off the wife and children of the enfranchised Indian from any further participation in the annuity. He suggested the plan of only enfranchising the father, but let the wife and children still be numbered with the Tribe and share in their privileges. In this way it would place the enfranchised Indian in a middle position between the Indian and the White. He would be the advocate for the rights of the tribe to which his family belonged. He would not advise his people to enfranchise all at once—this should be done gradually, according to competency. He considered that according to chief Wm. Wawanosh's proposal only one in a thousand would accept enfranchisement. The terms were too severe. As regards the locating the enfranchised Indian, he would suggest that he be located among his people, in his own Reserve, so as to place him and his family in the midst of their tribe.

Chief Henry thought there were not a great many qualified for enfranchisement. He referred to the Six Nation Indians, on the Grand River, who numbered about 3,000. Many of them were very intelligent and greatly advanced in civilization, but his[?] estimation is that only two per cent of the population are competent to be enfranchised.

Chief Wm. Wawanosh stated that Indians can always get lawyers and others to assist them in their affairs. The enfranchised Indian can always be at liberty to assist his tribe at any time. He did not favor the suggestion of J. Henry in placing the enfranchised Indian in a middle position.

Jas. Ashquabe—None of my people on Snake Island wished for enfranchisement. They think it would be the means of bringing them to poverty. He spoke of the permanency of the Reserves. They wished to remain as they were. He spoke of the great advancement in civilization, as having been made by the Indians during the last 20 years. The late General-Superintendent, Mr. Howe, spoke very favorably of the progress made in agriculture by the Indians in Ontario. He could not see the necessity of a change from our present position. He saw sufficient progress as we are. He did not favor enfranchisement.

Rev. Allan Salt—We have rejected the Act on enfranchisement. Let our Council then act wisely. The Government wants to know whether we will allow our educated Indians to become citizens, like the whites. I would say yes. After an Indian has been examined by the Council of his Tribe, and if found competent, then we can memorialize the Government on behalf of the applicant. If we say "No" to the Government, then we shall be looked upon as children.

Council adjourned until Thursday morning.

———————————

GENERAL COUNCIL, SARNIA RESERVE

July 2nd, 1874.

The President, Rev. H. P. Chase, in the chair.

C. Halfmoon offered up prayer.

Moved by Dr. Jones, seconded by Rev. A. Salt, that in the opinion of this General Council some plan or scheme is necessary for the enfranchisement of the educated and temperate Indians.

Carried unanimously.

Chief N. H. Burning—There were, he said, some among his people who were wealthy, educated and civilized. One young man in their community wished to be enfranchised. They granted him the privilege. He received a share of their money. He went over to the States and squandered it all. He came back again to us in utter poverty, and wished to be taken back into our community. He referred to the Sarnia Reserve. He had not seen much progress in agriculture, there were no barns, &c., &c. There was not enough to indicate that the Sarnia Indians were qualified to be enfranchised. Although they, the Six Nations, were greatly in advance in agriculture, still only two per cent of their population were competent to be enfranchised. He advised the young men not to leave their Reserves. There was a great deal of progress to be seen in our midst as we are. He referred to one young man in their midst who was a merchant and was prosperous. It would be foolish in us to cast away the privileges we enjoy in our present condition.

Rev. Allan Salt—To be a British citizen was an important thing, there were many privileges connected with it. He alluded to the British citizens in Africa who were made prisoners. When this came to the knowledge of the English Government, troops were immediately sent for their release.[143] And why? because they were

———————————

143 It seems likely that Salt is referring to a British expeditionary force sent to Abyssinia (Ethiopia) in 1868. In an attempt to cause Britain to reconsider its decision not to provide military assistance to Emperor Tewodros II (known as Theodorus or Theodore to Europeans), the emperor ordered the imprisonment of several British officials and missionaries. Britain responded by sending a combined force of British and South Asian soldiers to both punish Tewodros and rescue the hostages. See, for example, Darrell Bates, *The Abyssinian Difficulty: The Emperor Theodoros and the Magdala Campaign, 1867–68* (Oxford: Oxford University Press, 1979).

British Citizens. St. Paul, as we read in the New Testament, was ordered to be scourged, but when the Government authorities knew that Paul was a Roman citizen he was liberated at once. And why: it was because he was a Roman citizen. St. Paul, as we all know, was a Jew, but he had been made a Roman citizen. In our present state we are minors, we are right therefore in working to become higher than this. St. Paul's advice is :—That if there is any way of gaining a freedom the advantage should be taken.

Chief Moses Brown—In his tribe there were young men who were educated. He will not keep them back from becoming enfranchised. He wished them all prosperity and happiness. He was proud of their education. He considered the educated were those who were elevating his tribe. The venerable Abram Sickles for instance, had been for many years engaged in teaching his people the way to progress and happiness. In his reserve they had very little money wherewith they might assist those who were being enfranchised, but they had a good portion of land.

The President, Rev. H. P. Chase, spoke as follows :—In order to become a citizen it is necessary to take an oath of allegiance. I have never yet taken this oath, therefore I am not yet a real citizen. When a man has been initiated into a citizen, and if he is wealthy, then his property as well as his person is protected by the laws of the country. If he happens to be a poor man, he is taken care of, the poor house and the hospital are open for his relief. So the rich and poor are both honored and protected. Now although I have never yet taken the oath of allegiance, I have, nevertheless, been paying for taxes on my property in the town of Sarnia for several years. My money has gone to assist in building the jail, the high school, &c. And if he was to be assaulted or injured at any time, he felt sure of a general protection, and since I have been paying for taxes I have been privileged to sit with the Jury in Courts. I allude to this in order to convey the idea that an Indian may pay taxes, and still not be a real or complete citizen— by paying for taxes does not necessarily make a citizen. I have alluded also to the privileges I now enjoy even in my present position in order to make the impression that when a man becomes a complete citizen he will receive great protection, privileges and honors—this is what we want. When we have become enfranchised and have taken the oath of allegiance, then we shall enjoy all these privileges. He did not advocate for all to become citizens, only those who were competent.

John Sumner—He was in favor of opening a door to enfranchisement to those who were qualified. But if all became enfranchised poverty and ruin would be the consequences.

Joseph Wawanosh—He spoke favorably of the advantages enjoyed by citizens. He himself was not competent to be enfranchised. He coincided with the proposal of John Henry, that the enfranchised Indian's family should still participate in the privileges of their tribe.

John Elliott, New Credit—A door was about to be opened to enfranchisement for the educated and of temperate habits. He could now foresee some of the troubles that will likely arise in the future—say for instance, an enfranchised Indian living in the midst of his people, should at any time sell his land to a white man, and if this white man happened to be a person of a quarrelsome disposition, then there will be a good deal of trouble in the Indian community. Unless an Indian was out of debt when enfranchised his property would never be safe, but liable to seizure at any time. He leaves it to the General Council to draw up some plan or scheme to carry out enfranchisement.

David Sawyer—He spoke of Chief Wm. Wawanosh's proposal of cutting off the enfranchised Indian from the benefits of the annuity, &c. In this case, he favored the plan of giving a portion of the principal money instead. He spoke also of John Henry's proposition, which did not at all suit his views. We may as well remain as we are rather than adopt J. Henry's proposal. If we adopt Chief Wawanosh's plan then we shall be elevated and benefitted. He spoke of the permanency of the Reserves at the present time. If we once receive our deeds we can easily dispose of our lands. This is the very reason why the Government in former days placed us as we are, and made our Reserves permanent.

After this lengthy and interesting debate it was moved by the Rev. John Jacobs, seconded by Andrew Jacobs, that a Committee of one from each Reserve be appointed to draw up a plan or scheme for the enfranchisement of Indians, and to present the same before the General Council.

Moved in amendment by J. Sterling, seconded by Philip Gerlow, that a Committee of five of the most intelligent in the Council draw up a plan or scheme for enfranchisement and to lay the same before the Grand Council.

Moved, in amendment to the amendment, by Chief N. H. Burning, seconded by Chief Clench, that no plan or scheme be drawn up by this General Council, but to lay the subject before our respective Tribes or bands for action on our return home.

The vote being taken, the original motion was carried by a large majority.

This important Committee was composed of the following :—

1. CHIEF DR. PETER E. JONES, New Credit.
2. REV. JOHN JACOBS, Rama.
3. REV. ALLAN SALT, Alnwick.
4. CHIEF WILLIAM WAWANOSH, Sarnia.
5. JOHN HENRY, Muncytown.
6. CHARLES HALFMOON, Lower Muncey.
7. CHIEF WILLIAM JACOBS, Cayuga.
8. CHARLES KIYOSHK, Walpole Island.
9. JOSEPH SKY, Caughnawaga.
10. JAMES SNAKE, Moraviantown.
11. JAMES ASHQUABE, Snake Island.
12. ADAM SHAWNOO, Kettle Point.
13. JOHN SICKLES, Oneidatown.
14. P. J. KEGEDOONCE, Cape Croker.
15. SIMPSON QUAKEGESHIG, Saugeen.
16. J. PORTER, Grand River.
17. JAMES JOHNSTON, Sauble.

The Committee then met together for consideration; and the General Council adjourned.

...

Chief Dr. Jones then presented his proposition, which was as follows—

"The Governor-General-in-Council may, on the favorable report of the Chiefs and the majority of the Council of the Tribe to which such Indian applying belongs, through the Superintendent-General of Indian Affairs, order the issue of Letters Patent granting to any Indian, who from the degree of education and civilization to which he has attained, and the character for integrity and sobriety which he bears, to be a safe and suitable person for becoming a proprietor, in fee simple, of the land which has been allotted to him, within the Reserve belonging to the Tribe, Band or body of which he is a member; and in each case, such Indian shall have the power to dispose of the same by will or otherwise; and if he dies with a will, as to any such lands, the same shall descend to his children or heirs, according to the laws of that portion of the Dominion of Canada in which such lands are situated. That the lands to be thus located should be selected by the Chiefs and Council of each Band; and also the quantity apportioned to each Indian or his family should receive. Every such Indian shall, before the issue of the Letters Patent mentioned in the foregoing section, declare to the Council the name and surname by which he wishes to be enfranchised, and thereafter known; and on his receiving such Letters Patent, in such name and surname, he and his wife and minor children shall be held to be enfranchised; and from the date of such Letters Patent the provisions of any such Act or law making any distinction between the legal rights or liabilities of any Indian and those of Her Majesty's other subjects, shall cease to apply to any Indian, his wife or minor children as aforesaid, so declared to be enfranchised, who shall no longer be deemed Indians within the meaning of the laws relating to Indians, except in so far as their rights to participate in the annuities and interest money, and rents and councils of the Tribe, Band or body to which they belong is concerned."

This proposition was adopted by the Committee almost unanimously.

After the Committee had presented their Report to the General Council considerable discussion ensued.

Moved by J. Sterling, seconded by A. Jacobs, that the report of the Committee on enfranchisement be adopted by this General Council.

Moved, in amendment, by J. Elliott, seconded by Nelson Beaver, that the motion for the adoption of the Committee's Report be deferred until to-morrow, so as to give the Council time for consideration.

The amendment was carried unanimously.

Council adjourned until Friday morning at 9 a.m.

GENERAL COUNCIL, SARNIA RESERVE

Friday, July 3rd, 1874.

The President, Rev. H. P. Chase, in the chair.

The Rev. Abram Sickles offered up prayer.

The debate on the Committee's Report was resumed by J. Sterling, J. Sumner, Nicholas Plain, Lawrence Herkimer, Nelson Beaver, &c, &c.

Some maintained that when an Indian became enfranchised, he and his family should be cut off from further participation in the annuities of the Tribe, such person, however, to receive such portion of the principal money, as may be fixed upon by the Tribe. Others maintained that no land belonging to the Reserve should be allotted to an enfranchised Indian, but that a sufficient sum of the principal be given him, so that he can purchase land elsewhere. Others again advocated for the adoption of the entailed deed system, as proposed by the Rev. Allan Salt.

After the discussion, and when the vote was taken for the adoption of the Committee's Report, it was carried by a very large majority.

3.3 Memo on Enfranchisement

The memo reproduced below is undated and unsigned. It would, though, have been within the duties of Deputy Superintendent General of Indian Affairs Duncan Campbell Scott to pen such a missive to his immediate superior, Minister of the Interior Arthur Meighen. The tone and perspective also seem to fit with Scott's views of the issues presented but you can judge that for yourself by comparing this document with Scott's 1920 testimony before the Special Committee of the House of Commons excerpted in this chapter too. As for the timing, there are hints and traces within the document that could be further researched to help pin down the exact date it was written. A researcher could also examine other documents in the Library and Archives Canada file that contains this memo for additional hints and traces. But even after engaging in all the corroboration possible, the provenance of the document remains rather more uncertain than we might like. The question then is how a historian who comes across this document in the course of her or his research might use it, or if it should be simply disregarded.

Source: Unsigned, undated memo on "Enfranchisement," LAC, Department of Indian Affairs fonds, RG 10, vol. 6810, file 470-2-3, pt. 7.

Enfranchisement.

The proposed amendments repeal sections 107 to 122.[144] These clauses have stood upon the Statute Books since 1857. Under them it has been found possible to enfranchise only 25 Indian families of 102 persons since Confederation or during a period of 53 years.

If the ultimate object of our Indian policy is to merge the natives in the citizenship of the country, it will be seen that these clauses are most inadequate. They were framed with such a refinement of caution and are so wholly dependent upon the consent of the Indian band whereof the Indian is a member, that they are practically inoperative. Under these clauses, presuming that the band is willing, it takes six years for an Indian to become enfranchised, and the applicant is wearied by the additional six years of tutelage before he is deemed fit to handle his own property and take his place among the citizens of the country.

In the Session of 1918 we obtained from Parliament a clause which enables the Governor General in Council to enfranchise, on application, all Indians who have no land on reserves and who are willing to accept their share of the funds of the band and to abrogate any title to the lands on the reserve. This clause has served to show that numbers of Indians desire to take the final step towards citizenship, as to date we have enfranchised 97 families of 258 individuals under its provisions. We have further evidence bearing in the same direction, consisting of individual applications for enfranchisement from Indians who are holders of property on reserve. Under the date of January 7, 1920, an application was received from 33 Indians of Walpole Island asking for enfranchisement for themselves and their families.

The proposed new sections give the Superintendent General power to report from time to time on Indians who are qualified for enfranchisement, and they give the Governor General authority, acting on such reports, to enfranchise an Indian and his wife and minor unmarried children. The clauses provide adequately for the treatment of lands and monies, and while the departure from the spirit of the existing Act is radical, it is in all respects desirable that we should have legislation enabling us to enfranchise Indians without the preliminary application from themselves and without the consent of the band.

There is on the reserves in Ontario and Quebec a class of Indians who are living the life of ordinary citizens, but who have the special protection of the Indian Act; they have reached a point of progress where they are stationary, and where it will require an impetus from without if they are to make any further advancement. The reserves themselves are, as they stand, in many cases, an obstacle to the progress of the white communities, and they require to be broken up in the interests of these communities and of the Indians themselves. The complete enfranchisement of a band carries with it a certain amount of risk and responsibility; no one can

---

144 These clauses allowed for more individual choice and community authority in determining who would become enfranchised than did subsequent clauses related to enfranchisement.

forecast exactly what will happen. The only experience the Department has had in such an experiment was satisfactory. The enfranchisement of Wyandottes of Anderdon was carried out successfully and without hardship to the Indians, but this band had undeniably reached a fair level of civilization. There are certain other bands in Ontario and Quebec who would, I think, come through the trial of enfranchisement as favourably as did these Indians, namely, the Huron band of Lorette, the Caughnawaga band, the Iroquois of St. Regis, in the province of Quebec, and the Tyendinaga, and a large number of the Six Nations and the Sarnia band in the Province of Ontario.

Last summer Mr. C. M. Barbeau, of the Anthropological Division, Geological Survey, carried out an investigation at Lorette at our request, and his report will be in my hands in a few days. Mr. Barbeau tells me that the result of his investigation shows that these Indians are ready for enfranchisement.

I would anticipate that placing this legislation on the statute book would have an excellent effect on the Indians whose pleasure it is now to make claims for special privileges; for instance, the Six Nations, who say they are not British subjects but allies of the Crown and a separate nation within a nation, and not subject to the laws of this country. It would also check the intrigues of smart Indians on the reserves, who are forming organizations to foster these aboriginal feelings, and to thwart the efforts and policy of the Department. As evidence of what I refer to, I am sending herewith a copy of a circular issued by an Indian of the Six Nations, F. O. Loft who is earning his living outside the reserve. This may be merely a clever scheme to put him in funds, but it has the effect of disquieting the Indians and stirring up suspicion of the Department and the Government. Such a man should be enfranchised.

Finally we must come close to the heart of the subject and provide legislation which will carry out the ultimate aims and objects of the policy which has governed the administration of this Department since Confederation. It is illogical to develop a policy, spend money on it, and to achieve results without possessing ourselves of the power to make a final disposition of the individuals who have been civilized and to despatch them into the ordinary life of the country with the knowledge that they have every chance to succeed.

3.4 Evidence of D. C. Scott to the Special Committee of the House of Commons, 1920

By the end of World War I, it had become clear to officials of the Department of Indian Affairs that Indigenous people were not willingly going to give up their rights and identity as Indians in order to accept Canadian citizenship. In 1918 and 1919, amendments were made to the Indian Act meant to both facilitate enfranchisement and reduce community control over reserve lands. Even with these revisions, though, the senior civil servant in the department, Duncan Campbell Scott, argued that even more drastic measures were required if Canada's long-standing goal of assimilation was to be realized. Scott's boss, Minister of the Interior Arthur Meighen, agreed, and a further amendment to the Indian Act was introduced in the spring of 1920 as Bill 14. The bill faced resistance from both Indigenous and settler communities, so the House of Commons referred the bill to a special committee. Scott's testimony before the committee is excerpted below. After hearing this and other testimony, the special committee recommend acceptance of the bill with virtually no modifications.

Source: Evidence of D. C. Scott to the Special Committee of the House of Commons Examining the Indian Act Amendments of 1920, LAC, Department of Indian Affairs fonds, RG 10, vol. 6810, file 470-2-3, pt. 7, pp. K-4, L-1 to L-4, M-1 to M-4, N-1 to N-4, mf C-8533.

. . .

MR. [DUNCAN CAMPBELL] SCOTT: It has been stated that the franchise provided for under this Bill is a compulsory franchise, and I have been asked the question whether that is so. I have been asked that question in the hope apparently that I would endeavour to conceal that fact, but it is a compulsory system, and I hope the Committee will support it. The present law as it exists has not been satisfactory, it placed it too much in the hands of the band. In the first place when an Indian wished to be enfranchised he had to undergo a probationary period which is imposed upon the Indian by the Act, and it forced them out. Under the present system he has to apply for enfranchisement, but he has to be located for a certain piece of land, then his application has to go before the band at a certain time, to see whether or not they approve of his being enfranchised. After all these preliminary steps, and after three years' probation he gets his share of the capital money of the band, and after another probationary period of three years, during which he must behave himself, he gets a patent on his land. That is to say it is six years before he can take his position as a citizen of the country. The result has been that since confederation we have only been able to enfranchise about 150 individuals, and it is a crying shame that people should not be able to be enfranchised immediately, when they desire to do so. During 1917, I recommended to the Minister that any Indians who have any land located on the reserve may apply for enfranchisement and become immediately enfranchised if they have the proper qualifications.

Since the passage of that Act, and it has been in operation less than two years, we have enfranchised nearly three hundred individuals. That shows that there is a class which that amendment certainly reaches, and that they are men who are willing and anxious to take their places as Canadian citizens. It shows that there is such a class of reserves, there is no doubt about it whatever. You have heard evidence from people who are, in all respects, thoroughly qualified to be enfranchised, no matter what their reasons are for not being enfranchised, sentimental and other reasons. You have had oral and visible evidence that there are Indians in the Country who are perfectly able to stand alone, whether they are willing or not. The Bill empowers the Superintendent to appoint an officer or person to make enquiry and report, and when that report is satisfactory, the Governor in Council may enfranchise, and from that date the Indian is a Canadian citizen; that is, he takes his place free of any disabilities of the Indian Act as a citizen after having received his equitable share of the property and funds. The clauses of the Act have been carefully thought out, and I think they would be easily operated. There is no doubt about it. We provide that the Governor in Council may make regulations for any special cases that may arise. There will be minute differences in the franchise of an individual or of a whole band. We intend to take that step. The Governor in Council shall have the power to make regulations. It is not the intention of the Department that there should be any wholesale enfranchisement. What I want is to have on the statute books a progressive franchise, so that when any Indians ask for it I will have the privilege, or the Department will have the privilege, of saying to the Indian, "Don't you think it is time you should be enfranchised?" To my mind, the word "investigation" carries with it consultation. They say that there is no measure of consultation in this Bill. There is, because you cannot investigate without consulting. You must consult the Indian. You must know all about his personal affairs, and how he is fixed before you allow him to go out.

MR. [MICHEL-SIMÉON] DELISLE: On that very point, it does not seem very clear that it is on your initiative that you have the power to declare that I should be enfranchised. I would be the first one to suffer.

MR. [DUNCAN CAMPBELL] SCOTT: What do you mean by that?

MR. [MICHEL-SIMÉON] DELISLE: I will be the first one to be enfranchised, and from my point of view I will suffer.

MR. [DUNCAN CAMPBELL] SCOTT: The Bill provides for investigation.

MR. [MICHEL-SIMÉON] DELISLE: Suppose I did not want it. I won't ask for it, but you know me, and you will say Mr. Delisle should be enfranchised because you consider him fit.

MR. [DUNCAN CAMPBELL] SCOTT: Yes.

MR. [MICHEL-SIMÉON] DELISLE: That is where I consider it is not right.

MR. [DUNCAN CAMPBELL] SCOTT: I will not say it; it is the Governor in Council.

MR. [JOHN] HAROLD: Our time is very limited, and I think Mr. Scott should be allowed to finish.

MR. [DUNCAN CAMPBELL] SCOTT: That is the purpose of the Bill, and if the Committee wish to ask me any questions or to express any opinion upon the evidence, I am at their service.

MR. WILSON: We are a new country and a great many people are coming to us. After a time they become enfranchised, but we have no law compelling these people to become enfranchised, and I would like you to give us the reason why you wish to obtain the enfranchisement of the Indian by compulsion.

MR. [DUNCAN CAMPBELL] SCOTT: I want to get rid of the Indian problem. I do not think as a matter of fact, that this country ought to continuously protect a class of people who are able to stand alone. That is my whole point. I do not want to pass into the citizens' class people who are paupers. That is not the intention of the Bill. But after one hundred years, after being in close contact with civilization it is enervating to the individual or to a band to continue in that state of tutelage, when he or they are able to take their position as British citizens or Canadian citizens, to support themselves, and stand alone. That has been the whole purpose of Indian education and advancement since the earliest times. One of the very earliest enactments was to provide for the enfranchisement of the Indian. So it is written in our law that the Indian was eventually to become enfranchised. It will be may [sic] years before this will apply to the Indians in the West, although I have a petition from the Moshelle Tribe to become enfranchised. They have a very good system by which under this Bill they will become enfranchised. While they are a race of half-breeds, it is quite possible that they will be able to stand alone, although I do not know that I am quite in favour of their enfranchisement. But they are progressive enough to ask for it.

MR. [FRANK BAINARD] STACEY: Your interpretation of the phrase is entirely different from my experience of some thirty years of the Indian peoples' meaning. Their idea of compulsion is literal, your interpretation is not. You suggest an initiation on the part of the Department, which will result in enfranchisement as a result of conversations, consultation, agreement.

MR. [DUNCAN CAMPBELL] SCOTT: Certainly that is my reading of the Act, and if the Act does not explain it properly, it is the Committee's privilege to suggest amendments.

MR. [FRANK BAINARD] STACEY: From all the evidence we have heard I am satisfied that their idea is that it is absolutely compulsory.

MR. [DUNCAN CAMPBELL] SCOTT: The compulsory power is in the Act, there is no doubt; but all the relations of the Indians are on that basis. There is very little compulsion exercised in the clauses of the Act that empower it.

THE CHAIRMAN: It would only be exercised after inquiry.

MR. [DUNCAN CAMPBELL] SCOTT: I don't want to give up the initiation. I would like this Bill to go through, and I would like the Committee to be unanimous. It would be a tremendous help to me and a tremendous advance if it could go through as it is.

MR. LICKERS: How far does that word "investigation" mean consultation?

THE CHAIRMAN: Perhaps we could insert the word "consultation".

MR. LICKERS: If you had a band of chickens and you go to feed them, that is investigation, but it is not consultation.

MR. [DUNCAN CAMPBELL] SCOTT: But you are not chickens.

MR. LICKERS: We are domestic animals.

MR. [DUNCAN CAMPBELL] SCOTT: All this feeling is pure fiction. There is no such relation between the Department and the Indians as Mr. Lickers tries to make out.

MR. LICKERS: How far does the word "investigation" carry consultation.

MR. [DUNCAN CAMPBELL] SCOTT: It carries it fully.

THE ACTING CHAIRMAN: It goes further—to make inquiry.

MR. LICKERS: So that there is no compulsion.

THE ACTING CHAIRMAN: After the inquiry the report was made, and no action is based on the report.

MR. [JOHN] HAROLD: Would it be well to put that word there.

THE ACTING CHAIRMAN: Yes.

MR. [DUNCAN CAMPBELL] SCOTT: As to the way the investigation should be made, we say the Superintendent General should appoint an officer or person. I have no objection to making a change there. I do not want to set up a commission, because it costs money, and I do not want to add to the staff of the Department a person to be specially assigned to conduct these investigations. I want to make use of my experienced officers in making these investigations. The Committee might think of that.

THE ACTING CHAIRMAN: That will be a detail.

MR. [FRANK BAINARD] STACEY: Will you tell us to what extent there have been requests similar to the one you have quoted?

MR. [DUNCAN CAMPBELL] SCOTT: There have been quite a few of them lately, from individuals from Moravian town. Albert Tobias spoke to is [sic] about that. A large number of them wished to be enfranchised. I have not investigated, and I cannot say whether they could stand alone. We have had a petition from Walpole Island, the reserve the Rev. Mr. Brigham came from, for enfranchisement.

MR. [JOHN] HAROLD: A point has been brought up several times that the old method of franchisement was too hard, and that the new one is going to another extreme, and it has always appealed to me that if this were framed along lines so that the Indian had not to make the application, or take the initiative, and have it arranged so that he could automatically become a citizen, it would be better. Why do you approach it the way you do instead of the other method.

MR. [DUNCAN CAMPBELL] SCOTT: Because if you understood the Indian mind you would know. Surely we have had enough illustrations of it here. These gentlemen are perfectly able to address the Committee—far better than I am—as far as the form goes. But these are the people who will never move.

MR. LAPOINTE: What do you say about the argument of the young gentlemen yesterday, Mr. Moses and Mr. Martin. They impressed me very much. They are in favour of the enfranchisement of the Indians but they do not want it compulsory. I think the proper way is to encourage them, because if you force them against their will, they will have a sense of wrong in their heads. The old Act requires the consent of the band. I would be opposed to that. There should not be any obstacle in the way of an Indian who wants to be enfranchised. He should be encouraged, but on the other hand if you compel him, it seems to [me] you are going to the other extreme.

MR. [DUNCAN CAMPBELL] SCOTT: We have not gone to the other extreme.

MR. LAPOINTE: They all know that as long as you are there they will be well treated.

MR. [DUNCAN CAMPBELL] SCOTT: That has nothing to do with it. I accept the responsibility of recommending the legislation, and for the few years that I have to remain here I will endeavour to carry it out. All the legislation is in the interest of the band. The purpose of the Act is not to rush in everywhere and enfranchise people. I do not believe it would be possible to enfranchise the Six Nations or the Caughawagas [sic].

MR. [JOHN] HAROLD: Or any person on those reserves.

MR. [DUNCAN CAMPBELL] SCOTT: Take the Caughnawagas Indians—I would not want to touch the thing at all. Their land rights and villages are in such an entangled condition that whoever takes that question up in future is going to have an awful time—we attempted to survey the reserves a few years ago and spent a whole lot of Indian money doing it, I think in an extravagant fashion, and the survey is not worth the paper it is written on.

MR. [MICHEL-SIMÉON] DESLISLE [DELISLE]: Why all that tangle?

MR. [DUNCAN CAMPBELL] SCOTT: All the lots are irregular, and it is very difficult to make a survey. But take the Caughnawagas, why is it that a judge of the Quebec Superior Court should be a Caughnawagas Indian? That is one thing. Judge Delemimiere has rights on your reserve just as much as you have.

MR. [MICHEL-SIMÉON] DESLISLE [DELISLE]: How did he get them?

MR. [DUNCAN CAMPBELL] SCOTT: There is no use in arguing about that. There was a time when a white man could sit down on a reserve and marry an Indian woman, or because [sic] associated with the tribe. Individual cases of that kind could be dealt with under the law.

MR. [JOHN] HAROLD: Your proposition is not to pass legislation now with the idea of going into the Six Nations and picking out a certain number of men and enfranchising them?

MR. [DUNCAN CAMPBELL] SCOTT: No. One of our intelligent Indians said "Give us notice" and this is just what I am doing. I am giving them notice "Here you are to be enfranchised", and I want to make it plain that this is a thing that is coming and has got to come. It has not arrived yet for the Caughnawagas and Six Nations, but it has arrive[d] for some reserves.

THE ACTING CHAIRMAN: The objection was raised that the Six Nations Indians were not ready for the enfranchisement now, and that has been considered by the Department.

MR. [DUNCAN CAMPBELL] SCOTT: Yes, and in reference to the provision that I spoke of, the amendment to the Act, nearly all these people who are enfranchised are members of the Six Nations Reserve. The Six Nations have got rid of that element that was living in Toronto and who would come under that amendment. Of cource [sic] they can be enfranchised under this provision as easily, but we have not gone to the furthest extreme in the matter of enfranchisement. The people who have gone the furthest are the Americans. Their new Bill of enfranchisement which has passed Congress, and which they intend to carry out, simply provides that two Commissioners shall be provided for the whole country. Those Commissioners will have to finish their business in two years. They are empowered to make lists of the different bands in the country showing who are t[h]e Indians belonging to that band.

When these lists are made up and filed with the proper authorities in Washington, ipso facto, all these people on these lists are enfranchised and become citizens of the United States.

MR. LAPOINTE: Are there any exceptions?

MR. [DUNCAN CAMPBELL] SCOTT: Yes, not because they were Six Nations at all, but because their affiars [sic] are in such a complicated condition that Congress has appointed a special commisssion [sic] to go into them.

MR. LAPOINTE: It is the law of the United States to-day?

MR. [DUNCAN CAMPBELL] SCOTT: It is the law of the United States, and the only reason why the Six Nations are exempt, not because they are Six Nation Indians, but because, I have the decision here showing that Congress has exempted them from the provisions of the Bill because their affairs, in the State of New York, are of such a complicated condition. There is no comparison between our Bill and that of Congress. Just as soon as the affairs of the Six Nations in New York have been adjusted, they will be enfranchised because the United States are determined not to continue their Indians in a state of tutilage [sic]. We are not going as far as that, but I want to safeguard the interests of every Indian and every band in this country, and, at the same time, put on the statute books a provision that will enable us to enfranchise them so that the Indian, well knowing that we have the power to go to him and say "Do you not think it is time to be enfranchised"? will prepare himself for it.

MR. [JOHN] HAROLD: It is not the desire to force any one to do anything against their own interests?

MR. [DUNCAN CAMPBELL] SCOTT: No.

THE CHAIRMAN: And it can only be done after thorough investigation by the Department and by an officer appointed for the purpose.

MR. DESLISLE [DELISLE]: On the application of the Indian?

MR. [DUNCAN CAMPBELL] SCOTT: No. I cannot give up the initiative which must be with the Government, because we have had the other way long enough and have made no progress.

MR. [JOHN] HAROLD: The idea of this enfranchisement is that it gets away from the point of the Indian being the ward of the nation, because as soon as he is enfranchised then he has got to stand alone, he is no longer a ward, and the Department will have no further responsibility.

MR. [DUNCAN CAMPBELL] SCOTT: No, he becomes thoroughly self-supporting and subject to the law of the country and it lifts him from under the shadow of the Indian Act; he exercises all his rights as a citizen. Mr. Cook mentioned the enfranchisement Bill of Wyandottes and I am glad he did so as it is an illustration of the time it takes to make a change such as proposed by this Bill. That Bill was passed 25 years ago, but we did not suceed [sic] in accomplishing it until 20 years afterwards. We were unable to distribute the funds of the band because one old woman called Laforest objected and we had to wait until she died. They were perfectly capable of looking after their own affairs and the reserve was divided amongst them. There was a great many difficulties in connection with this work and we had to get a man specially trained in order to straighten up the affairs of that band, I remember I was afraid he would die before we could get the work completed, but he didn't, and after ten years' delay we were able to get the funds distributed. The officer visited every member of the band individually and the facts in connection with it were published in the report because I wanted the public to read it. He found that at that time one member of the band was manager of a large factory in Detroit getting $6,000 a year, and at the bottom of the social scale, as you might say, was a char woman supporting herself, as hundreds of other women are supporting themselves here, and there was not one bit of hardship suffered by any member of the band. They had all been absorbed into the life of the country and had dissapeared [sic] in the mass. Our object is to continue until there is not a single Indian in Canada that has not been absorbed into the body politic. [A]nd there is no question, and no Indian Department, that is the whole object of this Bill.

MR. LAPOINTE: There was an argument made here that this Bill constituted an infringement of the rights of the Six Nations under the Treaty.

MR. [DUNCAN CAMPBELL] SCOTT: They had no treaty. In fact I think their own people criticize that argument, there were two or three Indians who spoke here yesterday and said they were British subjects. They hold their reserve, they surrendered all their lands to the Crown except the reserve at Brantford, there are two townships there, everything else they surrendered to the Crown, because they mismanaged their lands so horribly when handling it themselves by issuing title which they had no right to. [T]hey squandered their property and in 1841 they surrendered it to the Government and asked us to administer it, which we have done as well as we could since that date, but the rights of the Six Nations are just like those of the other Indians. They are under the Indian Act, they are just as all the other Indians are in every other respect, there is no difference whatever, their rights are thoroughly safeguarded, I do not think the progressive element of [t]he reserve will object to that sentiment at all. This is what I have always told the Indians, it is exactly what I have told them for ten years, I do not know what they want. The last thing I would like to see done is the splitting up of the Six Nations. I want to see them all live in peace and contentment, I will not live long enough perhaps to see it myself, but my aim is that they shall be absorbed in the county of Brant. I know there is a reactionary element on the reserve and it will probably take 30 years to accomplish the result.

The committee adjourned.

3.5 Indian Act Amendment, 1920

By the second decade of the twentieth century, Canada's Department of Indian Affairs, and especially its deputy superintendent general, Duncan Campbell Scott, had grown impatient with the slow pace of assimilation. In an effort to remedy the situation, Canada introduced several amendments to the Indian Act in the few years prior to 1920 that were designed to narrow the conditions under which Indigenous communities and their leadership could resist enfranchisement. With the amendment of 1920 below, Canada went even further in assuming authority over enfranchisement by removing the necessity of both individual consent and community approval.[145] While not included in the excerpt below, the 1920 amendment also included a provision for the mandatory attendance of Indian children in day or residential schools as determined by the federal minister responsible. This requirement, like the tightening federal control over enfranchisement, was designed to further expedite assimilation.

Source: Canada, An Act to Amend the Indian Act, *Statutes of Canada* 10-11 Geo. V (1919–20) c.50, s.3.

---

145 The forced enfranchisement provisions were withdrawn in 1922 but were back in the act from 1933 to 1951. Leslie and McGuire, *The Historical Development of the Indian Act*, 118–20 and 124–25.

An Act to Amend the Indian Act, 1920

ENFRANCHISEMENT 107 . . .

Governor in Council may enfranchise Indians, on approval of report of Superintendent.

(2) On the report of the Superintendent General that any Indian, male or female, over the age of twenty-one years is fit for enfranchisement, the Governor in Council may by order direct that such Indians shall be and become enfranchised at the expiration of two years from the date of such order or earlier if requested by such Indian, and from the date of such enfranchisement the provisions of the Indian Act and of any other Act or law making any distinction between the legal rights, privileges, disabilities and liabilities of Indians and those of His Majesty's other subjects, shall cease to apply to such Indian or to his or her minor unmarried children, or, in the case of a married male Indian, to the wife of such Indian, and every such Indian and child and wife shall thereafter have, possess and enjoy all the legal powers, rights and privileges of His Majesty's other subjects, and shall no longer be deemed to be Indians within the meaning of any laws relating to Indians.

3.6 A. G. Chisholm, "The Case of the Six Nations," *London Free Press*, March 20, 1920

Andrew Gordon Chisholm was a lawyer based in London, Ontario, who was engaged by the Six Nations (Haudenosaunee Confederacy) of the Grand River for almost 40 years. Prior to being called to the bar in 1888, Chisholm had served as an officer with the 7th Fusiliers in the 1885 North-West resistance and later made an unsuccessful bid for a seat in Parliament as a Conservative. In this letter to the editor of the *London Free Press*, Chisholm succinctly explains the basis for the Six Nations' understanding of their relationship as allies as opposed to subjects of Britain. As the letter indicates further, the Six Nations' position is that, as a result of this historic relationship, they are an independent people who should not be subject to the Indian Act. Finally, Chisholm hints at the differences between the Six Nations and some of their Indigenous neighbours in the ways they understand their association with Canada, and in the strategies and tactics they believe best to employ to further their interests.

Source: "The Case of the Six Nations," *London Free Press*, March 20, 1920.

THE CASE OF THE SIX NATIONS

Editor Free Press: Your correspondent, "A Delaware Indian," writes an interesting letter in this morning's paper, but I fancy even he scarcely understands the objection of the Six Nations to their compulsory enfranchisement. So far as the other Indians of Canada are concerned, that is not the concern of the Six Nations, these can do as they wish. The Six Nations were, and claim to be still, a perfectly independent people under the protection of the British crown. From 1664 they were in close alliance with Great Britain, and from that time till after the revolutionary war that country made constant use of this political alliance and of the predominating position of the Six Nations in the councils of the Indian peoples of North America, of whom they were the head, the "Eldest Brethren" to maintain her influence over the Indian nations. This influence, after the conquest, was extended to the Indians of Canada, and aligned them with their brethren to the south. From 1664 to the Conquest the British relied almost entirely on the Six Nations to protect their colonies from French attacks, and they did so protect them. For some time after the outbreak of the revolution the Six Nations remained neutral, but were finally appealed to in the terms of the alliance to assist the King's arms, and the promise was made them by the British Government to preserve them in all their rights.

It is matter of history what the Six Nations did, and the losses they suffered in those terrible years for them, 1776–1783. After the Treaty of Paris the British Government granted them territory along the Grand River, from its mouth to its source, covering some 1,200 miles, as a new home, where they were to continue in the enjoyment of all their national rights and privileges. These included that of self-government of their own internal and domestic affairs. Never a statute governed that nation, and till Canada took over the administration of Indian affairs, in 1859, was it sought to interfere with them by such a method. The Six Nations have constantly protested against the attacks made on their rights as a separate people by the Indian Act. They are not subjects of Britain but allies, and while, because of the old alliance, they sent practically every man among them physically fit to join the overseas forces of the C. E. F. [Canadian Expeditionary Force]; for the same reason they successfully resented the mistaken attempt of the Canadian Government to apply the compulsory clauses of the Military Service Act among them, on the plea they were liable thereto as subjects.[146]

The Six Nations are now taking the proper legal steps, in conjunctoin [sic] with the Indian department, to have their legal status in Canada recognized, and as full records of the treaties between themselves and the crown have been preserved, it is hoped this can be finally determined.

---

146 The government of Canada now estimates that about 4,000 Aboriginal people (Indian, Métis, and Inuit) served in the armed forces of Canada during World War I. INAC, "Aboriginal Contributions During the First World War," https://www.aadnc-aandc.gc.ca/eng/1414152378639/1414152548341 (accessed August 25, 2017).

Just a word as to the Delaware (Moravian) Indians, whom your correspondent speaks for. They did nobly in the war, but where all did, there is no need to compare. The Moravians should fight for Britain! When their forbears, in their old home in Ohio, were almost exterminated by the treacherous attack of an American party coming among them and received as friends one of the bloodiest pages in American history, it was Britain, their old protector, who came to their rescue and gave them a shelter in Canada, which they still occupy; but they should not make insinuations against their uncles, the Six Nations—probably it was not so intended.

Faithfully yours,
A. G. CHISHOLM
Solicitor for Six Nations.

Illustration 3.1: Onondeyoh (Frederick Ogilvie Loft) in military uniform, circa 1916–1919.

Source: Canada. Dept. of National Defence/Library and Archives Canada/ PA-007439

3.7 Letter from F. O. Loft to James Lougheed, February 9, 1921

Frederick Ogilvie Loft (Onondeyoh) was born in 1861 on the Six Nations Grand River Reserve in present-day Ontario. His parents spoke English fluently and were members of the Protestant Christian community on the reserve. Loft continuously worked to combine his Mohawk culture with a desire to participate in Euro-Canadian society, and at age 37, while living and working in Toronto, he married Affa Geare, a non-Indian of British descent. He applied for enfranchisement in 1906 but was turned down by his band council, which at that time still had some authority over the practice. After the commencement of hostilities in World War I, Loft misrepresented his age downward by over a decade to qualify as a lieutenant in overseas service. On his return from Europe, he was instrumental in forming the first country-wide Indigenous organization in Canada, the League of Indians, in 1918. The purpose of the league was to advocate for First Nations' interests, especially around questions related to education, the treatment of Indigenous veterans, and the Indian Act. In Loft's letter to James Lougheed, the federal cabinet minister responsible for Indian affairs, he outlines the reasons for his opposition to involuntary enfranchisement that had become part of the Indian Act in 1920.

Source: F. O. Loft to James Lougheed, Minster of the Interior, February 9, 1921, LAC, RG 10, vol. 3211, file 527,787, pt. 1, image 169–70 of 374.

75 Madison Ave.,

Toronto, February 9th, 1921.

Hon. Sir James Lougheed,

Minister of Interior,

Ottawa, Ontario.

Dear Sir:—

I have the honour to advise you that I am in receipt of a letter from Mr. J. D. McLean, Secretary and Assistant Deputy Superintendent General to the effect that the Department is considering the matter of my enfranchisement under the Act passed last Parliament.

It is my desire most respectfully to submit to you my most earnest dissent and disapproval of being enfranchised, on principle and ethics of it which involves denationalization. To be branded as an outcast from the bosom of my kin and native heath, would be to inflict a stigma on my conscience that could never be expiated. It is a proud privilege of mine to belong to a family, tribe, yes and a race who have never been found wanting to contribute their share in manhood to go to the aid of Government and our Country in times of stress and war. Added to my pride too is the fact that I am at the present moment on the reserve list of officers of the Militia Forces of Canada, being among those having served in the late war.

For the sake of my race, I hold exceptional pride in my present status; for the simple reason so few of our people are able to prove to the outside world the advantages of higher education and the possibilities in them if properly educated and trained. If it should serve nothing more than as an example to others, it is something. To this extent we should be encouraged rather than discouraged by being made alien by force of law to foreswear our nationality; to be forced to renounce the blood of a father and mother.

With me, it is not the lure of gold, franchise, distinction or anything else, but to live the few short years that God may be pleased to allot me, as I am now sixty years, to fight the good fight with might—not for myself only but for others too, and to breathe the air of freedom and liberty so dear to all mankind; to die in peace and without the pang, taunt or haunt to pass with me, that I was the subject of a law and power, that lay hands on me with the edict: You are my prisoner, henceforth you will be what I command, not what you think or say or choose.

An able jurist has said, "no legislative body should pass legislation to interfere with the liberties of the person." In accordance with British law and jurisprudence even the criminal at the bar of justice is allowed to plead his or her own defence and that such must be given every possible benefit of a doubt. So it is in military law.

You, Sir, are the judge and administrator of this law that is now in force; it is to you I plead for clemency, not for myself merely but for my fellow brethren of my race to treat with us in the spirit of justice equity and righteousness consistent with our deserving.

I beg to submit that the officers of your Department are not sufficiently informed at first hand as to the circumstances of individual, or family, whether or not capable of assuming the obligations to be imposed under the Act—quite apart from educational standards— to warrant promiscuous recommendation for enfranchisement founded on mere supposition. To be educated is one thing, but to be financially fit is quite another; and should be of serious concern and moment in all cases. I am forced to speak of this because I am conversant of the unfortunate plight of some families who have made the effort to live in the world of severe competition. I recall the case of an Indian family in Toronto that was compelled to appeal to the Department for assistance. I was asked by the Department to make a report. I found the bread-winner partially disabled; the family in evident distress and want. With no means, no home on their reserve, scarcely knowing where to go or what to do. The wife was willing to go out and work but could not because of the children whom I found in tatters and rags.

Though much against my conscience and will I was obliged to recommend the younger children to be taken away and be cared for in an orphanage. This was done by the Department. My heart and soul went out in pity for them. I often think of them and wonder what will eventually become of them in their old age. Will they eventually become a charity and on whom? This is what we have as a duty to seriously consider as a problem of our race. It is a matter of greater moment and real christian [sic] concern than all that the franchise or anything else material can imply or define.

This law has no popularity in principle or design, by in fact a large majority of our people. Neither was it in the Committee of the House or in the House of Commons last session.

To my way of looking at it, it is too open and too drastic; making it possible to send people inadequately equipped to face the rigors of the world of competition, seriously handicapped. It virtually interprets the swelling of the population of millions of homeless people to-day. Discontented elements who are contributing much of the unrest now rampant all over the world in fact. I pray for the protection of our poor innocent people. Whatever I might be able to contribute in my humble way for this cause, and the conservation of the Indians' homes to them, until such time as they are really competent to take care of themselves; to help in the great cause of their uplift morally, socially and industrially, as well as educationally is a duty I owe to them and my Maker. It is a charity; a practical religion that man owes to man and to God.

These are the principles of the new organization of the League of Indians of Canada. As law-abiding elements we have faith in the Government that it will treat with us as men aiming for the better status by and through the great brotherhood and fraternalism of mankind; believing in the rights and equalities of all, in all that pertains to Justice, Freedom and Liberty.

Thanking you, Sir, for your kind indulgence and with it the hope you may be pleased to consider my matter favorably,

I have the honour to remain, sir, in truth and regard,

Yours most respectfully,

[signed] F. O. Loft

Chapter Four

Gender

More than many pieces of legislation, the Indian Act has been explicitly gendered. Over the course of the act's history, this has had a profound effect on Indigenous communities. It has disrupted familial relationships. It has removed Indigenous women from their homes and barred them from active roles in governing. The Indian Act and its effects have tended to produce and confirm negative stereotypes of Indigenous women. It has made them vulnerable to violence both within and outside their communities. It does not take much imagination to envision how the Indian Act contributed to the conditions in which over 1,500 Indigenous women have been murdered or have gone missing in Canada.

Previous chapters have asked you to consider the documents in light of several key concepts of historical thinking and Indigenous methodologies, including change over time, relationship, context, responsibility, respect, and contingency. We can apply these concepts here too. Taking the chapter as a whole, consider how the Indian Act has changed over time in its treatment of women. Here we have an opportunity to consider the source of that change—how did it come about? What does that tell us about how and why the place of Indigenous women in Canada has changed over time? But we also need to recall Thomas King's warnings about being too drawn to finding change in the historical record. We need to remain alert to continuity as well. Particularly as you consider Sharon McIvor's case and the opinion of the Indigenous Bar Association, ask yourself about this continuity. What discriminatory measures remained unchanged in the Indian Act even after its revisions through Bill C-31 and Bill C-3?

Relationships too permeate these documents. As you examine the definitions outlined in An Act to Amend and Consolidate the Laws Respecting Indians (Indian Act, 1876), consider which relationships are legitimated and which undermined by the legislation? What bonds of responsibility are broken by the act? You might particularly consider the effects on relationships and multigenerational responsibility as you review the document entitled "Commutation of Annuity of Rosalie Howse née Ermineskin," issued on April 1, 1891. How does this form indicate how the act is applied in communities? How does knowing that the Ermineskin family had a long history of Cree-Métis intermarriage affect your reading of that document? Mavis Goeres expresses much of her frustration with the Indian Act in terms of relationships. What relationships did it enable, and which did it disrupt and, what does this tell you about how the Indian Act complicated life for Indigenous people?

In the court case involving Sharon McIvor, what is at stake for her personally? What relationships is she seeking to protect? What is the case made by the defendants (Indian and Northern Affairs and the attorney general of Canada)? How is their view of what is at stake different? How does the decision of Madam Justice Ross understand the relationships that emerge from the Indian Act, in particular the 1985 revision?

To our list of concepts explored in previous chapters, we can add reciprocity as a lens with which to view the documents in this chapter. Indigenous scholars tell us that reciprocity is an important value in all relationships—between nations, within communities, among genders. The Indian Act replaced reciprocal gender relations with hierarchical ones based on a patriarchal two-gender model. When you review the documents in this section, consider these hierarchical relationships. What heteronormative hierarchies were created through the Indian Act and maintained through its revisions? The *Report of the Aboriginal Justice Inquiry of Manitoba* very clearly explains the relationship between the victimization of Indigenous women, residential schooling, and the Indian Act. These modes of oppression worked intersectionally to replace gender reciprocity with gender hierarchy. Reviewing the documents in this section and using the report as a guide, list all the ways that the Indian Act undermined gender reciprocity, women's place in their own communities, and limited equality within Canadian society.

Fighting patriarchy and gender discrimination were causes that Indigenous and settler women shared in the late twentieth century. In the testimony of Mavis Goeres, we see that Indigenous women were joined by Indigenous and feminist organizations in their struggle. Yet Goeres notices a lack of reciprocity among these organizations, specifically between Indigenous women who marched on Ottawa and those from other groups who joined them. What do you think stood in the way of more enduring relationships between Indigenous women and feminist groups at the end of the twentieth century? What prevented Indigenous women from feeling truly included in either the larger Indigenous organizations, such as the Assembly of First Nations, or women's organizations, such as the New Brunswick Women's Council? How might true reciprocity among these groups and their members have been achieved?

The position paper of the Indigenous Bar Association goes beyond criticizing the existing status provisions within the Indian Act to envisioning a day when the "status system as a whole" might be overturned. In particular, it demonstrates the legal precedent that the Crown must consult with

Indigenous peoples whenever it "contemplates conduct that might adversely affect [Aboriginal right or title]." Further, it argues that determining membership is a "fundamental right" of all nations, including Indigenous nations. The association's call is for the government of Canada to treat Indigenous nations with respect by acknowledging their right and their ability to determine citizenship according to their own criteria. In a multi-juridical setting, such as Canada, such a move would embody the reciprocity of a long-standing relationship. As you review this document, you might wish to consider how the Inuit criteria for citizenship demonstrate the values of relationship, responsibility, respect, and reciprocity. What other values or behaviours do they encompass? How are these criteria different from those of the Indian Act?

Finally, these documents offer us opportunities to consider not just what is written but how is it written. Return to the Consolidated Indian Act (RSC, 1985, c.I-5). How easy is it to understand? If you had to interpret this act in order to ensure that your daughter or son had access to Indian status, would you feel fully confident in your interpretation? Contrast this with the language of the position paper of the Indigenous Bar Association. Who was the intended audience of the 1985 Consolidated Indian Act? And how might that have influenced the language used? Similarly, consider the intended audience and the goal of the Indigenous Bar Association's position paper. You might also want to think about the use of a form when you analyse the document that commutes Rosalie Howse's annuity. Why do bureaucracies produce forms? What does it suggest about the process in which the form is used? Can you envision the process by which this form was filled out? What did the use of a form in this case enable, and what did it prevent? Given the role that the courts play in determining Indigenous rights and title, look carefully at the form and language of the court documents related to the McIvor case. What did you learn?

Documents

4.1 An Act to Amend and Consolidate the Laws Respecting Indians [Indian Act of 1876], section 3

Section 3 of the 1876 Indian Act defined who was and who was not an Indian. This definition had been the subject considerable discussion and at least four other pieces of legislation. The earliest of these acts, An Act for the Better Protection of the Lands and Property of the Indians of Lower Canada (1850) had the broadest definition of Indian: "persons of Indian blood, reputed to belong to the particular Tribe or Body of Indians interested in such lands and their descendants; all persons intermarried with any such Indians and residing among them and the descendants of all such persons; all persons residing among such Indians, whose parents on either side were or are Indians of such Body or

Tribe or entitled to be considered as such and; all persons adopted in infancy by any such Indians, and residing in the Village or upon the lands of such Tribe or Body of Indians and their descendants."[147] Within the year, another act was passed that amended that definition, narrowing it to exclude those without Indian parents and adding a gendered element with the clause "all women, now and hereafter to be lawfully married to any of the persons included in the several classes hereinbefore designated; the children issue of such marriages, and their descendants."[148] This definition provided the basis for all subsequent definitions of "Indian" enacted in law. The 1868 Act Providing for the Organization of the Department of the Secretary of State extended that definition for the first time to the former colonies of Nova Scotia and New Brunswick, now part of the Dominion of Canada. In 1869 the Gradual Enfranchisement Act made it clear that "any Indian woman marrying any other than an Indian shall cease to be an Indian within the meaning of the Act, nor shall the children issue of such marriage be considered as Indians within the meaning of the Act," and it added an additional reference to blood quantum with the stipulation, "no person with less than ¼ Indian blood, born after the passing of the Act, shall be deemed entitled to share in any annuities, interest or rents."[149] Ideas about gender, marriage, and the family pervade these definitions.

Indigenous communities protested these definitions, and, in particular, the General Council of the Six Nations demanded that the section removing Indian women who married non-Indians be repealed on the grounds that it was "unjust in depriving woman of her birthright, has a very immoral tendency for the Indian women . . . and breaks an ancient and acknowledged custom."[150] The Grand General Council of Indians of Ontario repeatedly debated the effects of this legislation on women. In the end, the council supported the 1876 act despite these concerns.[151]

Source: Canada, An Act to Amend and Consolidate the Laws
Respecting Indians, *Statutes of Canada* 39 Vic. (1876) c.18.

---

147 Canada, "An Act for the Better Protection of the Lands and Property of the Indians of Lower Canada," *The Provincial Statutes of Canada* (Kingston [Ont.]: S. Derbishire & G. Desbarats, Law Printer to the Queen's Most Excellent Majesty, 1850), 1247–48.

148 Canada, "An Act to Repeal in Part and to Amend an Act, entitled, An Act for the Better Protection of the Lands and Property of the Indians of Lower Canada," *Statutes of the Province of Canada*, 1851, c. 59.

149 Leslie and Maguire, *The Historical Development of the Indian Act*, 53.

150 Six Nations, *The General Council of the Six Nations and Delegates from Different Bands in Western and Eastern Canada: June 10, 1870* (Hamilton: Spectator Office, 1870).

151 Shields, "Anishinabek Political Alliance in the Post-Confederation Period," 45–46.

TERMS . . .

Indians.   3. The term "Indian" means
             First. Any male person of Indian blood reputed to belong to a particular band;
             Secondly. Any child of such person;
             Thirdly. Any woman who is or was lawfully married to such person.

As to   (a) Provided that any illegitimate child, unless having shared
illegitimates.   with the consent of the band in the distribution moneys
                 of such band for a period exceeding two years, may, at
                 any time, be excluded from the membership thereof
                 by the band, if such proceeding be sanctioned by the
                 Superintendent-General:

Absentees.   (b) Provided that any Indian having for five years continuously
                 resided in a foreign country shall with the sanction of the
                 Superintendent-General, cease to be a member thereof and
                 shall not be permitted to become again member thereof,
                 or of any other band, unless the consent of the band with
                 the approval of the Superintendent-General or his agent,
                 be first had and obtained; but this provision shall not apply
                 to any professional man, mechanic, missionary, teacher or
                 interpreter, while discharging his or her duty as such:

Woman marrying (c) Provided that any Indian woman marrying any other than
other than an   an Indian or a non-treaty Indian shall cease to be an Indian
Indian.   in any respect within the meaning of this Act, except that
                 she shall be entitled to share equally with the members of
                 the band to which she formerly belonged, in the annual or
                 semi-annual distribution of their annuities, interest moneys
                 and rents; but this income may be commuted to her at any
                 time at ten years' purchase with the consent of the band:

Marrying   (d) Provided that any Indian woman marrying an Indian of
non-treaty   any other band, or a non-treaty Indian shall cease to be a
Indians.   member of the band to which she formerly belonged, and
                 become a member of the band or irregular band of which
                 her husband is a member:

As to half-breeds. (e) Provided also that no half-breed in Manitoba who has
                 shared in the distribution of half-breed lands shall be
                 accounted an Indian; and that no half-breed head of a
                 family (except the widow of an Indian, or a half-breed
                 who has already been admitted into a treaty), shall, unless
                 under very special circumstances, to be determined by
                 the Superintendent-General or his agent, be accounted an
                 Indian, or entitled to be admitted into any Indian treaty.

4.2 Amendment to the Indian Act, 1985, sections 5, 6, and 7

The 1951 amendment to the Indian Act codified the differential treatment of women in new ways. First, an Indian register was introduced. Second, section 12 (referred to below) introduced a new set of rules by which status could be denied. The specific portion of section 12 was this:

12 (1)   The following persons are not entitled to be registered, namely,
    (a) a person who
        (i)   has received or has been allotted half-breed lands or money scrip,
        (ii) is a descendant of a person described in sub paragraph (i),
        (iii) is enfranchised, or
        (iv) is a person born of a marriage entered into after the coming into force of this Act and has attained the age of twenty-one years, whose mother and whose father's mother are not persons described in paragraph (a), (b), (d), or entitled to be registered by virtue of paragraph (e) of section eleven (is the illegitimate child of a female person [who qualifies for membership], unless the Registrar had declared that the child is not entitled to be registered), unless being a woman, that person is the wife or widow of a person described in section eleven, and
    (b) a woman who is married to a person who is not an Indian.

Section 12(a)(iv) became known as the "double mother rule." You will see this referred to in subsequent sections of this chapter.

The 1960s and 1970s were an era of renewed protest, both within Indigenous communities and among women. New organizations formed and old ones took on renewed vigour. The 1970 Royal Commission on the Status of Women included recommendations that the discriminatory portions of the Indian Act be repealed.[152] Indigenous women organized two major national groups in this era: the Indian Rights for Indian Women (founded in 1969 by Kahnawá:ke's Mary Two-Axe Early) and the Native Women's Association of Canada (founded in 1974). Individual women brought a number of cases against the Indian Act: Jeanette Corbiere-Lavall (Anishinaabe from Wikwemikong) in 1971, Yvonne Bedard (Six Nations) in 1972, and Sandra Lovelace (Maliseet from Tobique) in 1981. Lavell and Bedard both argued that section 12 violated Canada's 1960 Bill of Rights. Both fought their cases right up to the Supreme Court.[153]

152 Florence Bird, *Report of the Royal Commission on the Status of Women in Canada* (Ottawa: Information Canada, 1970), 410, http://epe.lac-bac.gc.ca/100/200/301/pco-bcp/commissions-ef/bird1970-eng/bird1970-eng.htm (accessed August 1, 2017).
153 Joanne Barker, "Gender, Sovereignty and the Discourse of Rights in Native Women's Activism," *Meridians: Feminism, Race and Transnationalism* 7, no. 1 (2006): 127–61; Glen Coulthard, *Red Skin, White Masks*, 79–87.

Lovelace brought her case to the United Nations Human Rights Committee, which ultimately ruled that section 12(1)(b) violated the International Covenant on Civil and Political Rights by denying her the right to live in her own community.[154]

Women in communities were not idle while these court cases proceeded. In 1979, the women of Tobique marched from the Mohawk community of Kanesatá:ke to Ottawa, garnering considerable press coverage. Many Canadians were astounded that the Indian Act was being used to deny women a home in their own communities.

Then, in 1982, Canada repatriated the Constitution, which included a Charter of Rights and Freedoms. Three years later, Canada passed Bill C-31 and amended the Indian Act to conform to the Charter of Rights and Freedoms.

Source: Canada, An Act to Amend the Indian Act, *Statutes of Canada* 33–34, Elizabeth II (1985), Ch. 27. Reprinted by permission of the Government of Canada, 2018.

Amendment to the Indian Act, 1985

Definitions and Registration of Indians

Indian Register

Indian Register	5. (1)	There shall be maintained in the Department an Indian Register in which shall be recorded the name of every person who is entitled to be registered as an Indian under this Act.
Existing Indian Register	(2)	The names in the Indian Register immediately prior to April 17, 1985 shall constitute the Indian Register on April 17, 1985.
Deletions and additions	(3)	The Registrar may at any time add to or delete from the Indian Register the name of any person who, in accordance with this Act, is entitled or not entitled, as the case may be, to have his name included in the Indian Register.
Date of change	(4)	The Indian Register shall indicate the date on which each name was added thereto or deleted therefrom.
Application for registration	(5)	The name of a person who is entitled to be registered is not required to be recorded in the Indian Register unless an application for registration is made to the Registrar.

---

154 Coulthard, *Red Skin, White Masks*, 87.

Persons entitled
to be registered

6. (1) Subject to section 7, a person is entitled to be registered if

(a) that person was registered or entitled to be registered immediately prior to April 17, 1985;

(b) that person is a member of a body of persons that has been declared by the Governor in Council on or after April 17, 1985 to be a band for the purposes of this Act;

(c) the name of that person was omitted or deleted from the Indian Register, or from a band list prior to September 4, 1951, under subparagraph 12(1)(a)(iv), paragraph 12(1)(b) or subsection 12(2) or under subparagraph 12(1)(a)(iii) pursuant to an order made under subsection 109(2), as each provision read immediately prior to April 17, 1985, or under any former provision of this Act relating to the same subject-matter as any of those provisions;

(d) the name of that person was omitted or deleted from the Indian Register, or from a band list prior to September 4, 1951, under subparagraph 12(1)(a)(iii) pursuant to an order made under subsection 109(1), as each provision read immediately prior to April 17, 1985, or under any former provision of this Act relating to the same subject-matter as any of those provisions;

(e) the name of that person was omitted or deleted from the Indian Register, or from a band list prior to September 4, 1951,

(i) under section 13, as it read immediately prior to September 4, 1951, or under any former provision of this Act relating to the same subject-matter as that section, or

(ii) under section 111, as it read immediately prior July 1, 1920, or under any former provision of this Act relating to the same subject-matter as that section; or

(f) that person is a person both of whose parents are or, if no longer living, were at the time of death entitled to be registered under this section.

Idem

(2) Subject to section 7, a person is entitled to be registered if that person is a person one of whose parents is or, if no longer living, was at the time of death subtitled to be registered under subsection (1).

Deeming provision

(3) For the purposes of paragraph (1)(f) and subsection (2),

(a) a person who was no longer living immediately prior to April 17, 1985 but who was at the time of death entitled to be registered shall be deemed to be entitled to be registered under paragraph (1)(a); and

(b) a person described in paragraph (1)(c), (d) or (e) who was no longer living on April 17, 1985 shall be deemed to be entitled to be registered under that paragraph.

Persons not entitled to be registered

7. (1) The following persons are not entitled to be registered:

(a) a person who was registered under paragraph 11(1)(f), as it read immediately prior to April 17, 1985, or under any former provision of this Act relating to the same subject-matter as that paragraph, and whose name was subsequently omitted or deleted from the Indian Register under this Act; or

(b) a person is the child of a person who was registered or entitled to be registered under paragraph 11(1)(f), as it read immediately prior to April 17, 1985, or under any former provision of this Act relating to the same subject-matter as that paragraph, and is also the child of a person who is not entitled to be registered.

Exception

(2) Paragraph (1)(a) does not apply in respect of a female person who was, at any time prior to being registered under paragraph 11(1)(f), entitled to be registered under any other provision of this Act.

Idem

(3) Paragraph (1)(b) does not apply in respect of the child of a female person who was, at any time prior to being registered under paragraph 11(1)(f), entitled to be registered under any other provision of this Act.

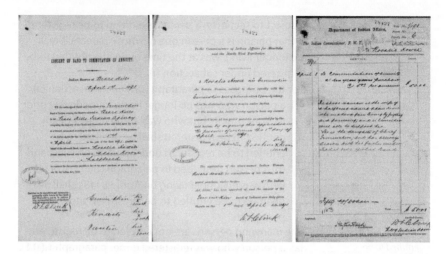

Illustration 4.1: Documents related to the commutation of the annuity of Rosalie Howse (née Ermineskin), 1891.

Source: PEACE HILLS AGENCY—ERMINESKIN BAND—COMMUTATION OF ANNUITY OF ROSALIE HOWSE NEE ERMINESKIN (PAY TICKET NUMBER 1), 1891. © Government of Canada. Reproduced with the permission of Library and Archives Canada (2017). Library and Archives Canada/Department of Indian Affairs and Northern Development fonds/e007850138/e007850139/e007850140

4.3 "Commutation of Annuity of Rosalie Howse née Ermineskin," April 1, 1891

In her family history, *The People Who Own Themselves*, historian Heather Devine amassed an impressive archive of Métis genealogy. One of the families that showed a remarkable degree of Métis-Cree intermarriage was the House family. Cree chief Mistawasis, a signatory to Treaty 6, was a member of a band known to comprise the House people (so named for their association with Hudson Bay Company posts known as "Houses," i.e., York House, Rocky Mountain House). He was the son of a Cree woman and a Métis man named Belanger. Mistawasis's daughter, Jane Belanger, married the Cree chief Ermineskin (Cree name: Sehkosowayanew) who also went by a Métis name, Baptiste Piche. In 1884, Rosalie Ermineskin, the daughter of Ermineskin and Jane Belanger, married Métis trader Adam Howse. Five years later, her father agreed to pay out 10 years of the annuities owed her under Treaty 6. Through her marriage to a non-status man, Rosalie had lost her status as an Indian, her right to live on reserve, and, through this commutation of annuity, all further claim to the benefits afforded her under Treaty 6.[155]

---

155 Devine, *The People Who Own Themselves*, Appendix 3, Genealogical Charts, accessed online at http://people.ucalgary.ca/~hdevine/naming.htm#29, August 1, 2017; see also Applications for Métis Scrip, RG 15-D-II-8-b, volume/box 1328, Claim of Adam Howse, 1885, LAC, Department of Interior.

Source: "Commutation of Annuity of Rosalie Howse née Ermineskin," April 1, 1891, LAC, Department of Indian Affairs fonds, RG 10, vol. 3853, file 78427, MIKAN no. 2061119.

CONSENT OF BAND TO COMMUTATION OF ANNUITY

Indian Reserve at Bears Hills
April 1st 1891

WE the undersigned Chiefs and Councillors of the Erminskin Band of Indians owning the Reserve at Bears Hills in the Peace Hills Indian Agency composing the majority of the Chiefs and Councillors of the said Band, have by vote at a Council, summoned according to the Rules of the Band, and held in the presence of the Indian Agent for the locality, on the 1st day of April in the year of Our Lord 18 91, granted on behalf of the aforesaid Band, consent to Rosalie Howse a former member thereof, who is married to Adam Howse a halfbreed to commute for the annuity payable to her at ten years' purchase, as provided for in sec. 12, the Indian Act, 1886.

Certified as to signatures and   Ermine Skin X His Mark
statements generally made herein
by the Chiefs and Councillors, and as
to nationality, as described herein, of
the above named woman's husband.
                    D. L. Clink   Kenwats X His Mark
                    Indian Agent.   Iwostin X His Mark

To the Commissioner of Indian Affairs for Manitoba and the North-West
        Territories.

I **Rosalie Howse nèe Erminskin** An Indian Woman, entitled to share equally with the Erminskin Band of Indians to which I formerly belonged, in the distribution of monies under Section [blank space in original] of "The Indian Act, 1880," hereby apply to have my income commuted to me at ten years' purchase as provided for the said Section, by signing this application in the presence of witnesses this 1st day of April . . . 1891.

Witness
D. C. Robertson   Rosaline Howse X Her Mark

This application of the above-named Indian Woman Rosalie Howse for the commutation of her income, at ten years' purchase, under Section [blank space in original] of "The Indian Act, 1880," has been approved of, and the consent of the Erminskin Band of Indians was duly given thereto on the 1st day of April A.D. 1891.
                                                                D. L. Clink

Vote No.   1/198
Farm No.
Treaty No.   6

Department of Indian Affairs,

The Indian Commissioner, N.W.T.

To: Rosalie Howse

Date 1891	Service	Amount.
April 8	*To Commutation of annuity at ten years* [years repeated in the original] *purchase @ 5.00 per annum*	$50.00
	The said woman is the wife of a halfbreed named Adam Howse who makes a fair living by freighting and farming; and is I consider well able to support her. She is the daughter of Chief Erminskin, and has always drawn with her father under Ticket no.1 of that Band.	
	Fifty °°Dollars—	
	Total ...	$50.00

Approved,		Hayter Reed	**Certified Correct**
		Commissioner	D. L. Clink
			Actg Indian Agent

Note – It is particularly requested that the number of the Vote under which the supplies named in the Voucher were purchased may be quoted on the upper right hand corner hereof, and that only such items shall be inserted herein as are properly chargeable to the vote quoted.

Form No. 12.

4.4 Mavis Goeres, *Enough Is Enough*

In the 1970s, Indigenous women across Canada were working together to improve living conditions on reserves, to advocate for Indigenous and women's rights, and to challenge the gender discrimination of the Indian Act. The

Indian Act had a profound effect on women's lives. For example, the Indian Act gave men—considered heads of household—sole possession of property on reserve through certificates of possession. Women had no housing rights. Furthermore, as we saw in the interview with Adam Solway in Chapter 1, women who lost Indian status through marriage could not return to their own communities when the marriage ended. In 1977, the eviction of one more woman from her marital home provoked Maliseet women from Tobique to band together. When their band council would not listen to their concerns, they occupied the band office. For four months, their collective action garnered intense public attention. The Tobique women looked closely at the Indian Act and found that its provisions violated the cultural norms and laws of the Maliseet people, who were traditionally matrilineal. Sandra Lovelace—a woman from Tobique—took the case against the Indian Act to the United Nations in 1977. The Tobique women carried on their lobbying for change, both at home on their reserve and nationally, as they raised public awareness of the discrimination faced by Indigenous women. In 1979, as the Tobique Women's Political Action Group, they organized a one hundred-mile march on Ottawa from Kanesatá:ke, near Montreal. Their rally on Parliament Hill attracted thousands. In 1984, the Tobique women agreed to work with Christian ethics doctoral student, Janet Silman, to tell their story of the events that unfolded between 1977 and 1984.[156]

Mavis Goeres, quoted in "Retrospective," in *Enough Is Enough: Aboriginal Women Speak Out, as Told to Janet Silman*, edited by Janet Silman (Toronto: Women's Press, 1987), 217–20. Reprinted by permission of Canadian Scholars / Women's Press. Copyright © Tobique Women's Group.

RETROSPECTIVE

Mavis Goeres

So we've had a long, hard struggle. I think what kept us going was our heritage and our sticking together. Maybe we didn't have all the same ideas, but we all had the one main goal in mind—equality for the women. We're just as good as the man. I think what really kept us going is our determination to seek what is rightfully ours. And that *is* our heritage. We all knew that no government agency—be it white or be it Indian—was going to tell us we were no longer Indian, when we *know* we are Indian.

156 Tobique Women's group, as told to Janet Silman, *Enough Is Enough: Aboriginal Women Speak Out* (Toronto: Women's Press, 1987): 9–16; the CBC Digital Archives includes a 1985 retrospective on Indigenous women's activism, "Our Native Land: Native Women Fight for Equal Rights," http://www.cbc.ca/archives/entry/our-native-land-native-women-fight-for-equal-rights (accessed August 1, 2017).

Here the Canadian government was making instant Indians out of white women. You might as well say they were trying to make instant white women out of us Indians. And it cannot be, because being Indian is our heritage—it's in our blood. I think that is our determination right there—it's because we are Indian. We were fighting for our *birthright*.

We had the demonstrations, the occupations, the women's walk to Ottawa. We got some housing for unwed mothers, but the band administration started giving that housing we got on account of the walk to unmarried men. Political promises. But still, we got something started, and we realized we'd been discriminated against for so long—Indian women in general—not just status or non-status . . . because I never liked that word, "non-status."

I knew I was Indian—nobody took the Indian blood out of me. Therefore I think all of us women decided there's this whole discrimination thing going on, and it's all geared against *the women*. The women had no rights. He could bring a white woman in, have children by her, and she had status. She had more to say than the Indian women did themselves. That's when the Tobique women *really* got involved.

We had obstacles along the way. Sadly, we had problems with Native organizations. I really feel that money has a lot to do with all these organizations— AFN, NCC, Métis, NWAC, even the New Brunswick Women's Council—straying from their original purpose. When they first organized it was to get Native people together, but then they would get monies which they were told to use for this purpose and this purpose only. But the money was coming in, people were getting paid—good pay that some of them never had before—and they forgot what they originally were going for. They get strayed.

I got an application from the New Brunswick Women's Council just yesterday to sign and send in my $2.00 as a member. I can't do it. I'm sorry, because I was on the executive and on the board of directors. I went to the First Ministers' Conference with the province under the women's council. I was fighting for equality and for the women, but once they started straying away from that objective, I gave up on that organization completely. I saw we weren't going anywhere.

A lot of those organizations were corrupted by money and greed and power; they really went down the drain. The difference with us was that, what money we had was donations. Nobody had control of us, nobody got any pay. We were lucky sometimes even to have a place to stay. In Montreal the other fall at the NAC meeting, there were five of us in one hotel room; whereas, the organizations all had rooms, meals provided. We ate at the YWCA.

Even on the women's walk to Ottawa, they were all donations. We slept on the bus or outside, let the elderly or sickly stay in whatever was offered. In Ottawa we even stayed in a jail that was turned into a hostel. A lot of us had blistered feet, but we went on. There was many times we'd be so discouraged, some would want to turn back—and some did—but most of us all kept each other going. The encouragement was there. It seems when everything is against you and you think you can't go on any longer, there's something that comes from within— something inside—gives you the added strength to go on some more.

Oh, it was a long, hard battle, and I pray there will be nothing standing in the way now to disillusion our happiness. Now that we've got our women's rights back now that the Indian Act is finally changed. I don't think Tobique will have any problems as far as reinstating their women, but I feel for other reserves, because I think they *are* going to have problems. We are okay here with our present administration, but with the wrong administration we could be in trouble again, too.

When I look back I see that we became more and more aware of the Indian Act standing behind a lot of our problems. Something I don't think other people are aware of, though, is the *hurt* that comes with it. No white woman actually came up and said anything to me personally, but there is one married to a man on this reserve that came up to my friend, Lilly Harris. Lilly had got up to say something at a band meeting, and this woman said, "Aw shut up! You non-status don't have nothing to say here." That hurt.

Another thing that hurt me regards my youngest daughter, Susan. She is very, very active in sports, very good in teams. When it came to Indian Summer Games, they said, "You can't play because you're non-status. You're not an Indian." I said, "My God, she's got as much Indian in her as a lot of them here." That's when I really got mad. I think the anger and hurt is what pushed us on, too. It wasn't only happening to my daughter, but to other women's daughters *and* sons. I protested and the *Toronto Star* did a story on my Susan and on Mary (Two-Axe) Early, showing how 12(1)(b) affected both their generations.

That Indian Act and the discrimination against women had such far-reaching effects—on relationships between people and on little day-to-day things. It's a good thing no white women came and called me "non-status" like they did Lilly, because I would fight them—physically, I mean. Nobody ever had, thank goodness, because I don't want to fight, but I wouldn't back down from one, either. I would fight for that because I am an Indian, an Indian through and through. I wish I could sit here and talk to you in Indian because the meaning comes out so much better, so much stronger.

Now that we've got the Indian Act changed and the women back, our reserve will be so much the stronger for it. Because Indian people will off-balance all the whites who have married in. Not just whites, either. Do you know that even Indian women from other reserves who married, feel they have more right to voice their opinions than our own women? But they don't have the same feelings for this reserve we do—that were born and brought up here. They don't.

We that grew up on Tobique know what the reserve used to be like. As an Indian person born and living here, you don't like some of the things that have been happening. But when you remember, then you can see that, yes, it can be different again. When you have twenty-two grandchildren like I have, and many live here, you want a better future. It *can* be better. That's what I mean when I say, now with the women back, our reserve will be so much the stronger. I know it.

4.5 Manitoba Justice Inquiry, "Cultural Changes—The Impact upon Aboriginal Women"

The Public Inquiry into the Administration of Justice and Aboriginal People was the result of tragedy. In 1971, 19-year-old high school student Helen Betty Osborne (Cree-Norway House) was brutally murdered in The Pas, Manitoba. The police focused on Osborne's friends in their initial investigation. Within the year, however, an anonymous informant wrote to the police implicating three local settler men in the crime. For years, rumours circulated in the community. At least one of the men spoke openly about the case in local bars. Finally, in 1987, Lee Colgan agreed to testify against two others in exchange for immunity. Dwayne Archie Johnston and James Robert Paul Houghton were charged with Osborne's murder. Johnston was found guilty and sentenced to life imprisonment, but Houghton was acquitted. A fourth man, whom the RCMP believed was involved in the murder, Norman Manger, was never charged. Indigenous people in the region wondered why it had taken 16 years for Osborne's killers to be brought to trial. Many alleged that The Pas and its police were indifferent to the fate of Indigenous women and unwilling to investigate crimes against them fully.

Within the year of the resolution of the Osborne case, yet another violent death of an Indigenous person provoked grief and outrage. Executive director of the Island Lake Tribal Council, J. J. Harper, was shot dead by police on the streets of Winnipeg. Indigenous and settler Manitobans called for an inquiry into how Indigenous people were being treated by the justice system. A provincial order in council called the Public Inquiry into the Administration of Justice and Aboriginal People into being on April 13, 1988. Its mandate was to investigate "all aspects of the way Aboriginal people are dealt with by the justice system in Manitoba."[157] This is part of what it had to say about how Indigenous women were treated.

Source: Manitoba, Public Inquiry into the Administration of Justice and Aboriginal People, *Report of the Aboriginal Justice Inquiry of Manitoba*. Vol. 1, *The Justice System and Aboriginal Peoples* (Winnipeg: Queen's Printer for Government of Manitoba, 1991– 1999), chapter 13 ("Aboriginal Women"), see section "Cultural Changes—the Impact upon Aboriginal Women."[158]

---

157 Aboriginal Justice Implementation Commission, "The Death of Helen Betty Osborne: The Aboriginal Justice Implementation Commission," *Report of the Aboriginal Justice Inquiry of Manitoba*, June 29, 2001, http://www.ajic.mb.ca/volumell/chapter1.html (accessed August 1, 2017).

158 For the context of this inquiry see A. C. Hamilton and C. M. Sinclair, "The Inquiry and the Issues," in *Report of the Aboriginal Justice Inquiry of Manitoba*, vol. 1, *The Justice System and Aboriginal Peoples* (Winnipeg: Queen's Printer for Government of Manitoba, 1991–1999), http://www.ajic.mb.ca/volumel/chapter1.html#3 (accessed February 25, 2017).

Cultural Changes—The Impact upon Aboriginal Women

For Aboriginal women, European economic and cultural expansion was especially destructive. Their value as equal partners in tribal society was undermined completely. The Aboriginal inmates in Kingston Prison for Women described the result this way:

> The critical difference is racism. We are born to it and spend our lives facing it. Racism lies at the root of our life experiences. The effect is violence, violence against us, and in turn our own violence.[159]

It is only in the past decade that writers have acknowledged the very important role Aboriginal women played in the first centuries of contact with Europeans and their descendants. Yet, while their role within Aboriginal society remained relatively stable for some time after contact, all that changed completely with the advent of the residential school system.

The victimization of Aboriginal women accelerated with the introduction after Confederation of residential schools for Aboriginal children. Children were removed from their families and homes at a young age, some to return eight to 10 years later, some never to return. The ability to speak Aboriginal languages and the motivation to do so were severely undermined. Aboriginal students were taught to devalue everything Aboriginal and value anything Euro-Canadian.

Many Aboriginal grandparents and parents today are products of the residential school system. The development of parenting skills, normally a significant aspect of their training as children within Aboriginal families, was denied to them by the fact that they were removed from their families and communities and by the lack of attention paid to the issue by residential schools. Parenting skills neither were observed nor taught in those institutions. Aboriginal children traditionally learned their parenting skills from their parents through example and daily direction. That learning process was denied to several generations of Aboriginal parents. In addition to the physical and sexual abuse that Canadians are now hearing took place in residential schools, emotional abuse was the most prevalent and the most severe.

Not only did residential schools not support the development of traditional parenting roles among the children, but they taught the children that they were "pagan"—an inferior state of being—and should never use their language or honour their religious beliefs. These messages were imparted to Aboriginal children in a sometimes brutal manner. Several presenters also pointed out that residential schools not only removed children from their families, but they also prevented closeness, even contact, from occurring between siblings and relatives at the same school.

---

159 Fran Sugar and Lana Fox, *Survey of Federally Sentenced Aboriginal Women in the Community* (Ottawa: Native Women's Association of Canada, 1990), 18.

The damage done by residential schools is evident today as Aboriginal people, long deprived of parenting skills, struggle with family responsibilities and attempt to recapture cultural practices and beliefs so long denied.

Grand Chief Dave Courchene Sr. put the experience succinctly:

> Residential schools taught self-hate. That is child abuse. . . . Too many of our people got that message and passed it on. It is their younger generations that appear before you [in court].

We believe the breakdown of Aboriginal cultural values and the abuse suffered by Aboriginal children in the schools contributed to family breakdown. This began a cycle of abuse in Aboriginal communities, with women and children being the primary victims.

The Canadian government also undermined equality between Aboriginal men and women with the legalization of sexist and racist discrimination in successive pieces of legislation. In 1869 it introduced the concept of enfranchisement, whereby Indian people would lose their status as Indians and be treated the same as other Canadians. For Aboriginal women, this process of enfranchisement had particularly devastating consequences, because the role assigned to Canadian women was one of inferiority and subjugation to the male.

Upon being enfranchised, Aboriginal people lost their status under the *Indian Act*. An Indian woman lost her status automatically upon marrying a man who was not a status Indian. This was not true for Indian men, whose non-Indian wives gained status as Indians upon marriage. Under subsequent *Indian Acts*, Indian agents could enfranchise an Indian if he were deemed "progressive." In cases where a man became enfranchised, his wife and children automatically lost their status, as well.[160]

While Bill C-31 (1985) addressed many of these problems, it created new ones in terms of the differential treatment of male and female children of Aboriginal people. Under the new Act, anomalies can develop where the children of a status Indian woman can pass on status to their children only if they marry registered Indians, whereas the grandchildren of a status male will have full status, despite the fact that one of their parents does not have status. . . .

Aboriginal women traditionally played a prominent role in the consensual decision-making process of their communities. The *Indian Act* created the chief and council system of local government. The local Indian agent chaired the meetings of the chief and council, and had the power to remove the chief and council from office. Aboriginal women were denied any vote in the new system imposed by the Indian Affairs administration. As a result, they were stripped of any formal involvement in the political process.

The segregation of Aboriginal women, both from wider society and from their

---

160 Kathleen Jamieson, *Indian Women and the Law in Canada: Citizens Minus*, Canadian Action Committee on the Status of Women (Ottawa: Supply and Services Canada, 1978).

traditional role as equal and strong members of tribal society, continues to the present day. This is due partly to the fact that the effects of past discrimination have resulted in the poor socio-economic situation applicable to most Aboriginal women, but it is also attributable to the demeaning image of Aboriginal women that has developed over the years. North American society had adopted a destructive and stereotypical view of Aboriginal women.

...

Example 1 6(1) Marries 6(1) ▼ Child is 6(1)	Example 2 6(1) Marries 6(2) ▼ Child is 6(1)
Example 3 6(1) Marries non-Indian ▼ Child is 6(1)	
Example 4 6(2) Marries 6(2) ▼ Child is 6(1)	Example 2 6(2) Marries non-Indian ▼ Child is non-Indian

Bill C-31, 1985

Figure 4.1: The Effects of Bill C-31.

Source: Adapted from Mary C. Hurley and Tomina Simeone, *Legislative Summary of Bill C-3: Gender Equity in Indian Registration Act* (Ottawa: Library of Parliament, 2010), Appendix C—Effects of Bill C-31

Illustration 4.2: Sharon McIvor speaking at a press conference, 2013.

Source: The Canadian Press/Sean Kilpatrick

Parliament's amendments (Bill C-3)

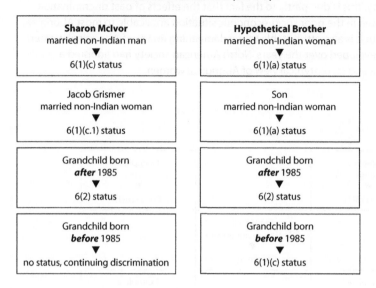

Figure 4.2: The Effects of Bill C-3.

4.6 Excerpts from the "Reasons for Judgment," *McIvor v. The Registrar, Indian and Northern Affairs Canada*

The 1985, Bill C-31 did not end gender discrimination in the Indian Act. It replaced section 12 with the equally complicated sections 6(1) and 6(2), that produced two categories of Indian status, one that was inheritable in perpetuity and one that was limited to two generations. The descendants of women who had lost status under the old discriminatory sections were still liable to lose status in the future. In 1989, Nlaka'pamux woman Sharon McIvor launched a challenge under the 1982 Charter of Rights and Freedoms on the grounds that the Indian Act amended by Bill C-31 still discriminated on the basis of gender. Her grandchildren, the sons of her son Jacob Grismer, could not be registered under the new rules even though their cousins, who had status Indian grandfathers, but otherwise identical Indigenous genealogies, were. It took seventeen years for the case to go to trial at the British Columbia Supreme Court. In 2007, Madam Justice Ross offered these "Reasons for Judgment" in the case (see the excerpts below).

Source: *McIvor v. The Registrar, Indian and Northern Affairs Canada, and The Attorney General of Canada*, 2007 BCSC 827. Reprinted by permission of the Superior Courts of British Columbia.

IN THE SUPREME COURT OF BRITISH COLUMBIA

Citation: McIvor v. The Registrar, Indian and Northern Affairs Canada,
                    2007 BCSC 827

Date: 20070608
Docket: A941142
Registry: Vancouver

Between:

Sharon Donna McIvor, Charles Jacob Grismer

Plaintiffs

And

The Registrar, Indian and Northern Affairs Canada,
The Attorney General of Canada

Defendants

Before: The Honourable Madam Justice Ross

Reasons for Judgment

Counsel for the Plaintiffs	Robert W. Grant
	Gwen Brodsky
Counsel for the Defendants	Sarah P. Pike
	Glynis Hart
	Brett C. Marleau
Date and Place of Trial:	October 16 to November
	10, 2006
	Vancouver, BC

INTRODUCTION

[1] In this action the plaintiffs, Sharon Donna McIvor ("Sharon McIvor"), and her son, Charles Jacob Grismer ("Jacob Grismer"), challenge the constitutional validity of ss. 6(1) and 6(2) of the *Indian Act*, R.S.C. 1985, c. I-5 (the "*1985 Act*"). These provisions deal with entitlement to registration as an Indian, or status as it is frequently termed. The plaintiffs do not challenge any other provisions of the *1985 Act*, and in particular, do not challenge the provisions relating to entitlement to membership in a band.

[2] Under previous versions of the *Indian Act*, the concept of status was linked to band membership and the entitlement to live on reserves. In addition, under previous versions of the *Indian Act*, when an Indian woman married a non-Indian man, she lost her status as an Indian and her children were not entitled to be registered as Indians. By contrast, when an Indian man married a non-Indian

147

woman, both his wife and his children were entitled to registration and all that registration entailed.

[3] For years there were calls for an end to this discrimination. Eventually in 1985, the government introduced and parliament subsequently passed Bill C-31, *An Act to Amend the Indian Act*, S.C. 1985, c. 27 (*"Bill C-31"*). Part of the purpose of the legislation was to eliminate what was acknowledged to be discrimination on the basis of sex from the criteria for registration. Another significant aspect of the amendments introduced as part of *Bill C-31* was that for the first time the issue of eligibility for registration or status was separated from the issue of membership in a band.

[4] The plaintiffs submit that this remedial effort was incomplete and that the registration provisions introduced in *Bill C-31* that form the basis for registration in the *1985 Act* continue to discriminate contrary to ss. 15 and 28 of the *Canadian Charter of Rights and Freedoms* (the *"Charter"*). The plaintiffs submit that the registration provisions continue to prefer descendents [sic] who trace their Indian ancestry along the paternal line over those who trace their Indian ancestry along the maternal line. The plaintiffs submit further that the provisions continue to prefer male Indians who married non-Indians and their descendents [sic], over female Indians who married non-Indians and their descendents [sic].

[5] In this action the plaintiffs seek the following relief:

1. A declaration that section 6 of the *1985 Act* violates section 15(1) of the *Charter* insofar as it discriminates between matrilineal descendants and patrilineal descendants born prior to April 17, 1985, in the conferring of Indian status.

2. A declaration that section 6 of the *1985 Act* violates section 15(1) of the *Charter* insofar as it discriminates between descendants born prior to April 17, 1985, of Indian women who had married non-Indian men, and descendants of Indian men who married non-Indian women.

3. A declaration that section 6 of the *1985 Act* violates section 15(1) of the *Charter* insofar as it discriminates between descendants born prior to April 17, 1985, because they or their ancestors were born out of wedlock.

4. An order that the following words be read in to section 6(1)(a) of the *1985 Act*: "or was born prior to April 17, 1985, and was a direct descendant of such a person".

5. In the alternative:
   An order that for the purposes of section 6(1)(a) of the *1985 Act*, section 11(1)(c) and (d) of the *Indian Act*, S.C. 1951, c. 29, as amended (the *"1951 Act"*), in force immediately prior to April 17, 1985 shall be read as though the words "male" and "legitimate" were omitted.
   And a further order that for the purposes of section 6(1)(a) of the *1985 Act*, s. 12(1)(b) of the *1951 Act* in force immediately prior to April 17, 1985, shall be read as though it had no force and effect.

6. A declaration that the plaintiffs are entitled to register under s. 6(1)(a) of the *1985 Act*.

7. . . .

8. An order that the relief granted in this proceeding applies exclusively to registration under section 6 of the *1985 Act* and does not alter sections 11 and 12 of the *1985 Act* or any other provision defining entitlement to Band membership.

. . .

[6] The defendants' response to the plaintiffs' claims can be organized around three principal themes:

(a) granting the relief sought by the plaintiffs would constitute an impermissible retroactive or retrospective application of the *Charter* in that it would require the court to apply the *Charter* to pre-1985 legislation and to amend repealed provisions of prior versions of the *Indian Act*;

(b) the plaintiffs suffered no injury. The only difference between the plaintiffs and Indians entitled to registration pursuant to s. 6(1)(a) of the *1985 Act* is in relation to the status of their children. There is no right to transmit Indian status, which is purely a matter of statute. Accordingly, there has been no denial of the plaintiffs' rights; and

(c) any infringement of the plaintiffs' rights is justified in light of the broad objectives of the 1985 amendments to the *Indian Act* which was a policy decision, made after extensive consultation, balancing the interests of all affected and which is entitled to deference.

[7] For the reasons that follow, I have concluded that the registration provisions contained in s. 6 of the *1985 Act* discriminate on the basis of sex and marital status contrary to ss. 15 and 28 of the *Charter* and that such discrimination has not been justified by the government. The following conclusions form the crux of my decision:

(a) The plaintiffs' claim, properly understood, requires neither a retroactive nor a retrospective application of the *Charter*. It is rather an application of the *Charter* to the present registration provisions of the *Indian Act*.

(b) Although the concept "Indian" is a creation of government, it has developed into a powerful source of cultural identity for the individual and the Aboriginal community. Like citizenship, both parents and children have an interest in this intangible aspect of Indian status. In particular, parents have an interest in the transmission of this cultural identity to their children.

(c) The registration provisions of the *1985 Act* did not eliminate discrimination. The registration provisions contained in s. 6 continue to prefer descendents who trace their Indian ancestry along the paternal line over those who trace their Indian ancestry along the maternal line and continue to prefer male Indians who married non-Indians and their descendents, over female Indians who married non-Indians and their descendents. This preference constitutes discrimination on the basis of sex and marital status contrary to ss. 15 and 28 of the *Charter*.

(d) This discrimination has not been justified by the government pursuant to s. 1 of the *Charter*. In that regard, as part of the 1985 amendments, the government elected to sever the relationship between status and band membership. Status is now purely a matter between the individual and the state. There are no competing interests. No pressing and substantial objective has been identified with respect to the discriminatory provisions in the registration scheme.

. . .

Conclusion Regarding Discrimination

[288] I have concluded that the registration provisions embodied in s. 6 of the *1985 Act* continue the very discrimination that the amendments were intended to eliminate. The registration provisions of the *1985 Act* continue to prefer descendants who trace their Indian ancestry along the paternal line over those who trace their ancestry through the maternal line. The provisions prefer male Indians and their descendants to female Indians and their descendants. These provisions constitute discrimination, contrary to ss. 15 and 28 of the *Charter* based on the grounds of sex and marital status.

. . .

VIII. REMEDY

[343] I have concluded that s. 6 of the *1985 Act* violates s. 15(1) of the *Charter* in that it discriminates between matrilineal and patrilineal descendants born prior to April 17, 1985, in the conferring of Indian status, and discriminates between descendants born prior to April 17, 1985, of Indian women who married non-Indian men, and the descendants of Indian men who married non-Indian women. I have concluded that these provisions are not saved by s. 1.

[344] The final issue is that of remedy.

[345] The defendants seek a suspension of any relief for a period of 24 months. Such a suspension would, in their submission, serve two purposes. First, an immediate declaration of invalidity would "deprive deserving persons of benefits without providing them to the applicant": see *Schacter v. Canada*, [1992] 2 S.C.R. 679 at 715–716. A suspension would enable the registration process to continue and afford Parliament time to seek input from Aboriginal groups in its development and implementation of a scheme consistent with the courts ruling. In this regard, I agree with the defendants' submission with respect to the concern over judicial scrutiny of legislation as expressed in *Hunter v. Southam Inc.*, [1984] 2 S.C.R. 145 at 169 as follows:

> While the courts are guardians of the Constitution and of individuals' rights under it, it is the legislature's responsibility to enact legislation that embodies appropriate safeguards to comply with the Constitution's requirements. It should not fall to the courts to fill in the details that will render legislative lacunae constitutional.

[346] However, further delay for these plaintiffs must be measured against the backdrop of the delays that they have already experienced. The record discloses

that from the late 1970's forward, successive governments recognized that the registration provisions discriminated on the basis of sex. It was not until 1985 that legislation was passed to remedy this discrimination, legislation that I have found continued to perpetuate the problem.

[347] Ms. McIvor applied for registration pursuant to the *1985 Act* on September 23, 1985. The Registrar responded some sixteen months later by letter dated February 12, 1987, granting her registration under s. 6(2) and denying registration to Jacob. Ms. McIvor protested the decision by letter dated May 29, 1987. The Registrar confirmed his decision some twenty-one months later by letter dated February 28, 1989. These proceedings were then initiated.

[348] At the time these proceeds came under case management in April 2005, the defendant's position was, and continued to be, that a substantial adjournment was required to afford the Crown sufficient time to prepare. This position was maintained notwithstanding the fact that the statutory appeal had been commenced in 1989 and the claim under the *Charter* in 1994. The defendants also asserted at that time that up to six months would be required for the trial of this action.

[349] The defendant's concession with respect to the plaintiffs' registration status, was made shortly before trial. It was based on an interpretation of the legislation and in my view could have been advanced at any time following the 1989 Decision of the Registrar. Having made the concession, the defendants immediately applied to strike the plaintiffs' claim.

[350] Against this backdrop, I conclude that the plaintiffs should not be told to wait two more years for their remedy.

[351] Plaintiff's counsel submitted that the course adopted in *Benner* should be followed, and that is the approach that I have decided to adopt. It is the intention of these reasons to declare that s. 6 of the *1985 Act* is of no force and effect insofar, and only insofar, as it authorizes the differential treatment of Indian men and Indian women born prior to April 17, 1985, and matrilineal and patrilineal descendants born prior to April 17, 1985, in the conferring of Indian status. The court remains seized of the case in order to give the parties the opportunity to draft appropriate relief in light of these reasons. Should the parties fail to reach agreement, I will hear further submissions on the issue of remedy.

"Ross J."

4.7 Indigenous Bar Association in Canada, "Position Paper on Bill C-3—Gender Equity in Indian Registration Act," 2010

In 2009, the British Columbia Court of Appeal heard the appeal of the BC Supreme Court decision in the McIvor case. It determined that the government of Canada must amend the Indian Act in order to remove the gender discrimination within it. Minister of Indian Affairs and Northern Development Chuck Strahl duly introduced Bill C-3 in 2010; it was entitled the "Gender Equity in Indian Registration Act." Sharon McIvor herself spoke out against the bill. Bill C-3 retained two categories of status—6(1) and 6(2)—from the previous legislation; both were based on gender and marriage. By keeping these two categories, Bill C-3 continued to discriminate against Indigenous women. The bill passed in 2011 but continues to be tested in the courts. In 2015, the Superior Court of Québec, in a decision of the case *Descheneaux v. Canada (The Attorney General)*, found that sections of the current Indian Act continue to treat Indigenous men and women (and their descendants) differently. The following year, the government of Canada introduced a new legislative amendment (Bill S-3). The Standing Senate Committee on Aboriginal Peoples is not, as of the summer of 2017, fully satisfied that Bill S-3 will end gender discrimination in the Indian Act.[161] Meanwhile, Indigenous legal scholars indicate that there are also larger issues of sovereignty at stake in any attempt by Canada to determine the "status" or citizenship of Indigenous peoples. This brief addresses these issues in some detail.

Source: Indigenous Bar Association in Canada, "Position Paper on Bill C-3—Gender Equity in Indian Registration Act," Submitted to the Senate Committee on Human Rights on December 6, 2010, http://www.indigenousbar.ca/pdf/IBA%20Submissions%20on%20Bill%20C3%20Gender%20 Equity.dec%202010.pdf. Reprinted by permission of the Indigenous Bar Association.

Indigenous Bar Association in Canada

Position Paper on Bill C-3—Gender Equity in Indian Registration Act[162]

Submitted to the Senate Committee on Human Rights

December 6, 2010

INTRODUCTION

The Indigenous Bar Association in Canada (IBA) is a non-profit organization representing Indigenous peoples involved in the legal profession across Canada, including judges, lawyers, academics, and students-at-law. The IBA was established in 1988 as a successor to the Canadian Indian Lawyers' Association

---

161 An update on the current legislation to amend the Indian Act can be found here: Government of Canada, Indigenous and Northern Affairs Canada, "Eliminating Known Sex-Based Inequities in Indian Registration," *Indian Status*, https://www.aadnc-aandc.gc.ca/ eng/1467214955663/1467214979755 (accessed August 1, 2017).

162 In the section reproducing the report from the Indigenous Bar Association, all further notes are from the original document unless otherwise stated. This document uses legal citation and cross-references notes using note numbers, which have been modified here. We have removed the "*supra* note" references that direct readers to where a source is first mentioned. But the reader can find that first reference through the shortened form of the source that the authors of the original document placed in square brackets. (See the next note for an example: [*Indian Act*].)

(CILA). The IBA relies on the voluntary contributions of its members and its goals and objectives include the following:

i) establishing a nation-wide community of Indigenous lawyers;
ii) providing ongoing education to its members with respect to principles rooted in Indigenous law;
iii) providing a forum for the exchange of information and experiences of Indigenous lawyers, academics, and students; and
iv) advancing legal and social justice for Indigenous peoples across Canada by engaging in law and policy reform.

The IBA continues to promote the recognition and respect for Indigenous laws, customs and traditions in carrying out all of its objectives.

ISSUE

In 1951 substantial amendments to the *Indian Act*[163] created a centralized register of all people eligible to be registered as Indians.[164] Sections 11 and 12 of the 1951 *Indian Act* perpetuated the federal government's long-standing practice of enfranchisement, whereby Indian women lost Indian status if they married a non-Indian male. Also, section 12(i)(a)(iv) of the 1951 *Indian Act* established the "double mother" rule which dictated that an Indian born after 1951 would lose their Indian status at the age of 21 if their mother, and their paternal grandmother, both acquired Indian status by virtue of marrying an Indian male. This legislative scheme was discriminatory and was arduously opposed by Indigenous communities.

In response, the Parliament of Canada passed Bill C-31, *An Act to Amend the Indian Act*, on June 28, 1985. Sweeping changes were made by amending status, membership and other provisions within the 1951 *Indian Act*. For instance, Indians who had lost their status as a result of the "double mother" rule were reinstated under section 6(1)(c).

On the other hand, section 6 of the 1985 *Indian Act* gave rise to a new form of gender discrimination. Section 6(1)(a) stated that a person is entitled to be registered if "that person was registered or entitled to be registered immediately prior to April 17, 1985."[165] Thus, if a male status Indian had children with a non-status Indian female prior to 1985, those children were entitled to 6(1) status. If a female was enfranchised under the 1951 *Indian Act*, she was entitled to be reinstated under section 6(1)(c), however, if she had a child with a non-status partner prior to 1985, her child was only entitled to 6(2) status. An individual with 6(2) status cannot pass

---

163 *Indian Act*, R.S.C. 1985, c. I-6 [*Indian Act*].
164 The term "Indian" is employed in the *Indian Act* and as such, the term "Indian" is only used in these submissions for the purposes of referencing the provisions contained with the *Indian Act*.
165 *Indian Act* at s. 6. 4.

their status on to their children if the other parent is non-status Indian. As a result, in some circumstances females reinstated under section 6(1)(c) were unable to pass their status on to their grandchildren; in every case, Indian males who had children before 1985 could pass their status on to their grandchildren.

This situation was faced by Sharon McIvor in *McIvor v. Canada (McIvor)*,[166] where Ms. McIvor, an Indian woman reinstated under section 6(1)(c) of the 1985 *Indian Act*, sought a declaration of invalidity of sections 6(1) and 6(2) of the *Indian Act* due to the fact that they violated section 15 of the *Charter of Rights and Freedoms*. Ms. McIvor's son, Jacob Grismer, was born prior to 1985 and was recognized as a 6(2) Indian. Jacob had a child with a non-status Indian and as a result, Ms. McIvor's grandchild was unable to acquire status. As previously illustrated, males in Ms. McIvor's position had the ability to pass their status on to their grandchildren in all cases.

The British Columbia Supreme Court ("BCSC") . . . held that section 6 of the *Indian Act* gave rise to differential treatment on the grounds of sex and ordered that the section be declared of no force and effect "only insofar, as it authorizes differential treatment of Indian men and Indian women born prior to April 17, 1985, and matrilineal and patrilineal descendants born prior to April 17, 1985, in the conferring of Indian status."[167] The decision was appealed to the British Columbia Court of Appeal ("BCCA") in April of 2009. The BCCA allowed the appeal in part. While the BCCA agreed that certain registration provisions of the *Indian Act* are unconstitutional, the court focused solely on the impact of the "double mother" rule and how it promoted gender inequality under the 1985 *Indian Act*. The Court held that . . . Ms. McIvor was the recipient of an "enhanced status" under the 1985 *Indian Act* and that in order to remedy the discrimination experienced in her case, a number of provisions could be employed; the BCSC was not necessarily required to augment Jacob's position by granting him section 6(1) status. Therefore, the BCCA ordered that section 6 of the *Indian Act* be amended within 12 months—i.e. April 6, 2010. Parliament was granted an extension to January 31, 2011.

Bill C-3 was introduced at first reading in the Senate on November 23, 2010 and was debated at second reading on November 25, 2010. This is a Bill to promote gender equality in Indian registration by responding to the BCCA decision in *McIvor*. If Bill C-3 receives Royal Assent in its current form, it will fail to address the legacy of colonial and assimilationist policies that can be traced to the earliest forms of the *Indian Act*.

While the IBA believes that Bill C-3 is a step towards addressing the gender discrimination inherent within the *Indian Act*, attention must be drawn to the fact that the amendments are a patchwork solution to the fundamentally flawed provisions dealing with status and citizenship in Indigenous communities. Bill C-3 does not address questions pertaining to citizenship, Indigenous jurisdiction and the long-term viability of the status system as a whole. Parliament has been afforded an opportunity to meaningfully recognize and implement systems

---

166　*McIvor v. Canada (Registrar, Indian and Northern Affairs)*, [2007] BCJ No. 1259 (SC)(QL) [*McIvor*].

167　*McIvor* at 351.

of membership based on Indigenous legal traditions. By disregarding the opportunity to address their broader issues, the Crown is depriving Indigenous nations of their ability to exercise their aboriginal, treaty, and international rights to govern their own citizens.

THE DUTY TO CONSULT

The Supreme Court of Canada in *Haida v. British Columbia*[168] made it clear that the Crown owes a duty to consult whenever it has "knowledge, real or constructive, of the potential existence of the Aboriginal right or title and contemplates conduct that might adversely affect it."[169] While the Crown may invoke its authority under section 91(24) of the *Constitution Act, 1982* to legislate with respect to "Indians and Lands reserved for Indians,"[170] this power must be read together with section 35 of the *Constitution Act, 1982*.[171] As such, the power to legislate with respect to First Nations is explicitly qualified by the need for adequate, meaningful consultation that is consistent with the honour of the Crown.

In this case, the amendments to the *Indian Act* trigger the honour of the Crown and the duty to consult. First, the Court in *Mikisew Cree First Nation v Canada (Minister of Canadian Heritage)*[172] clearly held that while First Nations do not have a veto when they are being consulted, the Crown cannot act unilaterally when it makes decisions that potentially adversely affect Aboriginal interests.[173] Bill C-3 must be viewed against a backdrop of persistent unilateral legislative attempts to assimilate Indigenous populations. By perpetuating the paternalistic regime effected by the *Indian Act* and failing to acknowledge the rights of Indigenous nations to govern their own membership, the Crown is impairing their ability to meaningfully exercise such rights. This in turn clearly gives rise to a duty to consult.

Second, the right to determine membership according to traditional and historical practices is a fundamental right of every Nation. Indigenous nations in Canada have been repeatedly characterized by the court as "collective" entities. The rights that accrue to these bodies can only be exercised as a community; individuals cannot claim an aboriginal right. As such, prudent policy demands that these entities have a voice when legislative change fundamentally alters the terms dictating who belongs to these collective entities.

FIRST NATIONS JURISDICTION OVER CITIZENSHIP

Indigenous nations across Canada have vehemently asserted that membership is a core area of self-government. These assertions are buttressed by major studies such as the 1983 Penner Report on Indian Self-Government in Canada

---

168 *Haida v. British Columbia (Minister of Forests)*, [2004] S.C.J. No. 70 (QL) [*Haida*].
169 *Ibid* at 35.
170 *The Constitution Act, 1982*, being Schedule B to the *Canada Act 1982* (U.K.), 1982, c. 11 s. 91(24).
171 *R. v. Sparrow*, [1990] 1 S.C.R. 1075 [*Sparrow*] at 62.
172 *Mikisew Cree First Nation v. Canada (Minister of Canadian Heritage)*, [2005] S.C.J. No. 71 (QL)
173 *Ibid*.

and the 1995 Report of the Royal Commission on Aboriginal Peoples. Further, the right to determine membership was an integral component of the "pre-existing sovereignty" historically exercised by Indigenous nations.[174] It is beyond dispute that Indigenous nations in Canada traditionally exercised the right to determine their own membership and that this right is now firmly entrenched in section 35 of the *Constitution Act, 1982*. In the view of the IBA, the status system under the *Indian Act* is an unjustifiable infringement of the inherent right of Indigenous nations to determine their own membership. In light of these factors, it is clear that the over-arching injustice to Indigenous nations stems from the imposition of an unwelcome, beleaguered status system and that Bill C-3 circumvents this issue by adopting a narrow-sighted view of Indigenous citizenship.

While Bill C-3 aims to address gender discrimination effected by the *Indian Act*, the larger issue illustrated in *McIvor* is that the colonial mindset which laid the framework for the *Indian* Act has failed time and again to fulfill the needs of Indigenous nations. Since the inception of Indian status within the *Indian Act*, the Crown has repeatedly amended the same to include a complex set of criteria for determining who is and who is not an "Indian." The limited relief offered by Bill C-3 is only the latest chapter in an ongoing effort by the Crown to undermine the ability of Indigenous communities to determine their own members.

It is important to mention that Indian status cannot be confused with the system of band membership contained within sections 8 to 14 of the *Indian Act*. For instance, under Bill C-31, sections 8-14 were amended to permit bands to determine their own criteria for membership according to custom; however, the federal government retained the discretion to determine for status. As a result, the rights of status Indians (as opposed to "band members") were segregated. Following Bill C-31, status Indians can access programs such as post-secondary funding, non-insured health benefits, and funding for housing. On the other hand, band members only have access to communal and political rights such as rights to live on reserve land, participate in elections, and access band assets. In *McIvor*, the BCSC made it clear that the designation of status and the right to receive corresponding benefits has become a powerful source of identity within Indigenous communities.[175] As such, the power to determine band membership is trivial in the face of the Crown's overwhelming power to dictate status designations in Indigenous communities.

The recognition of the right of Indigenous nations to exercise jurisdiction over membership is also consistent with Canada's status as a multi-juridical state. Canada's legal apparatus embraces common law, civil law and Indigenous legal traditions. For instance, the Supreme Court of Canada has stated that the common law has always recognized "the ancestral laws and customs of the aboriginal peoples who occupied the land prior to European settlement."[176] Renowned Indigenous legal scholar and IBA member, Dr. John Borrows, suggests that the

---

174 *Haida* at para. 20.
175 *McIvor* at para. 133.
176 *R. v. Van der Peet*, [1996] 2 S.C.R. 507 (QL) at para. 263.

multi-juridical platform is a strong basis to strengthen and unify the ties within Canada. With respect to Indigenous legal traditions, he states that the same can "have great force in people's lives despite their lack of prominence in broader circles. Indigenous legal traditions are a reality in Canada and should be more effectively recognized."[177] At its most basic level, the right to determine citizenship is an expression of the values and traditions embedded in Indigenous legal traditions.

These sentiments were echoed by Sebastien Grammond, a Canadian scholar who points to the beneficiary provisions of the James Bay Northern Quebec Agreement ("JBNQA") as an example of Indigenous autonomy in the area of membership. Grammond suggests that the principles embodied in sections 3A.3.1 of the JBNQA is recognition of the Inuit legal order as part of the composition of Canada's legal institution. Grammond goes on to state that the criteria adopted for the purposes of determining who is and who is not Inuk:

> ... effectively emphasize the individual's connection with the community, most notably when it is based on ancestry, residence in Nunavik, concern for the welfare of other beneficiaries (to be clear, sharing), and family and social connections. The criteria also encompass those factors which are traditionally seen by Western eyes as being "typical Inuit," such as respect for the land and animals, and knowledge of Inuktitut. *Furthermore, these criteria are to be applied by local communities entirely composed of Inuit, who are certainly better positioned than a bureaucrat, to determine if a person is a member of their community.*[178] [Emphasis added]

The system for determining membership within the JBNQA, which emphasizes communal ties and participation, is a favourable approach which, in the view of the IBA, could be replicated in other Indigenous jurisdictions across Canada. This is consistent with commonly shared views of Indigenous peoples in Canada that race-based formulae, such as those instilled by Bill C-3, 10 should be abolished. John Borrows argues that, "We should not deny people citizenship if they are willing to abide by First Nations citizenship laws and be fully participating members in our communities ... Indigenous laws should flow from the political character of our societies; they should not apply because of society's racialization of Indigenous peoples."[179] Until this point, it is clear that the current *Indian Act* has been the source of many grievances between status, non-status, on-reserve, and off-reserve Indigenous peoples. Such arbitrary, archaic distinctions need to be abandoned in favour of a more principled, community-based approach.

Finally, the Parliament of Canada formally endorsed the *United Nations Declaration on the Rights of Indigenous Peoples* ("UNDRIP") on November 12, 2010. UNDRIP is a comprehensive document which sets internationally agreed

---

177 John Borrows, *Canada's Indigenous Constitution* (Toronto: University of Toronto Press Incorporated, 2010) at 23 [*Borrows*].

178 Sébastien Grammond, "L'appartenance aux communautés inuit du Nunavik: un cas de réception de l'ordre juridique inuit?" (2008) 23 *Canadian Journal of Law and Society* 93 at 117 [translated by author].

179 Borrows at 157.

upon standards for protecting the rights of Indigenous Peoples all over the world. Article 33.1 of UNDRIP states that "Indigenous Peoples have the right to determine their own identity or membership in accordance with their customs and traditions." The recognition of Indigenous peoples' right to govern their own membership in Canada is an important step to ensure compliance with UNDRIP.

A status system that undermines the legitimacy of band governments cannot be characterized as one that promotes the honour of the Crown. Deficiencies that plague the band membership and status systems severely offend the goals of reconciliation sought by s. 35 of the *Constitution Act, 1982* and UNDRIP. Also, it is likely that Indigenous nations could advance a strong argument that sections 6–14 of the *Indian Act* unjustifiably infringe their Aboriginal right to have and maintain societal relationships in accordance with traditional principles, laws, customs and practices, including the right to determine their own members. Thus, reactive, short-sighted 11 remedial approaches to the *Indian Act*, such as those contained within Bill C-3, will only precipitate the injustice faced by Indigenous nations in Canada.

LEGISLATIVE REFORM

Bill C-31 introduced a formula outlining qualifications for Indian status in Canada which is preserved in Bill C-3. Sections 6(1) and 6(2) of the amended *Indian Act* created two distinct categories of Indians pursuant to the *Act*. "Full Blooded" Indians are alluded to in 6(1) while Indians with only one status parent would fall into the category outlined in 6(2). The distinction becomes important when one analyzes the effects of this provision on eligibility for registration. Effectively, only persons registered under s. 6(1) can pass their status on to their children. If children of a person registered under 6(2) are to be registered, the other parent must be registered under either s. 6(1) or 6(2). This creates a "two-parent" system, dictating which individuals can pass on their status and severely limiting status where non-status individuals become involved in the equation.

One of the most urgent concerns of First Nations people across Canada is the need for legislative reform to prevent vanishing status populations in some communities. If a status Indian in Canada wishes to pass on their status to their children, the *Indian Act* discourages any relationships with non-status society members because it reduces the resulting children's ability to inherit status. If a 6(1) status Indian decides to have children with a non-status individual, their legacy may be that their status may fail to pass to their grandchildren. If a person of 6(2) status wishes to have children with a non-status individual, their status will not pass to their children or grandchildren at all.

The rapid influx of status Indians to urban communities has had the effect of reducing the status Indian population as a whole. Any on-reserve status Indians who enter relationships with people outside of their own communities will forfeit their children's ability to pass on that status. This will inevitably produce a legislated extinction of status communities. It is beyond dispute that the *Indian Act* was predicated on a platform of assimilation and integration. Against this historical backdrop, it is clear that a legislative regime that systematically reduces the number of First Nations peoples in Canada without their consent will only prolong this antiquated platform of assimilation.

The status quo continues to perpetuate inequality within First Nation families. Families may have members that are registered as 6(1) or 6(2) or as non-Status Indians. Regardless if they are a family under the same household and if their community recognizes them as deserving citizens their Indian status is still legally defined by the *Indian Act*. This hinders their access to programs and services in their community. Funding to First Nations is allocated by the amount of registered band members not by the actual amount of population.

RECOMMENDATIONS:

1. The IBA recommends that the federal government of Canada move away from defining "Indians," to supporting an approach that recognizes First Nations' jurisdiction to determine citizenship

The federal government's ongoing interference in First Nation jurisdiction through the determination of who can be registered as an Indian under the *Indian Act* arguably contravenes s.35 of the *Constitution Act, 1982*. It is not palatable for the federal government acting on behalf of Canada to continue to interfere in this core area of First Nation jurisdiction. Moreover, the federal government's continued insistence to interfere with First Nation jurisdiction to determine First Nation membership is inconsistent with international norms. The fact that these legislative sections still exist . . . [is] inconsistent with current international conventions, most notably Article 33.1 of the United Nations Declaration on the Rights of Indigenous Peoples which reads:

> Indigenous peoples have the right to determine their own identity or membership in accordance with their customs and traditions. This does not impair the right of indigenous individuals to obtain citizenship of the States in which they live.[180]

---

180 See also: Article 4, 9, 18, 19.

  Article 4: Indigenous peoples, in exercising their right to self-determination, have the right to autonomy or self-government in matters relating to their internal and local affairs, as well as ways and means for financing their autonomous functions.

  Article 9: Indigenous peoples and individuals have the right to belong to an indigenous community or nation, in accordance with the traditions and customs of the community or nation concerned. No discrimination of any kind may arise from the exercise of such a right.

  Article 18: Indigenous peoples have the right to participate in decision-making in matters which would affect their rights, through representatives chosen by themselves in accordance with their own procedures, as well as to maintain and develop their own indigenous decision-making institutions.

  Article 19: States shall consult and cooperate in good faith with the indigenous peoples concerned through their own representative institutions in order to obtain their free, prior and informed consent before adopting and implementing legislative or administrative measures that may affect them.

2. The IBA recommends that Canada establish another Special Parliamentary Committee to act as a Parliamentary Task Force on the broader issue of self-government, membership and citizenship in conjunction with sections 6–14 of the *Indian Act.*

Previously, CILA had provided recommendations to the Penner Committee on Indian Self-government in Canada which addressed important related issues like membership and citizenship. One recommendation made by CILA (adopted by the Penner Committee) was that constitutional change was not required to implement self-government. The federal government was already in a position to take the broader steps necessary. CILA recommended:

> Under Section 91(24) of the Constitution Act, 1867 . . . the federal government is given exclusive jurisdiction over Indians and Indian lands. This means that the federal government has the power to pass legislation with respect to Indians and Indian lands without respect to the provinces. This is well illustrated in the Indian Act, which deals with areas that are within provincial jurisdiction. Areas such as wills and estates, motor vehicles, marriage, property, creditors' rights, and liquor are all included in the Act. It can therefore be concluded that the federal government has the authority to legislate in all respects of Indians dealing with an area under Section 92 of the Constitution Act, 1867.[181]

We understand that the Assembly of First Nations has also made this recommendation to this Committee. Given our conclusion that the scope of Bill C-3 does little to address the broader important issues, we recommend that you include such a recommendation to Parliament.

3. With respect to Bill itself, the IBA agrees with the CBA, that section 9 be removed from Bill C-3.

---

181 House of Commons, Special Committee on Indian Self-Government, Second Report to the House, October 20, 1983, p. 59.

Chapter Five

Land

The significance of land to both Euro-Canadian settlers and Indigenous communities cannot be overstated. It is in land that culture, economics, and identity coalesce into a complex whole. Yet, until relatively recently, students of history and popular audiences alike were presented with a story of Canada that tended to ignore the intricacies of the relationship between Indigenous peoples and their territories. Instead, they were offered a single narrative arc or plot-line, usually the history of nation building, that showed waves of intrepid Europeans moulding an empty, or at least underdeveloped, land mass to create a happy and prosperous present.[182] Within this narrative, liberal capitalist understandings in which land is owned by individuals rather than communities are presented as the natural and only imaginable way of things. Certainly there were others who, even decades ago, saw this as a national myth that is both arrogant and unsuitably restrictive, but until not long ago, they were but a small minority.[183]

The way we frame the past, what we consider to be important, and the kinds of questions we seek answers to shape our understanding of history. When we explore the documents presented in this chapter, then, it is important keep the discussion outlined above in mind. We would like you to consider the ways in which each of these documents either echoes the narrative of natural and unassailable Euro-Canadian progress through land and resource development or challenges that notion and demonstrates rather that history is better seen

---

182 For this longstanding interpretation of Canadian history, see, for example, Stephen Leacock, *Canada, the Foundations of its Future* (Montreal: n.p., 1941), 19; A. R .M. Lower, *Colony to Nation: A History of Canada* (Toronto: McClelland and Stewart, 1981); and J. L. Granatstein, *Who Killed Canadian History?* (Toronto: Harper Collins, 1998).

183 Among others, see Sherene Razack, "When Place Becomes Race," in *Race, Space, and the Law: Unmapping a White Settler Society* (Toronto: Between the Lines, 2002), 1–4: Ian Mackay, ed., *The Challenge of Modernity: A Reader on Post-Confederation Canada* (Toronto: McGraw-Hill Ryerson, 1991), xvii–xviii; and Ian McKay "The Liberal Order Framework: A Prospectus for a Reconnaissance of Canadian History," *Canadian Historical Review*, 81, no. 4 (December 2000): 616–45.

as a set of relations that were constantly being challenged and realigned. In other words, while context, contingency, responsibility, respect, change over time, and the other tools of analysis that we've already begun to employ continue to be critical, in this final chapter of *Talking Back to the Indian Act*, we encourage you to focus on the complexity or messiness of history that these documents, taken collectively, represent. We want you think about the complex and varied ways that land was perceived, valued, and utilized. Important too, of course, is the sometimes convoluted and incremental way land was transferred from Indigenous to settler control. We ask you further to consider the explanations presented to justify the displacement of Indigenous people and to reflect on the nature of any resistance that was mounted.

The selections from the 1876 Indian Act that we've included here make reference to the system of assigning location tickets, or sole occupancy rights, to individual Indigenous community members for small portions of reserve land. In what ways does this policy shift control of land from Indigenous to settler understandings of appropriate land holding regimes? In what ways might this policy further the long-term objective of assimilation? In what other ways are settler understandings about and related to land foregrounded while Indigenous understandings are ignored or silenced? Staying with the 1876 Indian Act, consider who is confirmed as the owner of the fragments of Indigenous territories known as reserve lands? In what ways do the 1911 revisions to the act further reduce Indigenous control of these lands? Under what conditions and by whom can reserve lands be appropriated without the consent of the resident First Nation?

Next, move to analyse the 1911 memo to the prime minister. What justifications does the author provide in support of the position that reserves near settler towns, like that of the Songhees (Lekwungen), should be relocated? The *Daily Colonist* article includes a bit of detail on the final chapter in the half-century-long negotiation for the removal of the Lekwungen from Victoria's city centre. It also hints at the long-standing dispute between the federal and provincial governments concerning which of them held underlying title to and reversionary interest in reserve lands in the province. As always, think about the language used to help you to determine the specific perspective of this newspaper and which party or parties it has the most affinity with. Even words such as "improvements" may include meaning that is culturally specific. What evidence of federal-provincial differences do you see here? Most often, the proceeds collected from the sale of reserve lands were controlled by Canada's Department of Indian Affairs, but from what you read here and in the 1911 Act Respecting the Songhees Indian Reserve, determine how the Lekwungen might be seen as challenging this policy or perhaps even the legitimacy of Crown title on their reserve.

These five documents present a pretty clear narrative of what Canadian authorities saw as problems and how they went about trying to solve them. Yet if you read these documents against the grain, the complexity of divergent interests and understandings in relation to land becomes more evident. For

Map 5.1: Territories of the Lekwungen

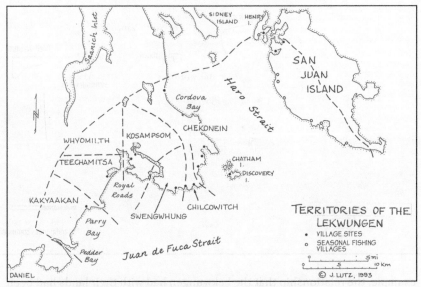

Source: Map originally created by Stuart Daniel and courtesy of John Lutz

Map 5.2: Lekwungen (Songhees) Reserves

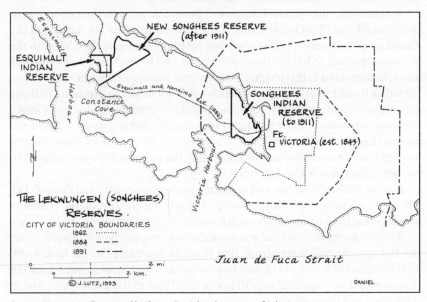

Source: Map originally created by Stuart Daniel and courtesy of John Lutz

Map 5.3: Burrard Inlet Indigenous Communities

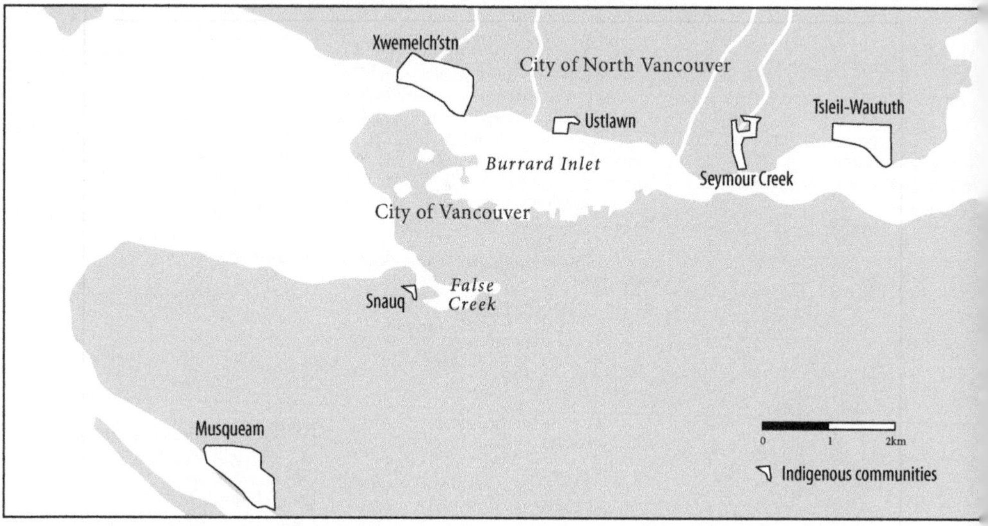

example, the relationship that the Lekwungen had with their lands had been under threat since the Hudson's Bay Company built Fort Victoria in the heart of their territory in 1843. In the decades that followed, village sites were combined and new ones were established, as the Lekwungen navigated unrelenting pressure from governments, commercial interests, and the growth of the City of Victoria. In the end, they were able to extract an arrangement that was far from perfect, but it was good enough that Canada did not want to see it repeated.

Resistance to the 1911 amendments to the Indian Act and their effects were widespread, but Chief Josiah Hill and the leadership of the Six Nations of the Grand River in Ontario present a specific set of objections in their letter to the governor general. What are these objections, and how do they make the land issue, as presented in this chapter's documents, even more complex? How does Canada's Department of Indian Affairs Secretary J. D. McLean respond to these objections? Reading against the grain, ask this question: In what ways might McLean be accused of attempting to smooth out what is a more complex situation than he is willing to admit by referring to the section 46 amendment as "right and reasonable" and by presenting the impact of the amendment to section 49 in the way that he does?

Back in British Columbia, and switching genres somewhat, read through Lee Maracle's narrative "Goodbye, Snauq." Maracle, by illustrating the transformations that have occurred through the process of colonization, adds nuance to the complexity of how land and its resources are perceived and used. What are the specific transformations that Maracle describes—to the land itself, to the resources it once held, and to who has access ? In what ways does the Squamish [Skwxwú7mesh] experience parallel that of the Lekwungen, and in what ways is it unique?

Documents

5.1 An Act to Amend and Consolidate the Laws Respecting Indians [Indian Act of 1876], sections 4 to 10, 25 to 28, and 59 to 60

Prior to the passage of the first Indian Act in 1876, legislation such as the 1869 Gradual Enfranchisement Act briefly mentions the breaking up of reserved lands into lots through the distribution of location tickets, today referred to as certificates of possession, to individual reserve residents. Sections 86 and 87 of the 1876 Indian Act, reproduced in Chapter 3 of this book, outline the conditions under which location tickets would be conferred, and we recommend that you have a look at those sections again now in the context of the theme presented here. Sections 4 through 10 of the act, excerpted below, provide more detail on the mechanics of allocating location tickets, the nature of the title that is granted, and how these holdings can be transferred or handed down. Sections 25 to 28 and 59 to 60 outline the methods by which reserve lands could be alienated and sold and what happens to the proceeds. Even though location tickets do not confirm actual fee simple title, think about how the selections below confirm both the Euro-Canadian understanding that land should be individually as opposed to collectively held and the settler view of land as a simple commodity. Consider how this last perception is just assumed. The selections below include other settler understandings too, such as appropriate gender roles, suitable political systems and decision-making processes, and the need for governmental intervention into the affairs of Indigenous communities.

Source: Canada, An Act to Amend and Consolidate the Laws Respecting Indians, *Statutes of Canada* 39 Vic. (1876) c.18, s.4–10, 25–28, and 59–60.

CHAP. 18.
An Act to amend and consolidate the laws respecting Indians.

[Assented to 12th April, 1876.]

RESERVES

Reserves subject to this Act.
4. All reserves for Indians or for any band of Indians, or held in trust for their benefit, shall be deemed to be reserved and held for the same purposes as before the passing of this Act, but subject to its provisions.

Surveys authorized.

5. The Superintendent-General may authorize surveys, plans and reports to be made of any reserves for Indians, shewing and distinguishing the improved lands, the forests and land fit for settlement, and such other information as may be required; and may authorize that the whole or any portion of a reserve be subdivided into lots.

What Indians only deemed holders of lots.

6. In a reserve, or portion of a reserve, subdivided by survey into lots, no Indian shall be deemed to be lawfully in possession of one or more of such lots, or part of a lot, unless he or she has been or shall be located for the same by the band, with the approval of the Superintendent-General:

Indemnity to Indians dispossessed.

Provided that no Indian shall be dispossessed of any lot or part of a lot, on which he or she has improvements, without receiving compensation therefor, (at a valuation to be approved by the Superintendent-General) from the Indian who obtains the lot or part of a lot, or from the funds of the band, as may be determined by the Superintendent-General.

Location ticket; in triplicate; how dealt with.

7. On the Superintendent-General approving of any location as aforesaid, he shall issue in triplicate a ticket granting a location title to such Indian, one triplicate of which he shall retain in a book to be kept for the purpose; the other two he shall forward to the local agent, one to be delivered to the Indian in whose favor it was issued, the other to be filed by the agent, who shall permit it to be copied into the register of the band, if such register has been established:

Effect of such ticket limited.

8. The conferring of any such location title as aforesaid shall not have the effect of rendering the land covered thereby subject to seizure under legal process, or transferable except to an Indian of the same band, and in such case, only with the consent of the council thereof and the approval of the Superintendent-General, when the transfer shall be confirmed by the issue of a ticket in the manner prescribed in the next preceding section.

Property of deceased Indian, how to descend.

Proviso.

9. Upon the death of any Indian holding under location or other duly recognised title any lot or parcel of land, the right and interest therein of such deceased Indian shall, together with his goods and chattels, devolve one-third upon his widow, and the remainder upon his children equally; and such children shall have a like estate in such land as their father; but should such Indian die without issue but leaving a widow, such lot or parcel of land and his goods and chattels shall be vested in her, and if he leaves no widow, then in the Indian nearest akin to the deceased,

but if he have no heir nearer than a cousin, then the same shall be vested in the Crown for the benefit of the band: But whatever may be the final disposition of the land, the claimant or claimants shall both be held to be legally in possession until they obtain a location ticket from the Superintendent-General in the manner prescribed in the case of new locations.

Indians in Manitoba, British Columbia or N. W. Territories, &c., having made improvements.

10. Any Indian or non-treaty Indian in the Province of British Columbia, the Province of Manitoba, in the North-West Territories, or in the Territory of Keewatin, who has, or shall have, previously to the selection of a reserve, possession of and made permanent improvements on a plot of land which has been or shall be included in or surrounded by a reserve, shall have the same privileges, neither more nor less, in respect of such plot, as an Indian enjoys who holds under a location title.

…

SURRENDERS

Necessary conditions previous to a sale.

25. No reserve or portion of a reserve shall be sold, alienated or leased until it has been released or surrendered to the Crown for the purposes of this Act.

On what conditions release or surrender to be valid.

26. No release or surrender of a reserve, or portion of a reserve, held for the use of the Indians of any band or of any individual Indian, shall be valid or binding except on the following conditions:—

Assent of band.

1. The release or surrender shall be assented to by a majority of the male members of the band of the full age of twenty-one years, at a meeting or council thereof summoned for that purpose according to their rules, and held in the presence of the Superintendent-General, or of an officer duly authorized to attend such council by the Governor in Council or by the Superintendent-General;

Proviso.

Provided, that no Indian shall be entitled to vote or be present at such council, unless he habitually resides on or near and is interested in the reserve in question;

Proof of assent.

2. The fact that such release or surrender has been assented to by the band at such council or meeting, shall be certified on oath before some judge of a superior, county, or district court, or stipendiary magistrate, by the Superintendent-General or by the officer authorized by him to attend such council or meeting, and by some one of the chiefs or principal men present thereat and entitled to vote, and when so certified as aforesaid shall be submitted to the Governor in Council for acceptance or refusal;

Superintendent-General may grant license to cut trees, &c.

3. But nothing herein contained shall be construed to prevent the Superintendent-General from issuing a license to any person or Indian to cut and remove trees, wood, timber and hay, or to quarry and remove stone and gravel on and from the reserve; Provided he, or his agent acting by his instructions, first obtain the consent of the band thereto in the ordinary manner as hereinafter provided.

No intoxicant to be permitted at council of Indians.

27. It shall not be lawful to introduce at any council or meeting of Indians held for the purpose of discussing or of assenting to a release or surrender of a reserve or portion thereof, or of assenting to the issuing of a timber or other license, any intoxicant; and any person introducing at such meeting, and any agent or officer employed by the Superintendent-General, or by the Governor in Council, introducing, allowing or countenancing by his presence the use of such intoxicant among such Indians a week before, at, or a week after, any such council or meeting, shall forfeit two hundred dollars, recoverable by action in any of the superior courts of law, one half of which penalty shall go to the informer.

Invalid surrenders not confirmed hereby.

28. Nothing in this Act shall confirm any release or surrender which would have been invalid if this Act had not been passed; and no release or surrender of any reserve to any party other than the Crown, shall be valid.

...

MONEYS

Governor in Council may direct investment of Indian funds.

59. The Governor in Council may, subject to the provisions of this Act, direct how, and in what manner, and by whom the moneys arising from sales of Indian lands, and from the property held or to be held in trust for the Indians, or from any timber on Indian lands or reserves, or from any other source for the benefit of Indians (with the exception of any small sum not exceeding ten per cent of the proceeds of any lands, timber or property, which may be agreed at the time of the surrender to be paid to the members of the band interested therein), shall be invested from time to time, and how the payments or assistance to which the Indians may be entitled shall be made or given, and may provide for the general management of such moneys, and direct what percentage or proportion thereof shall be set apart from time to time, to cover the cost of and attendant upon the management of reserves, lands, property and moneys under the provisions of this Act, and for the construction or repair of roads passing through such reserves or lands, and by way of contribution to schools frequented by such Indians.

Proceeds of
sales to Receiver
General.

60. The proceeds arising from the sale or lease of any Indian lands, or from the timber, hay, stone, minerals or other valuables thereon, or on a reserve, shall be paid to the Receiver General to the credit of the Indian fund.

5.2 An Act Respecting the Songhees Indian Reserve, 1911

The name Songhees was not applied to the Indigenous people residing on the southern tip of Vancouver Island until after Fort Victoria was established in their territory in 1843. The original inhabitants of the region lived in largely autonomous familial groupings but did refer to themselves collectively as Lekwungen, a term derived from the name of their common language. The establishment of Fort Victoria compounded the impact of population losses caused by introduced epidemic diseases to transform the lifeways of nearby Indigenous communities. Many moved from their winter village sites to create two new communities on Victoria's inner harbour. The smaller of the two was first set up at the present site of the BC legislature buildings and then, in the 1850s, relocated west to the Esquimalt waterfront. This and the remaining inner harbour site became known as the Esquimalt and Songhees reserves respectively. There had already long been pressure applied to residents of the latter, the Songhees reserve, to give up their land in the heart of Victoria. With the rapid growth of the city that began near the end of the first decade of the twentieth century, that pressure became profound, and, as the document below indicates, an arrangement was reached to move the community away from the inner harbour to a site adjacent to the Esquimalt reserve. As compensation, each head of family was awarded $10,000, or just over $240,000 in today's money. Department of Indian Affairs policy dictated that this money should be held in trust, but the Lekwungen were able to argue successfully to have it paid to them directly. Nonetheless, two years later, in contrast to what would likely have happened if they had been part of settler society, they were asked by the DIA to account for how the funds were spent.[184]

Source: Canada, An Act Respecting the Songhees Indian
Reserve, *Statutes of Canada* 1-2 Geo. V (1911) c.24.

---

184 Detail for this introduction was drawn from John Lutz, *Makuk: A New History of Aboriginal-White Relations* (Vancouver: UBC Press, 2008), 50–51, 100–103; John Lutz, "'Relating to the Country': The Lekwammen and the Extension of European Settlement, 1843–1911," in *Beyond City Limits: Rural History in British Columbia*, edited by R. W. Sandwell, 17–32 (Vancouver: UBC Press, 1999); Peter Baskerville, *Beyond the Island: An Illustrated History of Victoria* (Burlington, ON: Windsor Publications, 1986), 70–74; and Wilson Duff, "The Fort Victoria Treaties," *BC Studies* (Fall 1969): 4–5.

An Act respecting the Songhees Indian Reserve

[Assented to May 19, 1911]

His Majesty, by and with the advice and consent of the Senate and House of Commons of Canada, enacts as follows: —

Confirmation of agreement for sale of Songhees Indian Reserve

1 The agreement for the sale of the Songhees Indian Reserve contained in the schedule to this Act is hereby confirmed and, notwithstanding anything in *The Indian Act*, the whole of the amount payable to each head of an Indian family under the terms of the said agreement may be paid in the manner therein provided.

SCHEDULE

MEMORANDUM OF AGREEMENT made (in duplicate) between The Government of the Dominion of Canada, represented by the Honourable Frank Oliver, Superintendent General of Indian Affairs of Canada: and The Government of the Province of British Columbia, represented by the Honourable William Roderick Ross, Minister of Lands for the Province of British Columbia:

Witnesseth that it has been agreed between the parties hereto as follows: —

1: That the Songhees Indian Reserve, in the city of Victoria, in the Province of British Columbia, shall be conveyed or transferred to the Government of the Province of British Columbia for the consideration hereinafter mentioned as soon as the Songhees Band of Indians have surrendered the same under the provisions of the *"Indian Act"* and as soon as the necessary legislation has been obtained from the Parliament of Canada confirming this agreement.

2: That the Government of the Province of British Columbia will, in consideration of such conveyance or transfer: —

(1) Deposit in the Canadian Bank of Commerce in the city of Victoria the sum of ten thousand dollars ($10,000.00) to the credit and in the name of each head of a family of the said Songhees Band of Indians as set forth in the census of the said Band made November 21st to 25th, 1910, by Inspector Ditchburn, and any additional bona fide heads of families existing at the date of payment as the names of such heads of families are certified by the Superintendent General to the Minister of Lands, and will furnish the Superintendent General with the said Bank's receipt for each deposit countersigned by the Indian to whose credit such deposit has been made:

(2) Deposit the value of each Indian's improvements to his or her credit in the said Bank; and when the value of the schoolhouse, now used by the Indians

as a church, the water pipe, and any other Band improvements, is ascertained, will divide it equally among the heads of families and deposit the same to the credit of the respective heads, furnishing the Bank's receipt for each deposit as above. In case an agreement cannot be arrived at with respect to the value of such improvements, school-house and water pipe, the value shall be settled by arbitration, the Superintendent General and the Minister of Lands each to appoint an arbitrator and the two arbitrators so appointed to appoint a third arbitrator, and the decision of such arbitrators, or any two of them, to be final and conclusive:

(3) Convey in fee simple to His Majesty the King, represented by the Superintendent General, a piece or parcel of land at Esquimalt, being all that piece or parcel of land situate in and being part of Section two, Esquimalt District, Vancouver Island, and now known as Section 2A, and being more particularly described as follows: — Commencing at a post planted at high water mark on the northerly shore of Constance Cove, Esquimalt Harbour; thence in a direction north thirty-six degrees and twenty-eight minutes east, Magnetic (N. 36° 28' E. Mag.) a distance of eighty chains and ninety links (80.90.) more or less, to an intersection with the southerly boundary of the Craigflower Road; thence westerly along said southerly boundary to an intersection with the easterly boundary of the Admiral's Road; thence southerly following said easterly boundary to an intersection with the east boundary of the Esquimalt Indian Reserve; thence following the said east boundary of the reserve to its southeast corner; thence at right angles and westerly along the south boundary of the Indian reserve to its southwest corner on the shore of Esquimalt Harbour; thence following the shore line of the Harbour westerly, southerly and easterly to point of commencement, the whole containing by admeasurement one hundred and sixty-three and forty-two hundredths acres, more or less, and more particularly shown on the annexed tracing and thereon coloured red save and excepting that portion of the right of way (passing through Section 2A) conveyed to the Esquimalt and Nanaimo Railway Company by deed dated July 4, 1905, and registered in the Land Registry Office at Victoria in absolute fees book Vol. 22, Folio 385, No. 115080, and deposited in said office under No. 167:

Together with all mines royal and all mines and minerals and all rights, members and appurtenances whatsoever to the said hereditaments belonging, and all the estate, right, title and property whatsoever of the said Vendor in, to, and out of the said premises.

(4) Remove the dead, together with all monuments and tombstones from the said Songhees reserve in the city of Victoria to the new reserve at Esquimalt, and there re-inter and replace them in a manner satisfactory to the Superintendent General, the whole at the cost of the Government of British Columbia.

In witness whereof the parties have hereunto affixed and set heir hands and seals of office this 31st day of March, A.D., One thousand nine hundred and eleven.

Signed, sealed and delivered	FRANK OLIVER (Seal.)
by the Honourable Frank	Superintendent General of
Oliver in the presence of:	Indian Affairs.
FRANK PEDLEY	
Signed, sealed and delivered	WM. R. ROSS (Seal.)
by the Honourable William R.	Minister of Lands.
Ross in the presence of:	
R. F. CHILD	

5.3 "Last Chapter in Problem," *Daily Colonist*, March 17, 1911

Information that is today provided across multiple platforms was until very recently limited to printed newspapers. Like now, newspapers of the past included feature-length stories, editorials, obituaries, advertisements, photographs, cartoons, and other content that provides a unique window into a time and place. Like other primary sources, they offer information about particular episodes or issues, but they can also help us uncover long-term trends and provide specific detail and aspects of an event or time not available elsewhere. Whereas historians spend months or even years researching and producing their books and scholarly articles, newspapers contain much more immediate interpretations and windows into particular points in time. This immediacy is, of course, important for the reading public at the time the news was reported, but it also creates potential complications for historians to consider and navigate. Although it is unavoidable that a historian's subject position and political orientation will affect what she or he writes, newspapers more often openly display partiality or political orientation. Victoria's *Daily Colonist*, still in print today as the *Times Colonist*, has gone through numerous name and ownership changes since it was first published in 1858. The article from March 17, 1911, reproduced below, takes a clear position on the Songhees (Lekwungen) land sale and gives the reasons the author thinks it is important. It also provides specific detail on some elements of the final stages of the negotiations involving the Lekwungen, the federal and provincial governments, and the Hudson's Bay Company. Though the result of Lekwungen demands are evident in the article, it gives no information on internal Lekwungen discussions, how the $10,000 amount was arrived at, or what individual reserve residents thought about the move or the compensation. This perspective indicates who the *Colonist* saw as its primary constituency and whose interests were more clearly in line with its own. For those who want to read more from this newspaper, issues from the period of 1858 to 1951 are online and keyword searchable at http://www.britishcolonist.ca/.

Source: "Last Chapter in Problem," *Daily Colonist*, March 17, 1911, 1–2.

LAST CHAPTER IN PROBLEM

Songhees Reserve to Become Property of Provincial Government within the Next Few Weeks

FINAL ARRANGEMENTS ALMOST COMPLETE

Comprehensive Plans for Utilization of Land for Railroad Terminals and Other Purposes

It is confidently expected that the deed of conveyance from the Hudson's Bay Company to the Dominion Government (as trustees of the Indians) of the 163.42 acres of land fronting on Esquimalt Harbor and which are to form also the new home of the remaining members of the Songhees tribe, will be received from London in the course of the ensuing week; and immediately upon the arrival of this deed, the Provincial Minister of Lands, Hon. William R. Ross, will proceed to satisfy and extinguish the claims of the Indians by the payment to each family head of the sum of $10,000, and the removal of the tribe to its new reservation will thereupon take place.

The payment of the Indians, according to the agreement arrived at on the 25th of October last as a result of the negotiations successfully conducted in behalf of the Provincial Government by Mr. H. Dallas Helmcken, K. C. and Mr. J. H. S. Matson, would have been somewhat sooner accomplished but for the fact that the local government authorities have been obliged to await the execution of the deed for the chosen new home of the Songhees people by the Hudson's Bay Company, and this could not take place until the usual monthly meeting of the directorate of the historic vending company, held in London on the 8th instant.

Meanwhile, the former tenants of the fine property selected for the Songhees' future occupancy have vacated, and a mutually satisfactory understanding between the Federal and Provincial governments of the surrender to the latter of the old reserve in the heart of Victoria city has been reduced to the formal terms of an agreement on the precise lines of the announced arrangement with Chief Cooper and his people, which agreement will be attached as a schedule to short but sufficient ratifying legislation that will be forthwith submitted by Hon. Frank Oliver to the parliament at Ottawa for enactment.

Ceremony of Settlement

The settlement with the Indians on the basis of the cash payments mutually agreed upon will be made direct by the Provincial government, joint receipts being taken from the Indians and their bankers and the payment of the relinquishment money being witnessed by Indian Agent W. E. Ditchburn, and Alderman W. H. Langley, jointly representing the Dominion government, the receipts referred to being subsequently forwarded to the authorities at Ottawa.

The Federal government has also cordially concurred in the suggested method of providing for future Marine department patients at the Victoria local hospitals, in order that the old Marine hospital site may likewise be made available for new and larger usefulness in connection with the development of Greater Victoria, this method being embodied in provincial legislation of the just-past session, and affording mutually acceptable relief of the Dominion from the strict letter of its obligation to British Columbia in this behalf contained in the British North America Act crystallizing the terms of union under which British Columbia became one of the Federated provinces of Canada.

Railway Terminals

So soon as the present occupants—Indians and a few white tenants—have left the old reserve, careful consideration will be given by the provincial executive to comprehensive plans for its future utilization in such manner as to best promote the substantial development of Victoria and the general interests of British Columbia, of which this city is the capital. In this connection it is understood that an adequate area will most probably be set aside for railway terminal purposes, the Canadian Pacific Railway having already applied for approximately twelve acres as a site for car-building and repair shops, coal bunkers, etc. and it being understood that the Canadian Northern Pacific (and possibly other companies of continental importance) will also require similar and even larger allotments. The necessities of Victoria city in the premises will also be given full consideration, and the remaining acreage of the old reserve will, it is expected, be disposed of by auction or otherwise during the early summer—most probably before the close of June.

Government to Recoup

As intimated to the Provincial legislature during the recent session the extinction of the old reserve, meaning so much in relation to all plans for the development of Victoria, will involve an approximate expenditure by the province of $750,000, this including the money payments to the Indians and the $212,500 which has been agreed upon as the price to be paid to the Hudson's Bay Company for the accepted new reserve of 163.42 acres on Esquimalt Harbor. The House, it will be remembered, was assured that business-like arrangement would as quickly as possible be consummated by the government with a view to the recouping of the provincial treasury for these large advances; and having in view the exceptionally advantageous location of all the lands forming the to-be-abandoned reservation, with their extensive water-frontage and their marked centrality, it is confidentally [sic] to be expected that the province will be financially the gainer ultimately through its display of enterprise and diplomatic energy in bringing to a satisfactory consummation arrangement for the removal of the reserve which during so many years has most undoubtedly operated as a strong deterrent to Victoria's growth and progress.

Having in regard the expensive plans that are now taking definite form of augmentation of the transportation facilities of Vancouver Island and of its industrial enterprises, there can be no question but that the lands so soon to be made available for utilization within the limits of the old Songhees Reserve will be in strong demand not only by discriminating and far-sighted residents of this city and province, but also by investors from other parts who have been watching with interest the signs of the times which point so unmistakably to an early realization of the high destinies of this capital and this island.

Progress of Negotiations

Ever since the conclusion of the agreement between the provincial government and Chief Cooper and the members of his tribe, which brought into the realm of practical certainty a realization at last of the long-entertained desire of Victorians for the extinction of the reserve in the heart of the city, Lands Minister Ross has been doing everything within his power to facilitate and expedite the settlement of details with the authorities of the Indian department at Ottawa so that there should be no miscarriage of the agreement so heartily endorsed by all residents of British Columbia. In this the new member of the government must be accorded a very considerable share with the premier of the hearty approval of the interested public; nor should the constant and active endeavors of Mr. G. H. Barnard, M. P., Hon. William Templeman, Senator Riley and others at Ottawa to bring about the much desired result be over-looked or under-estimated.

For a short time, it may be admitted, fears were entertained that the execution of the agreement might be jeopardized or delayed by an apparent misunderstanding at Ottawa of the specific and fixed wishes of the Indians in the matter of the payment to them of their compensation money; their agreement to relinquish the reserve was secured, it will be remembered, upon a guarantee that there should be paid to the head of each family direct by the provincial government a sum of $10,000, in addition to a new home of their own selection being provided.

Of course the concurrence of the Dominion government, as guardians of the Indians, became imperative, and legislation in this connection was promised by the interested federal department. Referring to this understanding of the situation, Mr. Frank Pedley, deputy superintendent general of Indian affairs, in a communication of the 4th inst., advised that the Ottawa government proposed to pass a bill confirming the agreement with the Indians and authorizing the superintendent-general to pay the whole of the amount due to the head of each interested Indian family, under the terms of the agreement and at such time and in such proportions as might appear desirable.

Province's Stipulation

This communication indicating that the fixed position of the Indians was scarcely understood at Ottawa, a reply was sent explaining that the whole agreement rested upon explicit compliance with the understanding that the price of surrender was to be paid at once and in its entirety direct by the provincial government to the Indians; and in response to this a further message from Mr. Pedley was received on Monday last indicative of a desire on the part of the Dominion authorities to do all in their power towards facilitating a final settlement while properly watching each detail in the important transaction with due care, in their capacity as guardians of the Indians. In this telegram the deputy superintendent-general stated that "The department has no objection to the payment by the province of the moneys direct, but cannot divest itself of the responsibility attaching to it under the law of seeing that the Indians are paid as agreed. We are willing to consider any suggestions from you which will satisfy this department that the money is actually paid to the Indians, and for which action we can assume full responsibility as trustees for them."

Replying to this message, Hon. Mr. Ross telegraphed that upon his recommendation, and as providing a method which should meet the wishes and requirements of all parties, a minute-of-council had been passed by the provincial executive providing that the minister of lands for British Columbia should pay to each head of family of the Songhees tribe who might be found entitled thereto under the agreement of the 25th October, 1910, $10,000 for the extinguishment of their respective rights or interests in the reserve to be vacated, the minister when making payment, taking bankers' receipts for the moneys, countersigned by the Indians themselves in each instance, and forwarding these receipts to the superintendent-general of Indian affairs—the same course being adopted in payment to the federal department, as trustees for the Indians, of the money value of improvements, such as the school, water service, etc., on the reserve to be abandoned, in this case also certified copies of the minute-in-council being transmitted to Ottawa.

This proposal apparently has been accepted at Ottawa in the fair spirit in which it was advanced, a telegram from Mr. Barnard, M. P., yesterday stating that the minister was satisfied that the payments to the Indians should be made as proposed in the presence of Indian Agent W. E. Ditchburn and W. H. Langley, as representing the Dominion, duplicate receipts being sent from the provincial government to Ottawa.

A similar understanding of the concurrence of Ottawa is expressed in a message from Senator Riley.

Extinction of Marine Hospital

With respect to the extinction of the Marine hospital, the maintenance of which is by the Terms of Union made obligatory upon the Dominion, Hon. L. P. Brodeur in a communication of the 1st inst. to Mr. Barnard has intimated that the Dominion government is quite prepared to abandon the Marine hospital buildings to the provincial government if such action as the closing of the hospital could not at any time be construed as a violation of the Act by which British Columbia came into the Confederation. He added that this point might fairly be met by satisfactory provision being made in local hospitals for the care of sick mariners; and this arrangement to satisfy the only possible objections of the Dominion as to this detail in the extinction of the old reserve has now been fully covered by special legislation in this behalf enacted during the dying days of the late session of the provincial parliament.

With the payment of the surrender moneys agreed upon to the Indians and of the value of improvements to the Dominion in the Indians' behalf—if being necessary for the federal authorities to provide a new school, etc., on the Esquimalt Harbor reserve—the obliteration of the original Songhees reserve will be accomplished. Although the Indians were not absolutely unanimous in acceptance of the provincial offer, it was closed with by a very substantial majority of the tribe and the agreement in this behalf, now endorsed by the Dominion, is fully binding upon all.

The removal of the Indians will be hastened as much as possible and the government will also take measures to secure the immediate withdrawal of the few white tenants who have by consent occupied holdings within the reserve area. These, from a legal standpoint, are said to have no special claims for consideration, no more, allegedly than the Esquimalt & Nanaimo Railway, whose line has been run by courtesy through the reservation but without any bestowal of title for right-of-way.

The white tenants number about half a dozen including Mr. Patrick Everett who during more than forty years past has conducted a licensed house for the sale of intoxicating liquors within the confines of the reserve. The fact that such an occupancy for hotel or saloon purposes could be possible but emphasizes the unique position of this particular reserve. It being by law strictly non-permissible for liquor to be held or used or handled in any way within the boundaries of an Indian reserve.

Illustration 5.1: Paul Kane, *Return of a War Party*, 1847. Songhees village (left) and Fort Victoria (right).

Source: Credit: Royal Ontario Museum, Toronto, Canada/Bridgeman Images

Illustration 5.2: Growing City of Victoria from the Lekwungen (Songhees) Reserve, circa 1885.

Source: Image H-04833, courtesy of the Royal BC Museum and Archives

Illustration 5.3: View of Victoria from the Lekwungen (Songhees) Reserve, 1881.

Source: Image D-05453, courtesy of the Royal BC Museum and Archives

Illustration 5.4: Lekwungen (Songhees) Chief Michael Cooper and
BC Premier Richard McBride.

Source: Image E-00254, courtesy of the Royal BC Museum and Archives

5.4 Memorandum for the Prime Minister on an Act to Amend the Indian Act

Between 1871 and 1921, the non-Indigenous population of British Columbia swelled from just over 10,000 to nearly 500,000. In the decade that ended in 1911, settler population growth exceeded that experienced during the previous thirty years combined. In the Kamloops area of the BC interior, well away from the population centres of Victoria and the lower mainland, the non-Indigenous population more than tripled between 1891 and 1911. As dramatic as this influx of settlers was, it paled in comparison to the population explosion in western Canada east of the Rockies. This massive influx of newcomers witnessed a parallel escalation in pressure on Indigenous land and resources. In the short document below, a memorandum to the prime minister, the author explains how a proposed amendment to the Indian Act would help facilitate settler expansion by simplifying the process of alienating the fragments of land that remained under Indigenous control. The document also points to the role of Canada and its Department of Indian Affairs, the supposed "guardians of the Indians," in expediting that alienation. Like the memo on enfranchisement presented in Chapter 3 of this book, this memorandum to the prime minister is unsigned and undated. The original is typed on Department of Indian Affairs letterhead, though, which implies that it too was written by Deputy Superintendent Duncan Campbell Scott. The original also includes a date stamp of June 5, 1911, which reveals that it was written to Wilfrid Laurier, the prime minster of the day. Nonetheless, as with the memo reproduced in Chapter 3, we would, of course, prefer more direct evidence of provenance, like a signature and date in the body of the text. A question to keep in mind here too, then, is how this document and the information it contains should be used by researchers.

Source: "Memorandum for the Prime Minister," LAC, RG 10, vol. 6809, file 470-2-3 pt. 5.

MEMORANDUM FOR THE PRIME MINISTER with respect to Bill 177—an act to amend the Indian Act.

The amendment proposed in section 1 of this Bill is to enable a railway operating under a provincial charter to acquire lands in an Indian reserve with the consent of the Governor in Council.

While Section 46 of the Indian Act contains the following provision, namely,—

"if any act occasioning damage to any reserve is done under the authority of an act of Parliament or of the legislature of any province, compensation shall be made therefor to the Indians of the band in the same manner as is provided with respect to the lands or rights of other persons."

it [sic] is held, nevertheless, that this merely establishes conditions to the exercise of the right of acquiring where such right exists by virtue of competent legislation or otherwise, but does not, as a matter of fact, give to a railway operating under a provincial charter power to acquire.

The particular railway in question is The Prince Rupert and Fort Simpson Railway Company.

With respect to section 2 of this bill I may say that the proximity of Indian reserves to centres of population is becoming a matter of public concern on the ground that the development of such centres of population and adjoining country is being seriously retarded on account of the Indians holding large portions of uncultivated land, and, on the further ground of the detriment to the Indians themselves in being so situated. The location of the Songhees Indian reserve is a case in point. It is thought that each particular case of proposed removal ought to be determined on its merits after the fullest investigation before an impartial and competent tribunal, and it is proposed therefore to refer each case to the court, to determine whether it would be expedient to remove the Indians or not.

With respect to section 3 of this bill, the proposed repeal of section 171 of the Indian Act, the following information may be given.

At the First Session of the Dominion Parliament an Act was passed Cap.[?] 33, "Respecting the Governor General, the Civil List and the salaries of certain public functionaries." An item in this Act under the heading "Miscellaneous" was "Indian Annuities—Quebec and Ontario—$26,664.00 per annum." These were the annuities of the payment of which the Province of Canada was responsible, and by the Act they were charged upon the Consolidated Revenue. Almost immediately after an amount sufficient to produce these annuities was capitalized at 5% and charged as part of the debt of the Province of Canada. This amount is standing in the books of the Department of Indian Affairs, and the annuities have been, since the capitalization, paid from the interest. Section 171 was imported unnecessarily into the Revised Statutes of 1886. As it is now inoperative it may be repealed.

The Section to be substituted will enable the Department to pay all the other annuities which are at present voted by Parliament without the necessity of an annual vote, and hereafter the total annuities for which the Dominion is at present or will be in the future responsible, will be paid according to the Statute or from the proceeds of capitalized funds.

When enacted, the proposed amendment as regards annuities will make it possible to discontinue the annual vote for Indian annuities. They will become statutory payments and will disappear from the Indian appropriations. The Finance Department has several times suggested this informally. It was proposed to make a change when certain amendments to the Act were under consideration, and the Department of Justice approved of this clause as drafted in June, 1908.

With respect to section 4 of this bill I may say that there are many Indians in the Province of British Columbia, residing on parcels of land situated outside of the Indian reserves. They were not disturbed in their possession of these parcels until quite recently when the settlers began to come in and the question of the title is now at issue. In some instances the Indians were ejected from such parcels by white settlers who claimed the right to pre-empt these lands. Sub-section 1, of section 37A of the Indian Act as enacted by section 1, Chapter 28 of the Statutes of 1910, referred to "the possession of any lands reserved or claims to be reserved for the Indians" and it is thought that this is not comprehensive enough to embrace the claims of individual Indians to particular parcels of land as above referred to, and the proposed amendment is for the purpose of including these cases.

5.5 An Act to Amend the Indian Act (the Oliver Act), 1911

During the debate on proposed amendments to the Indian Act on April 26, 1911, Frank Oliver, the Liberal cabinet minister responsible for Indian Affairs, stood in the House of Commons and proclaimed that "it is not right that the requirements of the expansion of white settlement should be ignored,—that is, that the right of the Indian should be allowed to become a wrong to the white man." Oliver confirmed that amendments to the Indian Act were necessary due to the "pressure of population."[185] Those amendments, collectively known as the Oliver Act, were passed by the House of Commons, in large part, so that when the presence of Indigenous communities interfered with the interests of settler towns or businesses, remedial legislation such as the Act Respecting the Songhees Indian Reserve, with its cash settlement paid directly to reserve residents, would no longer be required. Even community consultation and consent would not be necessary to eliminate reserves or alienate portions of them. Both the Oliver and the Songhees Acts received royal assent on the same day, May 19, 1911.

Source: Canada, An Act to amend the Indian Act, *Statutes of Canada* 1-2 Geo. V (1911) c.14.

CHAP. 14.

An Act to amend the Indian Act.

[Assented to May 19, 1911]

His Majesty, by and with the advice and consent of the Senate and House of Commons of Canada, enacts as follows:—

R.S., c. 81, s. 46 amended. **1.** Subsection 1 of section 46 of *The Indian Act*, chapter 81 of the Revised Statutes, 1906, is repealed, and the following is substituted therefor:—

Compensation for lands taken for public purposes. "**46.** No portion of any reserve shall be taken for the purpose of any railway, road, public work, or work designed for any public utility without the consent of the Governor in Council, but any company or municipal or local authority having statutory power, either Dominion or provincial, for taking or using lands or any interest in lands without the

---

185 Canada, House of Commons, *Debates*, 11th Parliament, 3rd Session, Vol. 4, April 26, 1911, 7825–26.

consent of the owner may, with the consent of the Governor in Council as aforesaid, and subject to the terms and conditions imposed by such consent, exercise such statutory power with respect to any reserve or portion of a reserve; and in any such case compensation shall be made therefor to the Indians of the band, and the exercise of such power, and the taking of the lands or interest therein and the determination and payment of the compensation shall, unless otherwise provided by the order in council evidencing the consent of the Governor in Council, be governed by the requirements applicable to the like proceedings by such company, municipal, or local authority in ordinary cases."

Section added.　　**2.** The said Act is amended by inserting the following section immediately after section 49 thereof:—

Inquiry and report by Exchequer Court as to removal of Indians.　　"**49A.** In the case of an Indian reserve which adjoins or is situated wholly or partly with an incorporated town or city having a population of not less than eight thousand, and which reserve has not been released or surrendered by the Indians, the Governor in Council may, upon the recommendations of the Superintendent General, refer to the judge of the Exchequer Court of Canada for inquiry and report the questions as to whether it is expedient, having regard to the interest of the public and of the Indians of the band for whose use the reserve is held, that the Indians should be removed from the reserve or any part of it.

Order in Council.　　"**2.** The order in council made in the case shall be certified by the Clerk of the Privy Council to the Registrar of the Exchequer Court of Canada, and the judge of court shall thereupon *Notice of Inquiry.* proceed as soon as convenient to fix a time and place, of which due notice shall be given by publication in *The Canada Gazette*, and otherwise as may be directed by the judge, for taking the evidence and hearing and investigating the matter.

Powers of Court.　　"**3.** The judge shall have the like powers to issue subpoenas, compel the attendance and examination of witnesses, take evidence, give directions, and generally to hear and determine the matter and regulate the procedure as in proceedings upon information by the Attorney General within the ordinary jurisdiction of the court, and shall assign counsel to represent *Counsel.* and act for the Indians who may be opposed to the proposed removal.

Compensation for special loss and damage to be ascertained.　　"**4.** If the judge finds that it is expedient that the band of Indians should be removed from the reserve or any part of it, he shall proceed, before making his report, to ascertain the amounts of compensation, if any, which should be paid respectively to individual Indians of the band for the special loss or damages which they will sustain in respect of the buildings or improvements to which they are entitled upon the lands of the reserve for which they are located; and the judge shall, moreover, consider and report upon any of the other facts or circumstances of the case which he may deem proper or material to be considered by the Governor in Council.

Transmission of proceedings.

"**5.** The judge shall transmit his findings, with the evidence and a report of the proceedings, to the Governor in Council, who shall lay a full report of the proceedings, the evidence and the findings before Parliament at the then current or next ensuing session thereof, and upon such findings being approved by resolution of Parliament the Governor in Council may thereupon give effect to the said findings and cause the reserve, or any part thereof from which it is found expedient to remove the Indians, to be sold or leased by public auction after three months advertisement in the public press, upon the best terms which, in the opinion of the Governor in Council, may be obtained therefor.

Sale or lease of lands.

Disposition of proceeds.

"**6.** The proceeds of the sale or lease, after deducting the usual percentage for management fund, shall be applied in compensating individual Indians for their buildings or improvements as found by the judge, in purchasing a new reserve for the Indians removed, in transferring the said Indians with their effects thereto, in erecting buildings upon the new reserve, and in providing the Indians with such other assistance as the Superintendent General may consider advisable; and the balance of the proceeds, if any, shall be placed to the credit of the Indians: Provided that the Government shall not cause the Indians to be removed, or disturb their possession, until a suitable reserve has been obtained and set apart for them in lieu of the reserve from which the expediency of removing the Indians is so established as aforesaid.

Proviso.

New reserve.

Expropriation of lands for new reserve.

"**7.** For the purpose of selecting, appropriating and acquiring the lands necessary to be taken, or which it may be deemed expedient to take, for any new reserve to be acquired for the Indians as authorized by the last preceding sub-section, whether they are Crown lands or not, the Superintendent General shall have all the powers conferred upon the Minister by *The Expropriation Act*, and such new reserve shall, for the purposes aforesaid, be deemed to be a public work within the definition of that expression in *The Expropriation Act*; and all the provisions of *The Expropriation Act*, in so far as applicable and not inconsistent with this Act, shall apply in respect of the proceedings for the selection, survey, ascertainment and acquisition of the lands required and the determination and

R.S., c. 143.

payment of the compensation therefor: Provided, however, that the Superintendent General shall not exercise the power of expropriation unless authorized by the Governor in Council."

New s. 171.

3. Section 171 of the said Act is repealed and the following is substituted therefor:—

Payment of Indian annuities.

"**171.** The annuities payable to Indians in pursuance of the conditions of any treaty expressed to have been entered into on behalf of His Majesty or His predecessors, and for the payment of which the Government of Canada is responsible, shall be a charge upon the Consolidated Revenue Fund of Canada, and be payable out of any unappropriated moneys forming part thereof."

Section 37A amended.

4. Subsection 1 of section 37a of the said Act, as enacted by section 1 of chapter 28 of the statutes of 1910, is hereby repealed and the following is substituted therefor:—

Recovery of possession of reserves withheld or adversely occupied.

"**37A.** If the possession of any lands reserved or claimed to be reserved for the Indians, or of any lands of which the Indians or any Indian or any band or tribe of Indians claim the possession or any right of possession, is withheld, or if any such lands are adversely occupied or claimed by any person, or if any trespass committed thereon, the possession may be recovered for the Indians or Indian or band or tribe of Indians, or the conflicting claims may be adjudged and determined or damages may be recovered in an action at the suit of His

Damages.

Majesty on behalf of the Indians or Indian or of the band or tribe of Indians entitled to or claiming the possession or right of possession or entitled to or claiming the possession or right of possession or entitled to or claiming the declaration, relief or damages."

5.6 Letter from Chief Hill (and others) to Governor General Grey, May 1911

Resistance to the 1911 Indian Act amendments began soon after they were first introduced to Parliament. Opposition politicians argued that Oliver, as superintendent general of Indian Affairs, was given too much authority to expropriate reserve lands in an arbitrary manner. Indigenous leaders were rightly concerned that the amendments further reduced community control over reserve lands, the fragments of their traditional territories that remained to them. As presented in Chapters 1 and 3 in this book, the Six Nations (Haudenosaunee Confederacy) of the Grand River argued that they enjoyed a long-standing relationship with Great Britain, not as subjects but as allies of the Crown. The letter reproduced below is from representatives of the Six Nations to Governor General Albert Henry George Grey, the 4th Earl Grey, King George

V's representative in Canada. It was written after Parliament had passed the amendments but before they were given royal assent. The letter's authors present the basis for their unique relationship with the Crown, describe the rights and territorial protections provided by deeds and treaties, and give reasons that the governor general should intervene on behalf of the Six Nations.

Source: Chiefs Josiah Hill and others to Governor General Earl Grey, May 1911, LAC, RG 10, 470-2-3, pt. 5.

Six Nations Council House

Ohsweken Ont. May

To

His Excellency, the Right Honorable The Earl Grey P.C.G.C.M.G.G.C.V.O. Governor General of Canada, Ottawa, Ont.

May it please your Excellency—

We the undersigned Chiefs of the Six Nations Indians of the Grand River having been duly appointed and authorized by our colleagues of the Six Nations at their Council held on Tuesday 11th of April last a Committee to enquire into the nature of the bill introduced and submitted by the Premier (Sir Wilfred [sic] Laurier) to the House of Commons of Canada on the 10th of April last entitled (as it appears in the Toronto "Globe" and other newspapers) "Amendment to the Indian Act" Bill No 177, to Amend the "Indian Act."

The Chief provisions of which are that where a railway is run through an Indian Reserve the Governor in Council shall have power to authorize the building of the railway, also when an Indian Reserve is within ten miles of a City of over 10,000 people, application may be made to the Exchequer Court by the Superintendent General of Indian Affairs for enquiry and report as to whether it is expedient in the interests of the white population that the Reserve should be removed.

This bill having been assented to by the Parliament of Canada, we therefore on behalf of the Chiefs of the Six Nations Council and of the people of the Six Nations beg to request that your Excellency will be good enough not to give your assent or sign such Bill as the representative of His Gracious Majesty the King unless the said Bill is most distinctly amended so that the Six Nations are excluded, and protected from the operation of the provisions of the said Bill upon the following grounds:—

1st We hold that it is not within the Province of Canadian Parliament to nullify, alter or set aside a solemn Treaty or Compact entered into by the Imperial Government, and the King of Great Britain with the Six Nations Indians without the assent or consent of the Imperial Government and His Majesty the King of

Great Britain upon the one part, and His Majesty's Allies, the Six Nations upon the other.

2nd We are under the impression that the Governors General of Canada have instructions to veto "Any Bill the provisions of which shall appear inconsistent with oblications [sic] imposed upon us (the Crown of Great Britain) by Treaty."

We are of the opinion that the above Extract from instructions by the Home Government to His Excellency Lord Monk Governor General of Canada dated June 1st 1867 is specially applicable in this instance in which our rights and Treaties would be prejudicially affected and infringed upon by this legislation should it acquire the [missing word in original] of law by your Excellency's sanction.

3rd That this Bill infringes and tramples upon the conceded rights and privileges of the Six Nations Indians assented to by His Majesty King George the III with reference to their lands which were assured to them by His Majesty's special directions under His Royal will and pleasure in the two special Deeds known as the Haldimand's and Simcoe Deeds which secures to the Six Nations Indians forever their lands upon the Grand River under the protection of the King.

4th That this Amendment to the Indian Act jeopardizes our ownership of the lands set apart for our Reserve by order of His Majesty King George the III as compensation for the loss of lands in the United States sustained by the Six Nations while fighting for the British cause in the American revolutionary war, as this Bill aims to set aside our Deeds and title to our lands by placing into the hands of one man (the Superintendent General of Indian Affairs) the power of breaking up any Indian Reserve and removing the Indians therefrom.

5th It breaks faith with the Six Nations and tramples upon the solemn promise of King George III as set forth in our Deeds and Treaties.

We have the honor to be
Your Excellency's Obedient Servants
Chief Josiah Hill, Sec'y Six Nations Council
" David Jamieson
" J. W. M. Elliott, Secy Corr. Com S. N. Council

5.7 Letter from J. D. McLean to Chief Hill (and others), May 1911

Correspondence from Indigenous representatives to Crown authorities in the United Kingdom was most often simply referred back to the Department of Indian Affairs in Canada. The letter from Six Nations Chiefs Hill, Jamieson, and Elliot, reproduced above (document 5.6), was no exception. Consider how the short response from DIA secretary John D. McLean, reproduced below, completely ignores the Six Nations' long-standing assertions of sovereignty and downplays the effects of the increased authority to expropriate reserve lands without consent or consultation, an authority granted to the DIA by Bill 177, the 1911 amendments to the Indian Act.

Source: J. D. McLean, Assistant Deputy and Secretary, DIA, to Chiefs
Josiah Hill and others, May 30, 1911, LAC, RG 10, 470-2-3, pt. 5.

_____

Ottawa, May 30, 1911.

Chiefs,–

Having reference to your recent undated petition, addressed to His Excellency
the Governor General on the subject of Bill No. 177 of the House of Commons,
An Act to amend the Indian Act, I have by direction to inform you that, as
regards Section 1 thereof, the provisions of the amendment confer only a slight
enlargement of the powers conferred by Section 46 of the Indian Act, R. S. 43,
and do not affect Indian reserves to a greater extent, it is believed, than upon
consideration by the Six Nations Council will be found to be right and reasonable.

You will observe from the wording of Section 2 of the Bill that Section 49 as
amended only applies to reserves which are situated wholly or in part within an
incorporated town or city having a population of not less than eight thousand.

Incl. A copy of the Bill is inclosed [sic] for your information.

Your obedient servant,

J. D. McLean
Asst. Deputy and Secretary.
Chiefs Josiah Hill,
David Jamieson, and
J. W. M. Elliott,
Ohsweken, Ont.

5.8 Lee Maracle, "Goodbye Snauq," 2008

Lee Maracle is of S̲k̲wx̲wú7mesh, or Squamish, Tsleil-Waututh, and Métis
ancestry and is a member of the Stó:lō First Nation. She is also the grand-
daughter of Chief Dan George. Since she was first published in the early 1970s,
Maracle has been a prolific writer of novels, short stories, works of poetry,
and non-fiction texts. She is the recipient of numerous awards and honours,
and has held a variety of prestigious academic posts. In "Goodbye Snauq,"
Maracle explains how Snauq, now known as the False Creek area of Vancouver,
was transformed from a space shared by the Musqueam, Tsleil-Waututh, and
Squamish peoples and where gardens and shellfish beds proliferated to a site
of settler industrial and urban development, rife with the pollution attendant
to both. Most of the changes occurred during the lifetime of Squamish Chief
Khatsahlano, or X̲ats'alanexw, who lived between 1877 and 1971 and who has
a voice in Maracle's essay, as a witness to the settler appropriation of Snauq

and the forced relocation of the Squamish people. Through Khatsahlano's experiences and her own, Maracle explores both the myriad effects of the colonial complex and the ways in which colonial intrusion has been adapted to or resisted. Maracle does not refer directly to the Indian Act because neither the municipal government of Vancouver nor the provincial government of British Columbia used due process or even the mechanisms found within the Indian Act when they forced the Skwxwú7mesh residents of Snauq from their homes in 1913.[186] Nonetheless, the Indian Act's production of identity through status, the authority it confers to elected band councils, and its infringement on Indigenous land rights permeate Maracle's story. In 2002, the S̲k̲wx̲wú7mesh regained a portion of the land at Snauq and financial compensation for the illegal forced surrender of their land.[187]

Source: Lee Maracle, "Goodbye, Snauq," *West Coast Line: A Journal of Contemporary Writing & Criticism* 42, no. 2 (Summer 2008): 117–25. Reprinted by permission of Dr. Lee Maracle.

GOODBYE, SNAUQ

Raven has never left this place, but sometimes it feels like she has been negligent, maybe even a little dense. Raven shaped us; we are built for transformation. Our stories prepare us for it. Find freedom in the context you inherit; every context is different; discover consequences and change from within, that is the challenge. Still, there is horror in having had change foisted upon you from outside. Raven did not prepare us for the past 150 years. She must have fallen asleep some time around the first smallpox epidemic when the Tsleil Watuth Nation nearly perished and I am not sure she ever woke up.

The halls of this institution are empty. The bright white fluorescent bulbs that dot the ceiling are hidden behind great long light fixtures dimming its length. Not unlike the dimness of a Longhouse, but it doesn't feel the same. The dimness of the hallway isn't brightened by a fire in the center nor warmed by the smell of cedar all around you. There are no electric lights in the longhouse and so the dimness is natural. The presence of lights coupled with dimness makes the place seem eerie. I trudge down the dim hallway; my small hands clutch a bright white envelope. Generally, letters from the government of Canada, in right of the queen are threateningly ensconced in brown envelopes, but this is from a new government—my own government, the Squamish First Nation government. Its colour is an irony. I received it yesterday, broke into a sweat and a bottle of white

186 Jean Barman, "Erasing Indigenous Indigeneity in Vancouver," *BC Studies*, no. 155 (September 2007): 3–30.
187 The Indigenous Foundation's website hosts a mapping tool that documents the history of Snauq (the Kitsilano Reserve). It can be found here: http://indigenousfoundations.arts.ubc.ca/mapping_tool_kitsilano_reserve/.

wine within five minutes of its receipt. It didn't help. I already know the contents—even before the Canada Post managed to deliver it; Canadian mail is notoriously slow. The television and radio stations were so rife with the news that there was no doubt in my mind that this was my government's official letter informing me that "a deal had been brokered." The Squamish Nation had won the Snauq lawsuit and surrendered any further claim for a fee. The numbers are staggering—$92 million. That is more than triple our total GNP, wages and businesses combined.

As I lay in my wine soaked state, I thought about the future of the Squamish Nation—development dollars, cultural dollars, maybe even language dollars, healing dollars. I have no right to feel this depressed, to want to be this intoxicated, to want to remove myself from this decision, this moment or this world. I have no right to want to curse the century in which I was born, the political times in which I live, and certainly I have no right to hate the decision makers, my elected officials, for having brokered the deal. In fact, until we vote on it, until we ratify it, it is a deal in theory. While the wine sloshes its way through the veins in my body to the blood in my brain, pictures of Snauq roll about. Snauq is now called False Creek. When the Squamish first moved there to be closer to the colonial center, the water was deeper and stretched from the sea to what is now Clark Drive in the east; it covered the current streets from 2nd avenue in the south to just below Dunsmuir in the north. There was a sandbar in the middle of it, hence the name Snauq. I lay on my couch, Russell Wallace's music CD, *Tso'kam*, blaring in the background—Christ, our songs are sad, even the happy ones. Tears roll down my face. I join the ranks of ancestors I try not to think about. Wine soaked we howl out old Hank Williams crying songs, laughing in between, tears sloshing across the laughter lines. The fifties. My Ta'ah intervenes. Eyes narrowed she ends the party, clears out the house sending all those who had a little too much to drink home. She confiscates keys from those who are drunk, making sure only the sober drive the block to the reserve. "None of my children are going to get pinched and end up in *hoosegow*." My brain addled with the memory pulls up another drunken soiree, maybe the first one. A group of men gather around a whiskey keg, their children raped by settlers; they drink until they perish. It was our first run at suicide and I wonder what inspired their descendants to want to participate in the new society in any way shape or form. "Find freedom in the context you inherit." From the shadows Khahtsahlano emerges, eyes dead blind and yet still twinkling, calling out; "Sweetheart, they were so hungry, so thirsty that they drank up almost the whole of Snauq with their dredging machines. They built mills at Yaletown and piled up garbage at the edges of our old supermarket—Snauq. False Creek was so dirty that eventually even the white mans became concerned." I have seen archival pictures of it. They dumped barrels of toxic chemical waste from sawmills, food waste from restaurants, taverns and teahouses; thousands of metric tons of human sewage joins the other waste daily. I am drunk. Drunk enough to apologize for my nation, so much good can come of this . . . So why the need for wine to stem the rage?

"The magic of the white man is that he can change everything, everywhere. He even changed the food we eat." Khahtsahlano faces False Creek from the edge of Burrard Inlet holding his white cane delicately in his hand as he speaks to me. The inlet was almost a mile across at that time, but the dredging and draining of the water shrank it. Even after he died in 1967 the dredging and altering of our homeland was not over. The shoreline is gone; in its place are industries squatting where the sea once was. Lonsdale quay juts out onto the tide and elsewhere cemented and land-filled structures occupy the inlet. The sea asparagus that grew in the sand along the shore is gone. There is no more of the camas we once ate. All the berries, medicines and wild foods are gone. "The *womans* took care of the food," he says. And now we go to schools like this one and then go to work in other schools, businesses, in Band offices or anyplace that we can, so we can purchase food in modern supermarkets. Khahtsahlano is about to say something else. "Go away" I holler at his picture and suddenly I am sober.

Snauq is in Musqueam territory, it occurs to me, just across the inlet from Tsleil Waututh, but the Squamish were the only ones to occupy it year round; some say as early as 1821, others 1824, still others peg the date as somewhere around the 1850s. Before that it was a common garden shared by all the friendly tribes in the area. The fish swam there, taking a breather from their ocean playgrounds, ducks gathered, women cultivated camas fields and berries abounded. On the sand bar Musqueam, Tsleil Watuth and Squamish women till oyster and clam beds to encourage reproduction. Wild cabbage, mushrooms and other plants were tilled and hoed as well. Summer after summer the nations gathered to harvest, likely to plan marriages, play a few rounds of that old gambling game Lahal. Not long after the first smallpox epidemic all but decimated the Tsleil Watuth people, the Squamish people came down from their river homes where the snow fell deep all winter to establish a permanent home at False Creek. Chief George—Chipkayim—built the big long house. Khatsalanogh was a young man then. His son, Khahtsahlano, was born there. Khahtsahlano grew up [and] married Swanamia there. Their children were born there.

"Only three duffels worth," the skipper of the barge . . . is shouting at the villagers. Swanamia does her best to choke back the tears, fingering each garment, weighing its value, remembering the use of each and choosing which one to bring and which to leave. Each spoon, handles lovingly carved by Khahtsahlano, each bowl, basket and bent box must be evaluated for size and affection. Each one requires a decision. Her mind watches her husband's hand sharpening his adz[e], carving the tops of each piece of cutlery, every bowl and box. She remembers gathering cedar roots, pounding them for hours and weaving each basket. Then she decides, fill as many baskets as the duffels can hold and leave the rest.

Swanamia faces Burrard Inlet; she cannot bear to look back. Her son winces. Khahtsahlano sits straight up. Several of the women suppress a gasp as they look back to see Snauq's longhouses are on fire. The men who set the fires are cheering. Plumes of smoke affirm that the settlers who keep coming in droves have crowded the Squamish out. This is an immigrant country. Over the next ten days the men stumble about the Squamish reserve on the north shore, building homes and suppressing a terrible urge to return to Snauq to see the charred remains. Swanamia watches as the men in her house fight for an acceptable response. Some private part of her knows they want to grieve, but there is no ceremony to grieve the loss of a village. She has no reference post for this new world where the interests of the immigrants precede the interests of Indigenous residents. She has no way to understand that the new people's right to declare us non-citizens unless we disenfranchised our right to be Squamish is inviolable. The burning of Snauq touched of a history of disentitlement and prohibition that was incomprehensible and impossible for Swanamia to manage.

We tried though. From Snauq to Whidbey Island and Vancouver Island, from Port Angeles to Seattle, the Squamish along with the Lummi of Washington State operated a Ferry system until the Black Ball Ferry lines bought them out in 1930s. Khahtsahlano's head cocks to one side, and he gives his wife a look that says "no problem, we will think of something" as the barge carries them out to sea. We were reserved and declared immigrants, children in the eyes of law, wards of the government to be treated the same as the infirm or insane. Khahtsahlano determined to fight this insult. It consumed his life. We could not gain citizenship or manage . . . [our] own affairs unless we forwent who we were: Squamish, Tsleil Waututh, Musqueam, Cree or whatever nation we came from. Some of us did disenfranchise. But most of us stayed stubbornly clinging to our original identity fighting to participate in the new social order as Squamish.

Khahtsahlano struggled to find ways for us to participate. In 1905, he and a group of stalwart men marched all over the province of British Columbia to create the first modern organization of Aboriginal people. The Allied Tribes mastered colonial law despite prohibition and land rights to secure and protect their position in this country. He familiarized himself with the colonial relations that Britain had with other countries. He was a serious *rememberer* who paid attention to the oracy of his past, the changing present and the possibility of a future story. He stands there in this old photo just a little bent, his eyes exhibiting an endless sadness, handsomely dressed in the finest clothes Swanamia had made for him. A deep hope lingers underneath the sadness softening the melancholy. In the photograph marking their departure, his son stands in front of him, straight backed, shoulders squared with that little frown of sweet trepidation on his face, the same frown my sister wears [when] she is afraid and trying to find her courage. Khahtsahlano and his villagers face [the] future with the same grim determination that the Squamish Nation Band council now deploys. The wine grabs reality, slops it back and forth across the swaying room that blurs and my wanders through Snauq are over for today.

The hallways intervene again; I head for my office, cubby really. I am a Teaching Assistant bucking for my Master's Degree. This is a prestigious institution with a prestigious MA program in Indigenous Government. I am not a star student, nor a profound Teaching Assistant. Not much about me seems memorable. I pursue course after course. I comply day after day with research requirements, course requirements, marking requirements and the odd seminar requirements, but nothing that I do, say or write seems relevant. I feel absurdly obedient. The result of all this study seems oddly mundane. Did Khahtsahlano ever feel mundane as he trudged about speaking to one family head then another, talking up the Allied Tribes with Andy Paull? Not likely; at the time he consciously opposed colonial authority. He too studied this new world but with a singular purpose in mind—recreating freedom in the context that I was to inherit. Maybe, while he spoke to his little sweetheart, enumerating each significant non-existent landmark, vegetable patch, berry field, elk warren, duck pond and fish habitat that had been destroyed by the newcomers, he felt this way. To what end telling an eight year old of a past bounty that can never again be regained?

Opening the envelope begins to take on the sensation of treasonous behavior. I set it aside and wonder about the course work I chose during my school years. I am Squamish, descendent from Squamish chieftains—no, that is only partly true. I am descended from chieftains and I have plenty of Squamish relatives, but I married a Stó:lo, so really I am Stó:lo. Identity can be so confusing. For a long time the Tsleil Watuth spoke mainly Squamish—somehow they were considered part of the Squamish Band, despite the fact that they never did amalgamate. It turns out they spoke "Down River Halkomelem" before the first smallpox killed them. It was only later that many of them began speaking Squamish. Some have gone back to speaking Halkomelem while others still speak Squamish. I am not sure who we really are collectively and I wonder why I did not choose to study this territory, its history and the identity changes the above has wrought on us all. The office closes in on me. The walls crawl toward me, slow and easy, crowd me; I want to run, to reach for another bottle of wine, but this here is the university and I must prepare for class—and there is no wine here, no false relief. I have only my wit, my will and my sober nightmare. I look up: the same picture of Khahtsahlano and his son that adorns my office wall hangs in my living room at home. I must be obsessed with him. Why had I not noticed this obsession before?

I love this photo of him. I fell in love with the jackets of the two men, so much so that I learned to weave. I wanted to replicate that jacket. Khahtsahlano's jacket was among the first to be made from sheep's wool. His father's was made of dog and mountain goat hair. Coast Salish women bred a beautiful long and curly haired dog for this purpose. Every summer the mountain goats left their hillside homes to shed their fur on the lowlands of what is now to be the "sea to sky Highway." They rubbed their bodies against long thorns and all the women had to do was collect it, spin the dog and goat [hair] together, and weave the clothes. The settlers shot dogs and goats until our dogs were extinct and the goats were an endangered species. The object: force the Natives to purchase Hudson's Bay sheep-wool blankets. The northerners switched to the black and red Hudson's Bay blankets, but we carried on with our weaving using sheep's wool for a time; then when cash was scarce we shopped at local second hand shops or we went without. Swanamia put a lot of love in those jackets. She took the time to trim them with fur, feathers, shells and fringe. She loved those two men. Some of the women took to knitting the Cowichan sweaters so popular among non-Indigenous people, but I could not choose knitting over weaving. I fell in love with the zigzag weft, the lightning strikes of those jackets and for a time got lost in the process of weaving until my back gave out.

The injury inspired me to return to school to attend this university and to leave North Van. I took this old archive photo—photocopy really—with me. Every now and then I speak to Khahtsahlano, promise him I will return.

My class tutorial is about current events; I must read the letter—keep abreast with new events and prepare to teach. I detach, open and read the notice of the agreement. I am informed that this information is a courtesy; being Stó:lo, I have no real claim to the agreement, but because ancestry is so important, all descendants of False Creek are hereby informed . . .

I look at the students and remember: This memory is for Chief George, Chief Khahtsahlano and my Ta'ah, who never stopped dreaming of Snauq.

Song rolls out as the women pick berries near what is now John Hendry Park. In between songs they tell old stories, many risqué and hilarious. Laughter punctuates the air; beside them are the biggest trees in the world, 16 feet in diameter and averaging 400 feet in height. Other women at Snauq tend the drying racks and smoke shacks in the village. Inside them clams, sturgeons, oolichans, sockeye, spring salmon, are being cured for winter stock. Men from Squamish, Musqueam and Tsleil Watuth, join the men at Snauq to hunt and trap ducks, geese, grouse, deer and elk. Elk is the prettiest of all red meats. You have to see it roasted and thinly sliced to appreciate its beauty and the taste—the taste is extraordinary. The camas fields bloom bounteous at Snauq, and every spring the women cull the white ones in favour of the blue and hoe them. Children clutch at their long woven skirts. There is no difference between a white camas and a blue except the blue flowers are so much more gorgeous. It is the kind of blue that adorns the sky when it teases just before a good rain. Khahtsahlano's father, Khatsahlanogh, remembered those trees. On days when he carved out a new spoon, box or bowl, he would stare sadly at the empty forest and resent the new houses in its place. Chief George, sweet and gentle Chief George—Chipkaym—chose Snauq for its proximity to the mills and because he was no stranger to the place.

By 1907, the end of Chief George's life, the trees had fallen, the villagers at Lumberman's arch were dead, and the settlers had transformed the Snauq supermarket into a garbage dump. The newcomers were so strange. On the one hand, they erected sawmills in disciplined and orderly fashion and transformed trees into boards for the world market quickly, efficiently and impressively. On the other hand, they threw things away in massive quantities. The Squamish came to watch. Many like Paddy George bought teams of horses and culled timber from the back woods like the white man—well, not exactly like them; Paddy could not bring himself to kill the young ones—"space logging" they call it now. But still, some managed to eke out a living. Despite all the prohibition laws they found some freedom in the context they inherited.

"The settlers were a dry riverbed possessing a thirst that was never slaked." A film of tears fills Khahtsahlano's eyes and his voice softens as he speaks. "After the trees came down, houses went up, more mills, hotels, shantytowns until we were vastly outnumbered and pressured to leave. BC was so white then. So many places were banned to Indians, Dogs, Blacks, Jews and Chinamans." At one time

Khahtsahlano could remember the names of the men that came, first 100, then 1000; after that he stopped wanting to know who they were. "They were a strange lot—most of the men never brought womans to this place. The Yaletown men were CPR men, drifters, and squatters on the north shore of the creek. They helped drain one third of it, so that the railroad—the CPR—could build a station, but they didn't bring womans," he says as he stares longingly across the Inlet at his beloved Snauq.

The students lean on their desks, barely awake. Almost half of them are First Nations. I call myself to attention: I have totally lost my professional distance from subject; my discipline, my pretension at objectivity writhes on the floor in front of me and I realize we are not the same people anymore. I am not in a longhouse. I am not a speaker. I am a TA in a western institution. Suddenly, the fluorescent lights offend, the dry perfect room temperature insults, and the very space mocks. A wave of pain passes through me; I nearly lunge forward fighting it. Get a grip. This is what you wanted. Get a grip. This is what you slogged through tons of insulting documents for: Superintendent of Indian Affairs, Melville . . . alternatives to solve the Indian problem, assassination, enslavement . . . disease, integration, boarding school, removal . . . I am staggering under my own weight. My eyes bulge, my muscles pulse, my saliva trickles out the side of my mouth. I am not like Khahtsahlano. I am not like Ta'ah. I was brought up in the same tradition of change, of love of transformation, of appreciation for what is new, but I was not there when Snauq was a garden. Now it is a series of bridge ramparts, an emptied False Creek, emptied of Squamish people and occupied by industry, apartment dwellings, Granville Island tourist center and the Science Centre. I was not there when Squamish men formed unions like white men, built mills like white men, worked like white men and finally, unlike white men, were outlawed from full participation. I can't bear all this reality. I am soft like George but without whatever sweet thread of hope that wove its way through his body to form some steely fabric.

I awake surrounded by my students, their tears drip onto my cheeks. Oh my Gawd, they love me.

"It ok, I just fainted."

"You were saying you were not like Khahtsahlano, like Ta'ah. Who are they?" The room opens up; the walls stop threatening. I know how Moses must have felt when he watched the sea part, the relief palpable, measurable, sweet and welcome.

"That's just it. I thought I knew who I was. I know the dates. I know the events, but I don't know who they were and I can't know who I am without knowing who they were and I can't say goodbye to Snauq and I need to say goodbye. Oh Gawd help me."

"Well, I am not real sure that clears things up," Terese responds, her blond hair hanging close to my face. Some of the students look like they want to laugh; a couple of First Nations students go ahead and chuckle.

"Snauq is a village we just forfeited any claim to and I must say Goodbye."

"Doesn't that require some sort of ceremony?" Hilda asks. . . . She is Nu'chalnuth and although they are a different nation from mine, the ceremonial requirements are close.

"Yes," I answer.

"This is a cultural class—shouldn't we go with you?"

They lift me so tenderly I feet like a saint. This is the beginning of something. I need to know what is ending so that I can appreciate and identify with the beginning. Their apathetic stares have been replaced by a deep concern. Their apathy must have been a mask, a mask of professionalism, a mask covering fear, a mask to hide whatever dangers lurk in learning about the horrors of colonialism. The students must face themselves. I am their teacher. The goal of every adult among us is to face ourselves—our greatest enemy. I am responsible as their teacher to help them do that, but I am ill equipped. Still, Hilda is right. This is a cultural class and they ought to be there when I say goodbye. In some incomprehensible way it feels as though their presence would somehow ease the forfeiture and make it right.

I conjure the stretch of trees to the west and south of Snauq for the class, the wind whispering songs of future to the residents. The Oblates arrive singing Gregorian Chants of false promise. The millwrights arrive singing chants of profit and we bite, hook, line and sinker. How could we anticipate that we would be excluded if our success exceeded the success of the white man? How could we know that they came homeless, poor, unsafe and unprotected? Yaletowners accepted their designation as "squatters." This struck the Squamish at first as incredible. Chief George had no way of perceiving of "squatting." It took some time for the younger men like Khahtsahlano to explain to Chief George the perception of "ownership" of the white man, the laws governing ownership, the business of property. Sometimes he resorted to English because the language did not suffice. "BC is Indian land, but the government regarded Snauq's citizens as squatters until a reserve was established." Andy Paull explained the law, its hypocrisy and its strangeness to old Chief George. "Not all white men were granted land and not all were granted the same amount. But those who did purchase or receive land grants were white and they were men. The minimum land grant to white men during pre-emption was three hundred acres; for us it was a maximum of ten acres per family."

"What has this got to do with Snauq and more important with this class?" someone asks. I have been speaking aloud.

"There is so much more to history than meets the eye. We need to know what happened, and what happened has nothing to do with the dates, the events and the gentlemen involved; it has to do with impact." A sole student, eyes lifted slightly skyward, lips pursed innocent and inviting, strokes my arm.

They all pull their seats forward. "We need to finish this story." They nod, like for the first time they seem to know what's going on, even the white students nod, affirming that they too understand.

As I ready to head for the ferry terminal, it dawns on me that no one in this country has to deal with ancestry in quite the way we must. The new immigrants of today come from independent countries, some wealthy, some poor, but all but a few have risen from under the yoke of colonialism. They have nations as origins. Their home countries belong to the United Nations or NATO or other such international organizations. We do not, and this court case indicates we never will. The United Nations is debating an "Indigenous Right to Self-Government" bill, but Indigenous people will never be able to acquire the place other nations hold. Canadians do not have to face that they are still classically colonized, that because settlement is a fait accompli, we can only negotiate the best real estate deal possible. Indigenous people must face this while the eyes of our ancestors, who fought against colonial conquest and lost, glare down upon us.

"This is an immigrant nation," Prime Minister Chrétien said after the Twin Towers of the Trade Center in New York were felled. "We will continue to be an immigrant nation." How do we deal with this, the non-immigrants who for more than a century were rendered foreigners, prohibited from participation?

The money for Snauq will be put in trust. We must submit a plan of how we intend to spend it, to access it. The Squamish Nation gets to pick the trustees, but like our ancestors, we must have trustees independent of the nation. Our money is still one step removed from our control.

This story is somehow connected to another story, more important than the one going on now. Surrender or dig up the hatchet. The Squamish Nation has chosen surrender. Which way will my journey take me? Do I dare remember Snauq as a Squamish, Musqueam, Tsleil Watuth supermarket? Do I dare desire the restoration of the grand trees to the left and in the rear of Snauq? Do I dare say goodbye?

The ferry lunges from the berth. Students surround. We are on a mission. We travel to Snauq, False Creek, and Vancouver to say goodbye. In one sense I have no choice, in another, I chose the people who made the deal. In our own cultural sensibility there is no choice. There are 15,000 . . . non-Indigenous people living at Snauq, and we have never entitled ourselves with the right to remove people from their homes. We must say goodbye.

In this goodbye we will remember Snauq before the draining of False Creek. We will honour the dead: the stanchions of fir, spruce, cedar and the gardens of Snauq. We will dream of the new False Creek, the dry lands, the new parks and the acres of grass and houses. We will accept what Granville Island has become and honour Patty Rivard, the First Nations woman who was the first to forge a successful business in the heart of it. We will struggle to appreciate the little ferries that cross the creek. We will salute—Chief George—Chipkaym and Khatsahlanogh who embraced the vision of this burgeoning new nation. I will pray for my personal inability to fully commit to that vision.

The wind catches the tobacco as it floats to the water, lifts it, and as we watch it float, a lone Chinese woman crosses in front and she smiles. I smile too. Li Ka Shing, a multi-billionaire, rose as the owner and developer of False Creek. He is Chinese and he didn't live here when he bought it. I don't know if he lives here now, but for whatever reason I love the sound of his name. "Everything begins with song," Ta'ah says. His name is a song. It rolls of the tongue, sweetens the pallet before the sound hits the air: It is such an irony that the first "non-citizen immigrant residents" should now possess the power to determine the destiny of our beloved Snauq. I know it shouldn't but somehow it makes me happy, like knowing that Black Indians now people the Long Island Reservation in New York.

The Chinese were subjected to a head tax for decades. Until 60 years ago they were banned from living outside Chinatown, though I met Garrick Chu's mother, who grew up at Musqueam reserve. They were restricted to laundry businesses and teahouses economically. Once white men burned Chinatown to the ground. For decades Chinese men could not bring their families from China to Canada. Periodic riots in the previous century killed some of them and terrorized all of them. Underneath some parts of Chinatown they built underground tunnels to hide in as protection against marauding white citizens who were never punished for killing Chinese. Like the Squamish they endured quietly until assuming citizenship in 1948. For one of them to become the owners of this choice piece of real estate is sweet irony. "It was sold for a song by Premier Vander Zalm" the court records read. That too is a piece of painful, yet poetic, justice. I want to attend the Chinese parade, celebrate Chinese New Year, not for Li Ka Shing, but because one of life's ironies has given me hope. 5,000 miles from here, a group of Mi'kmaq bought land in Newfoundland and gained reservation rights. Another irony. They thought they had killed them all, and 350 years later, there they were, purchasing the land and setting up a reservation. There is hope in irony.

Yeah I am not through with Canada. I am not a partner in its construction, but neither am I its enemy. Canada has opened the door. Indigenous people are no longer "immigrants" to be disenfranchised, forbidden, prohibited, outlawed or precluded from the protective laws of this country. But we are a long way from being participants. I am not anxious to be a part of an environmentally offensive society that can preach "thou shalt not kill" and then make war on people, plants, and animals to protect and advance financial gain. The hypocrisy marring Canada's behavior toward us is still evident, but she struggles for maturity and while she struggles I accord myself a place. This place is still at the bottom as the last people to be afforded a place at the banquet table, the attendees of which have been partaking for over 500 years, but still there it is, the chair empty and hoping I will feel inclined to sit in it. The invitation is fraught with difficulties. Although today I must say goodbye, tomorrow I may just buy one of the townhouses slated for completion in 2010. Today, I am entitled to dream. Khahtsahlano dreamed of being buried at Snauq. I dream of living there.

We move to the unfinished Longhouse at the center of Granville Island, a ragged group of students and their teacher. I break into song: Chief Dan George's Prayer song. "Goodbye Snauq," I boom out in as big a voice as I can muster. The passing crowd jerks to a split second halt, gives us a bewildered glance, frowns, sidesteps us, and then moves on. The students laugh.

"Indians really will laugh at anything," I say as the tears stream across my face. The sun shines bright and turns [the] sky camas blue as we drift toward the co-operative restaurant to eat.

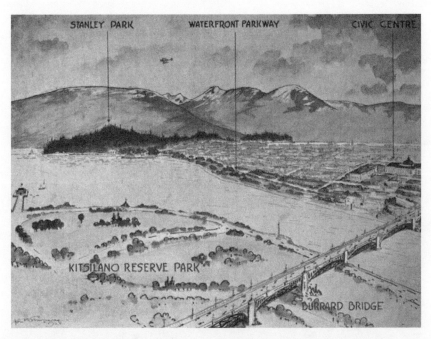

Illustration 5.5: Snauq and proposed park, 1929. Once Snauq had been evacuated and the longhouses burned, Vancouver proposed making the land into a park in 1929.

Source: From Harland Bartholomew and Associates, 1928, *A Plan for the City of Vancouver*

Illustration 5.6: Lee Maracle, circa 2017.

Source: Columpa Carmen Bobb, with permission from Lee Maracle

Appendix A

Reading Historically

You may wish to use this list of questions to stimulate your thinking. You will not be able to answer all questions for all documents, but these questions should get you thinking about how historical sources come to be, how they are formed, and what impact they have both at the time they are created and afterwards.

Reading Historically: Questions for Primary Sources

Contexts of Production

1. Who wrote or created the source?
2. What are the bases of the author's authority on the topic(s) presented in the source?
3. Why did the author or creator generate the source?
4. When and where was the source generated?
5. How much time had elapsed between the events depicted and when the source was created?
6. Did the author write about her or his own social, cultural, or gender group or another one?
7. How might the author's social position (including political orientation, geographic location, gender, class, culture, sexuality, and physical and mental ability) affect his or her ability to depict events or participants in events?
8. Are there any special circumstances that may have affected the author's ability to record what happened?

Questions of Content

1. What kind of language does the author use? Does the source include coded language (replacement words for less acceptable language), loaded language (words used to evoke emotion), or objective language (words used to conceal emotion or to convey an absence of personal involvement in the action or events or with the people depicted)?

2. Does the author overgeneralize? Does the author take a specific example and draw far-reaching conclusions about people, a place, or events? Is this generalization warranted?
3. Is the document obviously imbalanced in its presentation of facts?
4. Does that author use embellishments or rationalizations in the text?
5. Is opinion clearly expressed as opinion?
6. Does that author use words or phrases to indicate approval or disapproval?
7. What has the author left out?
8. How have the author's interests, intentions, or biases affected the content of this document, including what is left out?
9. Is the reasoning expressed in the article strong or weak?
10. How are hierarchies of power expressed in the document?
11. Are there contradictions, inconsistencies, or silences in the document? If so, what do these reveal?
12. What does the document tell us about the temper of the times?

Contexts of Reception
1. Who read this source in its original form?
2. Who was its intended audience? Who else might have read this source?
3. Was it intended to be published? Was it for limited distribution? Was it private?
4. Why and how is this source important historically? What does it tell us about the past?
5. How does the type of source (newspaper report, government report, oral history, petition, or memoir, just to take a few examples) affect how audiences read it at the time? And now?
6. How did the purpose of the source influence how it was written? How would the intended audience of the source affect its content, language, and tone?
7. How does the author's social position affect how a reader would read the source?
8. How would a reading of the source change over time?

The Indian Act in Historical Context—Timeline

1763	Royal Proclamation
1857	Gradual Civilization Act
1867	Confederation of the four colonies: Canada East, Canada West, New Brunswick, and Nova Scotia
1868	Act passed giving the superintendent general of Indian Affairs control over management of all Indian lands, property, and funds
1869	Gradual Enfranchisement Act
1869	Red River Resistance
1870	Canada acquires Rupert's Land from the Hudson's Bay Company
1870	Grand General Indian Council of Ontario and Quebec meets under this name for the first time
1871	Treaties 1 and 2 signed
1871	British Columbia joins Confederation
1873	Treaty 3 signed
1874	Treaty 4 signed
1875	Treaty 5 signed
1876	Treaty 6 signed
1876	Indian Act
1877	Treaty 7 signed
1880	Amendment (election and expansion of cause for removal of chiefs)
1884	Indian Advancement Act (powers of agent at council meetings)
1884	Amendment (making it illegal to sell or give fixed ammunition or ball cartridges to Indians in Manitoba or the North-West, and making it illegal to incite a riot among Indians)

1885	North-West Resistance
1884–1885	Amendment prohibiting the potlatch and tamanawas (winter dances)
1894–1895	Amendment (Indian agents become ex officio justices of the peace; Indians caught intoxicated, gambling, or in the possession of liquor could be arrested; the superintendent general now must approve all wills; outlaws ceremonies such as the Sun Dance and tightens enforcement against the potlatch; Department of Indian Affairs enabled to educate Indian children with or without their parents' consent)
1899	Treaty 8 signed
1905	Saskatchewan and Alberta enter Confederation
1905	Treaty 9 signed
1906	Treaty 10 signed
1911	Act Respecting Songhees Reserve
1911	Amendment (Oliver Act)
1913–1916	Royal Commission on Indian Affairs for the Province of British Columbia (McKenna–McBride Commission)
1914	Amendment (further restriction on "Indian dances"; Indians now require permission to attend an exhibition or stampede if dancing in "aboriginal costume")
1916	Allied Indian Tribes of British Columbia forms
1919	League of Indians of Canada forms
1920	Amendment (involuntary enfranchisement, compulsory school attendance)
1921	Treaty 11 signed
1922	Dan Cranmer prosecution under anti-potlatch provision of Indian Act
1927	Amendment (illegal to raise funds to pursue land claims)
1933	Amendment (further restriction on "Indian dances" strikes out the phrase "in aboriginal costume," making all dances restricted; compulsory enfranchisement brought in again)
1936	Amendment (Indian agents oversee band council meeting and can cast deciding vote)
1939	Indian Association of Alberta forms
1946–1948	Special Joint Committee on the Indian Act (a joint committee involves both the Senate and the House of Commons)
1949	Union of Ontario Indians incorporated
1951	Amendment (drops potlatch ban; fundraising for land claims no longer prohibited; women can vote in band council elections; Indian Register established)
1969	White Paper
1969	Union of British Columbia Indian Chiefs (UBCIC) forms
1970	Red Paper
1973	*Lavell* and *Bédard* cases

1975–1981	*Lovelace* case
1979	Indigenous women march to Ottawa from Kanesatá:ke
1985	Amendment (Bill C-31)
1988–1991	Public Inquiry into the Administration of Justice and Aboriginal People (Manitoba), commonly known as the Manitoba Aboriginal Justice Inquiry
1990	Oka Resistance
1991–1996	Royal Commission on Aboriginal Peoples (RCAP)
1995	Resistance at Ipperwash
2007	*McIvor v. Registrar, INAC* (BCSC)
2008–2015	Truth and Reconciliation Commission
2010	Amendment (Bill C-3—Gender Equity in Indian Registration Act)
2016	Bill S-3—An Act to Amend the Indian Act introduced (further attempt to eliminate sex-based inequities in registration)
2016	National Inquiry into Missing and Murdered Indigenous Women and Girls launched

Index

Printed and bound by CPI Group (UK) Ltd, Croydon, CR0 4YY

13/04/2025

14656521-0002